Rationality
and
Collective Belief

Anthony R. Harris

University of Massachusetts, Amherst

EDITOR

MODERN SOCIOLOGY
A Series of Monographs, Treatises, and Texts
GERALD M. PLATT, Editor

ABLEX PUBLISHING CORPORATION
NORWOOD, NEW JERSEY

Library of Congress Cataloging-in-Publication Data

Main entry under title:

Rationality and collective belief.

  (Modern sociology)
  Includes bibliographies and index.
  1. Social status—Mathematical models. 2. Decision-making—Mathematical models. 3. Discrimination—Mathematical models. 4. Collective behavior. 5. Belief and doubt. I. Harris, Anthony R. II. Title. III. Series.
HM73.R37 1985   305'.01'51   85-20152
ISBN 0-89391-044-9

ABLEX Publishing Corporation
355 Chestnut Street
Norwood, New Jersey 07648

Contents

One

Bias in Status Processing Decisions*

Anthony R. Harris
University of Massachusetts,
Amherst

Gary D. Hill
North Carolina State University,
Raleigh

> In his classic analysis of the significance of numbers in social life, Georg Simmel (1950) argued persuasively that numerical modifications effect qualitative transformations in group interaction. . . . [Yet] . . . the matter of relative numbers, of proportions of interacting social types, was left unexamined. But this feature of collectivities has an impact on behavior. Its neglect has sometimes led to inappropriate or misleading conclusions. (Kanter, 1977:965)

> The influence of the defendant's sex could not be measured because there were too few females in the sample. (Clarke and Koch, 1976:57)

One of the great hallmarks of modern social life involves the child's basic question: "What shall I be when I grow up?" It is asked initially with simple curiousity, but eventually with heightened intensity and preoccupation. In its asking, the question provides the basis for a major bond between child and parent. In its unfolding, the answer ties the generations and gives continuity to their hopes and fears, their human and material resources, and their sense of personal and group identity.

Undoubtedly the question is not thoroughly modern. Children everywhere in history must have asked it. What is new, what gives the question a vastly different voice, involves the modern sense of how an answer to it is likely to unfold. Scholars of social life, notably Weber

---

*The senior author's work on this paper was supported by the Netherlands Institute for Advanced Studies and the junior author's by the Mellon Foundation.

1

(1930), have led us to see that the concept of choosing a personal "career" is relatively new in history. Of longer lineage, and supplied constant theological support, was the idea that children were born into a natural order which offered an uncomplicated answer to the question — "What shall I be when I grow up?" Children would "be" what their parents were. In modern terms, that is, their "statuses" would be assigned or ascribed by birth, not achieved by talent and work.

What seems now to us to have been a radical transition from the "ascribed" answer in pre-industrial society to the "you must choose a career" answer of post-industrial society was, at least in the Western world, smoothed by the Protestant Reformation. For its cannons provided the notion of "calling" — a brilliant but paradoxical concept which preserved elements of the belief that an individual's life work was chosen by nature, yet simultanteously stressed that an individual was free to meet, or not meet, that calling.

The same modern question which preoccupies parents and children has, in various forms, preoccupied a great deal of the attention of modern social science. But where parents and children often believe that the vast array of productive social statuses is plausibly within the reach of any dedicated individual's grasp, students of modern society tend to find the evidence far more mixed, if not downright perplexing. Much of this perplexity is in heated historical continuity with the doctrinal debates which followed Calvin's introduction of the notion of "calling." For much of the present-day consternation revolves, still, around the question of exactly "how free" status attainment is.

On the one hand, it is clear that, in post-industrial society, individual talent and achievement make a difference. A person's resources, or human capital, in all its forms — education, work experience, technical skill, aesthetic virtuousity — has or can have a major impact on the social statuses the person attains. On the other hand, it is equally clear at the aggregate level that (a) there are still strong empirical links between individual human capital and social origin, (b) there are still strong empirical links between individual human capital and biological sex, and (c) net of human capital, there are still strong empirical links between individuals' social origin/sex and their social status (cf. Blau and Duncan, 1967; Duncan et al., 1972; Featherman and Hauser, 1976; Featherman et al., 1981; Hauser and Featherman, 1976; Hauser and Daymont, 1977; Wright, 1979). Such links moreover, are not limited to valued social statuses. They are also observed between disvalued statuses and social origin, disvalued statuses and sex, and disvalued statuses and human capital — or its lack (cf. Dohrenwend and Dohrenwend, 1976; Elliot and Ageton, 1980; Hindelang et al., 1979; Hirschi and Hindelang, 1977; Jensen, 1976; Kessler and Cleary, 1980; Kessler and McCrae, 1981; Tudor et al., 1979). Thus, even though industrialization has witnessed sweeping gains in the freedom of individuals to find a calling or choose a career, it appears that powerful biases in status attainment still exist.

This paper attempts to help explicate the problem in a new way and at a broad theoretical level. It focuses on the relationship between the macro-social outcome of bias and the micro-social decisions of people we shall call "status processors." The paper begins with a brief overview of some problems common to present-day approaches to the study of bias. It proceeds to a rational model of the constraints on status processing decisions, but goes on to suggest that this rational model cannot work without some simplifying concepts, or heuristics. Such heuristics are found and identified as (a) deeply embedded in social order, and (b) prime culprits in the production of biased status processing decisions. Based on these conclusions, the broad contours of a general model of bias in status attainment are developed. The model is counter-intuitive and rather unique in that it focuses on bias in status attainment as a dynamic process. The model is applied to some presently paradoxical issues in the area of criminal justice, and it appears to make sense of them. The paper concludes with a discussion of the model's implications for social policy aimed at reducing bias.

BASIC ISSUES AND CONCEPTS

At the outset, some definitions and a sense of context are needed. It would be nice to nail down, once and for all, the concept of status. But we need not be that ambitious. In most social science contexts, the term "status" is preceded by an adjective, like "educational" or "marital" or "employment." In some of these contexts. the resulting concept is categorical — as in "marital status." But in many, if not most, of these contexts, the resulting concept is ordinal — as in "educational." In both cases, the noun "status" refers to an array of positions comprising a socially important demographic dimension. Socially important dimensions are usually tied to the two core collective processes, childrearing and work which produces goods and services. Perhaps because such processes are collective and their outcomes interdependent, most statuses related to them are hierarchically arrayed and differentially valued.

Collectively, status positions first and foremost distribute value, both economic and noneconomic, to individuals. But, by implication, status positions also convey bundles of information. Most of this information is of the probabilistic kind, as in "well, if she's a lawyer, she's probably a tough cookie," or "if he's a doctor, he's probably rich." In line with the point that socially important statuses are tied to core production processes, probably no status dimension distributes value or bundled information as thoroughly, or has been so carefully researched, as occupational status.

Unquestionably, peoples' occupational status is — as it almost certainly has always been throughout history — the central organizing feature of their lives (even if the term "occupation" is new). As such, occupational status attainment is usually what social scientists have in mind when they study the structure of status attainment in post-industrial society. And, in the following, occupational status is pretty much what we will have in mind when we use the term "status." But there is a reason to be more ambiguous. It is this: the key phenomenon we have in mind is not occupational status per se, but rather, *any* "attained" status which has the power to organize people's lives and perceptions the way occupational status does. Perhaps Hughes' use of the term "master status" (1945) does the trick. The final term, "attained master status," basically suffices, but only with a corollary stipulation: the attainment process must be, at least in part, officially regulated by formal social institutions. Thus identified, "wife" and "father" qualify about as well as "lawyer" and "carpenter." And, equally important, so do the statuses "ex-con" and "mentally ill."

At some point in his or her life, almost everyone has some role in generating the distribution of incumbents to such statuses. Those who do not play an official role are likely to play an informal one. Parents shape the career aspirations of their children. The reports of pleased faculty help in the selection of undergraduates for professional degrees. And the victims of crimes who actually step forward facilitate the eventual production of ex-convicts. In modern society there also exists, of course, a veritable army of people whose formal role (and master status) — exclusively or in large measure — is precisely to help direct others into, and out of, particular master statuses. This array includes teachers at all levels of education, police, admissions staffs, judges, psychiatrists, big league scouts, probation, parole, and social workers, managers, foremen, business executives, and personnel officers. By statute or convention, all are engaged in detecting, monitoring, and transmitting people into, along, or out of the enormous variety of valued and disvalued career paths and master statuses characteristic of highly differentiated societies. They are people, in short, in the business of status processing.

Elaborate written and unwritten rules and codes, goals and values, form the basic guidelines of everyday status procesing. A powerful conceptual correlate of the notions of career and individual achievement is the assumption that these guidelines, whatever their exact nature and regardless of their formal status, should act to produce equity and not bias. Yet, as noted, the best evidence is that high levels of macro-social bias exist in status attainment processes. How can this be understood? One broad answer is this: it is in some people's interests to produce bias. But this is surely not informative. Most major regularities in social life can be said to involve at least someone's self-interest. Besides, a flood of contemporary legislation, the proliferation of affirmative action policies and appropriate watchdog agencies, and organizations like the A.C.L.U., appear to have made it increasingly difficult for bias in status processing decisions to occur. It would thus seem increasingly difficult to see people's interests being served by following biased rules if they are increasingly penalized for doing so.

As we shall try to point out, the basic muddle in trying to understand biased outcomes in everyday status attainment, and in trying to purge these outcomes from social life by public policy, involves two critical pitfalls in simply conceptualizing the problem.

The first may be called the fallacy of attributing bad faith (multiple rules) to status processors. Indeed, many status processors may be in deliberate bad faith by using different rules to evaluate different kinds of people — i.e., rely on a goose-gander logic. But the key problem is that most status processing decisions do not need to use "goose-gander" rules in order to produce macro-social bias. Without the slightest shift in rules, simplifying heuristics from everyday social life amply allow for the outcome of biased decisions. This kind of conclusion is easily overlooked through the blurring of concepts in real need of sharp distinction. They are: (1) the outcome of processors' decisions, (2) processors' rules for decisions, (3) "objective" profiles of people to be processed, and (4) processors' subjective adjustments to these profiles.

The confusion occurs when bias in the outcome of processors' decisions (#1) is the basis for the automatic inference that the processors have use different rules (#2) for judging different kinds of people. An example illustrates the point: Two groups of people, C and T, show the same objective aptitude and achievement profile to a college admissions office. While 30% of T is admitted, only 10% of C is. There appears little doubt that outcome bias has occured (for it has). Perhaps because of moral indignation, helped a little by a desire to simplify cognition, there is a very stong tendency to assume that the admissions office necessarily used different rules for evaluting each group. Another approach, however, is possible and of greater theoretical interest. It involves the assumption that processors adjust objective profiles (#3) on the basis of subjective criteria (#4), with the result that the groups are not seen as equal. In effect, this means processors are likely to use the same decision rules on two differently perceived groups. How, in detail, this is probably the case, provides one major strand of the argument to follow. Its irony rests on the idea that processors' "transformation" of two equal-appearing groups into two unequal-appearing groups is not likely to reflect subjective bias so much as processors' need to simplify the decision problem, and the ability of the social order to provide the quasi-rational basis for that simplification.

The second basic pitfall in effectively studying bias seems more like a methodological problem, but is ultimately theoretical as well. It may be called the fallacy of one-transition. In a recent paper, Berk and Ray (1982) point to the extraordinarily pervasive problem of "selection bias" in sociological data. This is a problem with a potentially severe impact on our ability to estimate effect magnitudes in wide variety of datasets, even those with seemingly marginal selection biases. Berk and Ray's contribution is extremely important in more ways than one. For if selection bias is a problem in the most general sociological case, it is surely a magnitude more problematic in the study of bias itself!

As a research topic, bias has been studied in basically quite static terms. (This is possibly clearer in the case of disvalued status attainment, such as prison sentencing, than in the case of valued status attainment, such as admission to the bar.) Occasionally a researcher will compare simple population rates in a particular setting or at a particular point in a status attainment process; for example, the rate of females compared to males in an advanced high school algebra class. Perhaps more frequently, with some concession to the idea that social life, like biological life, is more likely to occur in process than in cross-section, such rates are compared across two temporally contiguous points; for example, the rate of Blacks compared to Whites sent to prison from the courtroom setting (with an appropriate ceteris paribus adjustment). From this traditional perch, the traditional question has been: from t1 to t2, do the (adjusted) rate distributions became more or less discrepant? Whatever the outcome, there has been a very strong tendency to conclude that it is likely to characterize the whole status attainment process leading up to it. But surely the observed contiguous nodes are simply embedded parts of a much longer antecedent process, of which, typically, the nodes researched represent a small, "tail-end" chunk.

The point is clarified by realizing that an enormous number of studies on the question of racial and socioeconomic bias in criminal justice processing look only at population rate comparisons at the point of sentencing, or at the rate transitions from a quilty finding to sentencing. Ironically, this is somewhat analagous to a hypothetical comparison of the rates of Black and White females graduating from medical school in 19th century America, thoughtfully calculated against their point-of-entry baselines, with the conceivably ludicrous finding that no racial bias existed then.

The obvious pitfall of this cross-sectional approach — occasionally noted (e.g., Arnold, 1971) but rarely corrected — lies precisely in the selection of the settings and points at which population rates are compared or outcomes regressed on demographics. Following Berk and Ray in the general case, and the problem of bias in status attainment in the particular, there is no question but that such selection is extremely likely to affect the degree of bias observed. Ironically, as we shall argue in detail later, it is exactly at the end points of status attainment where we should expect the least bias in processing outcomes to occur. (Unfortunately, this is often the general part of status attainment processes which is most easily viewed and, thus, the most convenient for sampling purposes.) The theoretical ground for this expectation provides the second major strand of the argument. It rests on the twin ideas that (a) bias is produced through subtle cumulative processing decisions, and (b) an intrinsic part of this subtlety comes from processor's precise realization that status attainment is a dynamic and cumulative — not cross-sectional — phenomenon. In effect this means that status processing decisions are self-reflexive, looking as much to past decisions as to future outcomes. This again tends to help simplify decision problems. Interestingly enough, it also creates some potentially instructive counter-intuitive predictions.

DEFINING BIAS

At this point we need (1) a definition of bias and a sense of how it and related concepts will be used in the analysis, and (2) an illustration of this usage.

(1) Elementary Terms

 a. Process Nodes: A set of states or steps in the process of attaining a master status (MS).

 b. Transitions: The movement of groups or classes of individuals from one node to the next.

 c. Transition Probabilities: The hypothetical or empirical chances that different groups of individuals will move from one node to the next.

 d. Traits/Trait Clusters: Attributes of individuals which are commonly identified as central to attaining or occupying an MS.

 e. False Groups: Groups, at any node, to whom MS-relevant traits are "incorrectly" attributed or "incorrectly" not attributed.

 False Passes: Groups "incorrectly" attributed the MS-relevant trait(s), thus being "falsely passed" in a Master Status Attainment Process (MSAP); analogous to a Type II error in statistics.

 False Drops: Groups "incorrectly" not attributed the MS-relevant trait(s), thus being "falsely dropped" in an MSAP; analogous to a Type I error in statistics.

f. Equity Baseline: The "true" frequency of traits or trait clusters in groups of individuals at the first node identified in an MSAP; alternatively, comparative group rates of MS-relevant traits at the first node of an MSAP.

g. Process Bias: Numerical inequality in the comparative transition probabilities of groups matched for "true" MS-relevant traits.

h. Outcome Bias: Numerical departures from the Equity Baseline.

(2) Illustration

Imagine a situation where, at some initially identified point in time (N_0), two groups of people, T and C, show quite different "true" rates of a particular trait or cluster of traits. As a concrete example, imagine that the trait(s) in question, X, was "very fast swimming" and that the rate of X among T was 100 per 1000 and among C was 50 per 1000 (Figure 1). Let us also imagine that becoming a gold medal winner in the Olympics had the character of an MSAP. Along the way to the Olympics, several major steps must be hurdled $(N_1$ to $N_4)$. Situational constraints demand that the transition probabilities across nodes, for both groups, get lower as additional nodes are crossed. Experience also shows that the transition probabilities are generally low for group C.

The Equity Baseline, initialized at N_0 establishes an equity expectation: a ratio of two members of T to one member of C at any node following N_0. And it establishes this expectation virtually no matter what the constraints on diminishing transition probabilities. Departures from the Equity Baseline result from unequal group transition probabilities. Thus, a cross-node trace of the ratio of group transition probabilities yields an explicit picture of the (potentially systematic) fluctuation of Process Bias.

Rates at Nodes:

Groups	"True" N_0:Rates	N_1:Local	Competition Nodes N_2:State	N_3:National	N_4:Jr.Olumpics
T	100	70	42	21	8
C	50	30	15	6	2

Transition Probabilities Across Nodes:

Groups	N_0 to N_1	N_1 to N_2	N_2 to N_3	N_3 to N_4
T	.7	.6	.5	.4
C	.6	.5	.4	.3

FIGURE 1.   Transitions to "Junior Olympics."

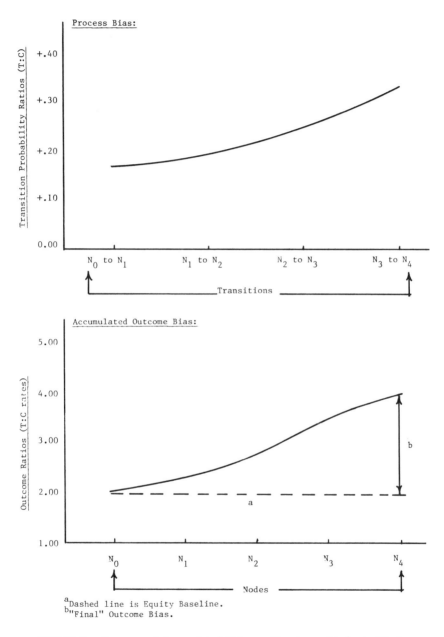

FIGURE 2.   Process and Accumulated Outcome Bias Across Nodes to "Junior
Olympics."

We are free to initialize Process Bias at 0.00 in the case of two-group comparisons, and calculate cross-node gains (or losses) in Process Bias by taking the ratio of the transition probabilities of the two groups and subtracting 1.00, or parity, from it. It is clear from Figure 2 that Process Bias is maximized (to +.33) in the last step of our hypothetical chain of nodes. This means simply that the "Olympic chain" shows its greatest transition bias occuring between Nodes 3 and 4, where 33% more T's than C's transit.

The initial population rates of X among T and C at N_0 — the starting point — were .10 and .05 respectively. That is, we initialized the Equity Baseline at a T/C ratio of 2:1. It is important to see that this choice, however hypothetical at the moment, has important consequences for any real world application. Given this particular starting ratio, 2:1, and a "final" ratio of 4:1, we can say that the little chain we observed produced a total Process Bias of 100% (the final ratio, 4:1, minus the starting ratio, 2:1, divided by the starting ratio, 2:1). Had we initialized (started) the chain at a later node, say N_2 then obviously we would have "officially" observed less process bias. The word "officially" is chosen carefully here, because it stresses the importance of the choice of starting points. "Telling" empirical arguments always begin from theoretical assumptions, and nowhere is this clearer than in the study of bias. We could well have taken the initial Equity Baseline ratio of 2:1 as the problem; that is, as the *last* node — the criterion phenomenon — of a T/C chain "initialized by nature" at 1:1!

For the moment, suffice it to say that we chose the "earliest" starting point, based on our data-gathering ability and our theoretical capacity to frame a social (and not biological) problem. Having found this point, we can thus — at least in theory — state more precisely how much bias in MSAP produces. In our Olympics example, the N_0 to N_4 chunk identified produced a total Process Bias of 100%. Very clearly, the final T/C ratio of 4:1 represents the initialized Equity Baseline parameter multiplied by the transition probability ratios in the chain. Outcome Bias for a particular process, therefore, is equal to the "final" ratio of group rates less their Equity Baseline (distance "b" in the lower portion of Figure 2). Hence Outcome Bias produced in the present example is 2:1 (4:1 less 2:1). But if we are willing to use the term bias coolly — that is, to see it as the result of the choices of "nature" and the choices of humans — than we can see that the Outcome Bias we are given is really 4:1. We have simply decided, in our example, to deal with half the problem.

Having identified a vocabulary and some imagery for approaching the problem of bias, we now turn to the role of status processors in helping create it. We begin with a discussion of the difficulty of making rational status processing decisions in contemporary society. A model is developed which helps clarify the enormous demands modern society places on status processors if they are to act rationally. The model is quite complex, in some ways innovative, but most of all presented as an "ideal type." That is, it attempts to model all the major elements of status processing decisions, were status processers to have a great deal of information and be capable of very complicated estimations. Eventually we will ask whether the basic demands of the model can be met in a much simplified form. The answer will be "yes" and will help understand why social bias is a likely outcome of status processing decisions.

THE DEMANDS ON RATIONAL STATUS PROCESSING DECISIONS

All social arrangements seem to produce personal costs, and modern social life is no exception. Large populations, occupational diversity, and the stress on universalistic rules for individual achievement all make some contribution to these costs. In large measure, nostalgia for simpler social arrangements, the pastoral dream, is nostalgia for higher levels of personal certainty, a clearer feeling for the guidelines of human behavior, a sharper sense of what a person can and should be. The great irony is that much of this loss results from a gain: the ascendancy of achievement over ascription. For, paradoxically, the great human vice of ascriptive rules is also its great human virtue, a world with major certainties for personal choice and identity.

Earlier we stressed the child's question. "What shall I be?" In parallel, though more mundane form, it the same question asked by status processors. "Who is s/he? What is s/he capable of?" In theory, vast stores of help are found lying in the largest single application of modern social science: battery upon battery of objective and psychological tests. And, clearly, these tests do help. But, equally clearly, they are commonly taken with a grain of salt (as, perhaps, they should be). Even after the tests are used, great uncertainties remain. That is, from the courtroom in New York to the admissions office at Harvard Law to the recruitment staff of a pro basketball team in Oregon, these tests are used to reduce uncertainty but end up reducing only part of it. Conventional wisdom (wisely) retains a preference for the "human element" and the ability to judge it over and above such tests.

The major basis for this preference seems to lie in the imprecision of the tests in predicting what they are supposed to predict. Related to the conclusion that the tests are imprecise, in the experience of every seasoned status processor there are dramatic statistical anomalies — cases of people who "made it" who theoretically shouldn't have, and cases of people who "didn't make it" who theoretically should have. These anomalies are often attributed unusually high or unusually low levels of what psychological tests seem to have the greatest difficulty measuring — old-fashioned "will power." Freedom to make this judgment over and above the tests is part of the reason to not be fully constrained by them. Another reason involves the stakes. Status processing is, at the minimum, a fairly serious business. Bad recruitment decisions can hurt a law school or a pro team; bad psychiatric or courtroom decisions can hurt families or new victims of crime on the streets. Good decisions can help raise the prestige of a law school or the success of a pro team; they can also minimize family problems or crime on the streets. Status processing decisions, in short, distribute important costs and gains to groups which rely on processing, as well as to those people who are themselves being "processed" by choice, accident, or violation.

Potentially high stakes and potentially high uncertainty are the key elements facing status processors. If, in general, they are to make fair decisions, there are many pieces of information to assess. If, in general, they are to make personally rational decisions, then there are many outcomes to consider. Consider an informal list of the possibilities facing, say, a pro scout:

1. He touts a college player, BW, very highly to the pro team's owner. BW is hired for a lot of money. BW plays very well for the team. In present terms, that is, he has been "passed" and has displayed the MS-trait in question. This helps the scout keep his job and perhaps get a raise.
2. He touts BW very highly to the team's owner. BW is hired for a lot of money. BW turns out to be a bust. In present terms, BW has been "falsely" passed — has not displayed the MS-trait in question. Because the scout was critical in the hiring decision, the outcome costs him a raise, if not his job.
3. He is strongly critical of BW's potential for pro ball and plays the decisive role in the team's decision not to hire BW. BW is hired by another team. BW plays badly there. Again, he has not displayed the MS-trait in question. But this time, for our scout, BW was "correctly" dropped. Such judgmental shrewdness builds the scout's usefulness to the team.
4. Again the scout is strongly critical of BW and plays the decisive role in the decision not to hire. BW is hired by another team and leads them to a lopsided victory against the scout's team in the league championship. In this case, BW has displayed the MS-trait in question but has been "falsely" dropped. A potentially very costly decision for our scout.

A rather symmetrical, 4-outcome analogy holds equally for disvalued status processing decisions (SPDs):

1. A District Attorney examines the case of an accused rapist. RS, very carefully. The evidence seems strong enough to warrant RS's being fully prosecuted. The D.A. makes this argument. At the ensuing trial, RS is found unequivocally guilty and sent to a maximum security prison. In SPDs where disvalued master statuses are produced, this outcome implies that the D.A.'s decision led to a correct "pass" — the trial documenting that RS had displayed the Master Status trait, rapist, in question. This furthers the D.A.'s plan to run for governor.

2. The D.A. examines RS's case very carefully. The evidence seems strong enough to warrant full prosecution, and the D.A. argues for it. At the ensuing trial, RS is fully exonerated and the prosecution somewhat embarrassed. This outcome implies that the D.A.'s decision led to a "false pass" — the trial documenting that RS did not display the trait in question. There is dollar costs to the state, and it is mirrored in the D.A.'s loss of credibility.

3. The D.A. examines RS's case very carefully. The evidence does not seem strong. The D.A. successfully argues for dismissal. Several months pass, and a confession from the true offender is obtained. In SPDs where disvalued statuses are at stake, this outcome implies a correct or "true" drop occured. While not dramatic, the D.A.'s local credibility is enhanced.

4. Again RS's case is examined very carefully; the evidence does not seem strong, and the DA successfully argues dismissal. Two weeks later, RS is re-arrested for rape and homicide. In present terms, the D.A.'s (and judge's) decision led to a costly "false drop" — very costly to the new victim and her family, and rather costly to the D.A.'s political ambitions as well.

Though these two examples are dramatic compared to the bulk of status processing decisions, they highlight the basic decision-making context and its intrinsic frailty. In particular, the examples illustrate the effects of "good" and "bad" SPDs on status processors themselves, rather than on other social beings (including the person actually processed). But this perspective is, at the moment, the sole perspective at issue. Or so it would seem.

The reason for the ambiguity is as follows. The problem at hand — bias in status processing decisions — is intrinsically a hall of mirrors. It is a process we shall call *highly self-referential* (cf. Hofstader, 1980). On the one hand, this means that status processors at particular nodes in MSAPs look at particular cases with a view toward prior decisions of other status processors and a view toward hypothetical decisions of future status processors. Here, complex "insider" knowledge and beliefs help distribute outcomes to processors, and help reduce apparent uncertainties. Thus, for example, in keeping RS in process, our imaginary D.A. should be assumed to be aware of the decisions which got RS there in the first place: decisions by the victim, her family, the police, the assistant D.A., and so on. And our D.A. should be assumed to be aware of how these decisions (and RS's dossier) will bear on the decisions of a judge and jury, and the judgments of an active public media. By itself, this process-specific self-referential problem is very complex.

On the other hand, we term SPDs "highly" self-referential because the demands on rational SPDs call for additional estimates of how cases themselves — the people being processed — are themselves self-referential vis-a-vis status processing decisions. For example, in looking at BW's prospects for pro ball, our imaginary scout took into account some estimate of BW's ability to "handle" the motivational issues of a big contract and league pressures. Would BW display the same driving qualities if given a huge salary? Would he still be "coachable"? Alternatively, in looking at RS's prospects for a "return to normal" life, our imaginary judge's sentence took into account some estimate of how RS's courtroom experience might, in itself, act as a strong deterrent against repeat offenses. Because disvalued status procesing is generally understood to be costly for those being processed, at various nodes along the way new processors reflect on the "rehabilitative" effect of prior SPDs. In order to do this, they must reflect on actual cases' responses to the process itself.

We can conceive of the first kind of self-referencing, in which processors think about what was on the minds of earlier processors and what will be on the minds of future processors, as first order estimates. These should be thought of as complex, but as well within the ken of the experienced and saavy status processor. We can conceive of the second kind of self-referencing, in which processors think about the process-referential motivational states of those being processed, as second order estimates. These should be viewed as even more complex than first order estimates, for they involve substantially higher levels of uncertainty for even the most highly experienced processors (though perhaps not for the most genuinely biased).

We shall eventually argue that both sorts of estimates, especially the second, are greatly simplified by everyday heuristics which are deeply embedded in social order, and that, in turn, this simplication leads to bias. For the moment, however, what has been said discursively needs to be said more formally. In the following section, we present the basic elements of a formal model of decisions made by status processors. Its basic structure incorporates the notion of processor's expected payoffs for processing decisions, which in turn incorporates processor's estimate of the motivational levels of those cases they process. The model should be seen as an "ideal-type" — a formalized accounting system for processing decisions — *were* processors to act fully rationally. Eventually, we shall find ourselves in the rather ironic position of overthrowing the model. (Though more in spirit than in form.) That is, because the model demands of processors such a complex and subtle calculus, the model would appear to be empirically viable only where these demands could be greatly reduced. We shall then argue that social heuristics meet this need, "save" the model, and, in so doing, provide the key basis for biased decisions by status processors.

A RATIONAL MODEL OF STATUS PROCESSING DECISIONS

In this section, we present the basic form of a rational model of status processing decisions. It is based on the idea of subjectively expected value or utility (cf. Slovic et al., 1977; Kahneman adn Tversky, 1982). This class of model attributes rationality to decision makers trying to operate in a world of uncertainty; but the "rationality" here is rational only with respect to the viewpoint of the decision maker. Subjective expected utility refers to the final outcome of a hypothetical cognitive review, in which possible goals and paths to these goals are evaluated in combination. More strictly, subjective expected utility (SEU) reflects the perceived utility of a choice, weighted by the subjectively estimated probability of obtaining that utility if the choice were actually made. The primary variant of the model expects that choices with higher SEU will be preferred over and acted upon before choices with lower SEU. It is possible to assume in addition, or alternatively, that a choice may involve a dis-incentive value or subjectively expected disutility. It is sometimes assumed that the minimization of subjectively expected disutility is the key rule in decision-making.

The model is first presented in simplified form in order to identify the major factors in processors' decisions or pass or drop the cases they receive. Following this, the model is discussed in greater detail. It is important to stress that the model carries an argument at the general level of status processing decisions (SPDs). Thus, the nature of decision-making, in *both* status "enhancing" or valuing processes *and* status "reducing" or disvaluing processes, is involved.

Because the character of processing outcomes depends initially on whether the status in question is valued or disvalued, the term "desired outcome" will be used temporarily to refer to the outcomes of both kinds of processes. (That is, where in processing for valued statuses, such as "Doctor," the desired outcome is the display of the trait(s) in question, but in processing for disvalued statuses, such as "Criminal," the desired outcome would seem to be the opposite — the non-display of the trait(s) in question.)

Several complex and unorthodox features mark the model. The first and perhaps most important is the assumption that in SPDs processors will consider two kinds of probabilities: (1) the probability that the person being processed will show (S) or not show ($\overline{S}$) the trait in question; and (2) the conditional probability, given S or $\overline{S}$, that utility or disutility will be returned to the processor after making the decision. Consider our imaginary pro scout: the first kind of uncertainty involves the estimated probability that a college player will succeed on the pro team, while the second kind of uncertainty involves the estimated probability that utility/ disutility will be returned to the scout, given the success or failure of the prospect. In the model, the first estimate is indicated by the term Prob' (the probability of S or $\overline{S}$) and the second by the term Prob" (the probability of utility/disutility given S or $\overline{S}$).

Figure 3 shows the decision model in simplified form. The decision to pass, P, is shown as a direct function of the SEU of a pass relative to the SEU of a drop (SEU p/d or, simply U*). U* is, in turn, shown as a joint function of the utility of a desired outcome to processor given a pass (U|p) and the two uncertainty estimates, Prob' and Prob". Finally, the terms U, Prob', and Prob" are shown as functions of 3 broad clusters of exogenous variables: (1) C, or Case characteristics; (2) PC, or Process characteristics; and (3), R or Role characteristics of the processor. These variables include such factors as the "objective" performance history of the case, what relative stage of the status attainment process the case is at, and the visibility/ accountability of the processor in the status attainment process.

The decision to drop or pass a case can be seen as function of relatively complex comparisons of the 4-outcome states identified earlier: the state where the case has been passed and the desired outcome occurs; the state where the case has been passed out the desired outcome does not occur; the state where the case has been dropped and the desired outcome occurs; and the state where the case has been dropped but the desired outcome does not occur. Consider, again, the case of the college prospect. If passed (hired) he may become a brilliant player and bring credit to the team and scout, or he may never play a game. If dropped (not hired), he may be hired for a lot of money by another team and fail there, or he may be the decisive factor in the championship game against the scout's team. Although there are important reasons for not expecting that all four outcome states will be weighed equally in any or most SPDs, the general functional form of the problem may be specified as follows:

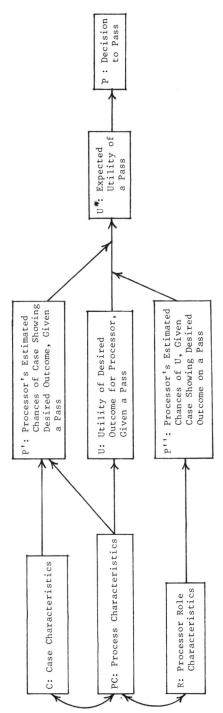

FIGURE 3.   Simplified model of processing decisions.

$$U^* = SEUp/d = U^*net \mid p - U^*net \mid d \tag{1.}$$

where

$$U^*net \mid p = U^*S \mid p - D^*S \mid p \tag{2.}$$

$$U^*net \mid d = U^*S \mid d - D^*S \mid d \tag{3.}$$

where

$$U^*S \mid p = (U \mid S \mid p) \cdot (P' \mid p) \cdot (P''(U) \mid p) \tag{4.}$$

$$D^*S \mid p = (D \mid S \mid p) \cdot (1 - P' \mid p) \cdot (P''(D) \mid p) \tag{5.}$$

and

$$U^*S \mid d = (U \mid S \mid d) \cdot (1 - P' \mid d) \cdot (P''(U) \mid d) \tag{6.}$$

$$D^*S \mid d = (D \mid S \mid d) \cdot (P' \mid d) \cdot (P''(D) \mid d) \tag{7.}$$

The most basic equation, (1.), states that the net subjective expected utility of passing a case (U^*) is equal to the net expected utility of a pass ($U^*net \mid p$) minus the net expected utility of a drop ($U^*net \mid d$). According to the maximization rule in SEU theory, if the resulting value is positive the case will be passed, and if the resulting value is negative the case will be dropped. Each of the these summary terms may be decomposed into a utility and a disutility component. Thus, the net expected utility of a pass ($U^*net \mid p$ in (1.)) is shown in (2.) as composed of an expected utility component (the utility of a Show given a pass decision or, simply, $U^*S \mid p$) and an expected disutility consideration (the disutility of a No Show given a pass decision or, simply, $D^*S \mid p$). These components are further decomposed in (4.) and (5.). The expected utility of a Show given a pass ($U^*S \mid p$ in (2.)) is shown as the product of three fundamental terms in (4.): the utility of S given a pass ($U \mid Sp$), the estimated probability of S given a pass ($P' \mid p$), and the estimated probabilty that utility for the S, given a pass, will be returned to the processor ($P''(U) \mid p$). Analagously, the expected disutility component of a pass ($D^*S \mid p$ in (2.)) is decomposed in (5.), and the net expected utility of a drop (($U^*net \mid d$ in (3.)) finds its building blocks in (6.) and (7.).

It will not be necessary for the reader to keep the precise details of (1.) to (7.) in mind. But it will be useful to remember the basic concept of the overall net expected utility of a pass relative to a drop (U^* in (1.)), and some basic ideas related to it.

First, SPDs are generally made in a world of two kinds of major uncertainty: one involves the uncertainty that the person being processed will actually display the Master Status-relevant trait(s) in question; the other involves the uncertainty that "correct" versus "incorrect" processing decisions will have positive or negative outcomes for a processor.

Second, and related, the question of the magnitude of these outcomes for processor is important. SPDs, at least initially, are best seen as being made in a world of consequentiality — a world where there are likely to be a least some costs for "incorrect" decisions and some rewards for "correct" ones.

Third, and tied to the first two points, the *possibility* of modeling these decision-making tensions for status-valuing and status-disvaluing processes simultaneously is attractive. In treating both kinds of MSAPs in the same model, there is already potential theoretical gain to be had in understanding the production of biased outcomes: having dropped a case, processors in both valuing and disvaluing MSAPs have some stake in cases not showing the trait(s) in question. This seems reasonable but perhaps not newsworthy. What *is* interesting is that the same valuing/disvaluing parallel holds for pass decisions. Having passed a case, processors in both valuing and disvaluing MSAPs have some stake in cases showing the trait(s) in question. In both cases, the interests of large social groups coincide with the personal interests of the processor. In the case of valuing processes, this is one thing: both interests "want"the admitted medical student to become a doctor, both "want" the hired college athlete to become a star — i.e., a valued social product. But in the case of disvaluing MSAPs, the parallel is another thing. For here, common goals tying processing and larger community act, paradoxically, to produce a socially disvalued product: both interests "want" the case on trial found guilty, both "want" involuntary commitments upheld. Thus, according to the model, but not according to the law, pass decisions in disvalued processes tend necessarily, and ironically, to align processors' interests with the hope of ensuring that disvalued outcomes — a "show" of criminality, the "existence" of mental illness — will eventually occur.

The basic model just discussed argues explicitly that uncertainty and self-interest characterize the decision problem for status processors. We now consider the issue of self-interest in more detail.

(1) Modeling U: Payoffs to Processor

Figure 3 indicates that the utility/disutility of SPDs to processors is a function of process characteristics, PC. Figure 4 further specifies this relationship. (To simplify matters, the complex bundle of subjective gains and costs shall be referred to by the summary term Utility, or U.)

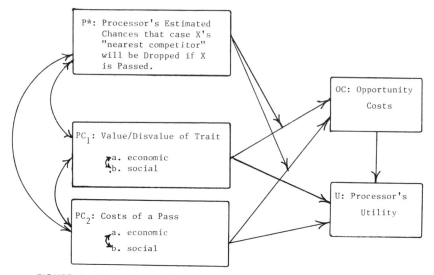

FIGURE 4.   Determinants of U, or Processor's Utility of Desired Outcome
Given a Pass.

Three major exogenous factors are shown as affecting the Utility of processing decisions. One, P*, involves the chances of paying what economists call opportunity costs. It is somewhat more complicated than the others, and we shall return to it momentarily. The other two factors are comprised of a social and an economic component:

1. The (objective) value of the MS-relevant traits for which the case is being processed.
2. The (objective) costs of processing a "pass" (i.e. forwarding a case.)

Objective Value is defined by two dimensions:

1. The economic or legitimate market value of the MS-relevant traits which could be commanded, in principle, at the point of the SPD in valuing processes; alternatively, the economic costs of the MS-relevant traits at the point of the SPD in disvaluing processes.
2. The noneconomic or social value of the traits at the point of the SPD in valuing processes (i.e, their prestige value); alternatively, the noneconomic costs of the trait at the point of the SPD in disvaluing processes.

These values should be thought of as statistical aggregates attributed to broad types of cases. For example, a "good mathematician"has a lower market value if not admitted to college than if s/he completes college; the prestige accrued for showing the trait follows suit. Alternatively, a "criminal" is assumed to produce lower economic and social costs if sent to prison than if s/he is dropped from further processing in the courts. Clearly, the greater the economic and social value of the trait, or the greater its potential economic and social disvalue, the greater the potential economic and social disvalue, the greater the potential Utility for a (correct) pass.

Processing costs are also defined by two dimensions: (a) the economic costs of passing a case on to the next stage of processing, and (b) the noneconomic or social costs of an erroneous or "false" pass. For example, the economic costs of transmitting a mathematics star through an accelerated high school program are lower than those incurred in transmitting the same person through M.I.T. The parallel holds for disvalued processing: the economic costs of transmitting a defendant through arrest are lower than those incurred in transmitting the same person through trial. And, in both valued and disvalued processing, processor's Utility for a (correct) pass decision is shaped by the noneconomic costs of a false pass. Thus, for example, prestige costs are higher for M.I.T. in failing to produce competent mathematicians than for special high school programs which fail to produce students scoring high on college placement exams. And such prestige costs are higher for D.A.s in failing to produce guilty findings than for police in failing to produce arraignments. (Clearly all such costs and gains are colinear.)

A third, more complex factor is represented as directly affecting U: DC or opportunity costs. To begin, note that OC is not shown as exogenous. Rather, it is somewhat mysteriously shown as a function of two product terms: $PC_1 \times P^*$ and $PC_2 \times P^*$, where P^* represents the chances of dropping case Y — case X's "nearest competitor" — if case X is passed.

In economics, the basic idea of an opportunity cost is that it represents the hypothetical value of a bypassed alternative. In SPDs, opportunity costs may also be conceived as occuring in two dimensions: (a) the economic opportunity costs of passing a case, and (b) parallel noneconomic opportunity costs.

In both valued and disvalued MSAPs, the opportunity costs of passing case X are best conceived in terms of the lost payoffs in having, therefore, to drop case Y. Prisons, pro teams, and M.I.T. have in common a limited number of vacancies. Any case may show strong enough absolute scores on a cardinal metric to justify a pass in valued or disvalued SPDs. But, given large supplies of incumbents and limited slots in the processing chain, choices are inevitably made on the basis of an ordinal reduction (as in "there is just not enough room to let all qualified candidates in!") Opportunity costs for passing case X are thus defined as the expected value of passing case Y, where Y is X's "nearest competitor," and where expected value is a weighted product of PC factors (Figure 4) and P^*, or the chances that Y will be dropped if X is passed. (But note two things here. First, no opportunity costs would therefore incur if P^* were zero, i.e., if all cases could be passed. And second, one major component of $OC - PC_1 \times P^*$ — could be construed as more properly contingent upon yet another probability element, P'/Y, or the chances that Y would actually Show the trait(s) in question if passed. Though eventually we shall consider the problem in this form, we do not represent it in modeling U.)

The modeling of Utility (U) in Figure 4 may be summarized as follows:

$$U = U \mid p = f(PC_1, PC_2, OC) \tag{8.}$$

where

$$PC_1 = p(PC_{1a}, PC_{1b}) \tag{9.}$$

$$PC_2 = q(PC_{2a}, PC_{2b}) \tag{10.}$$

$$OC = r(PC_1 \mid Y, PC_2 \mid Y, P^*) \tag{11.}$$

and

$$P^* = \text{Prob. of Y (X's ``nearest competitor'') being Dropped if X is Passed} \tag{12.}$$

The preceding discussion identified a set of factors determining U. It should also be clear that the discussion generated a fairly straightforward set of expectations for outcomes in status processing decisions. Imagine that we must choose one of two candidates for a Pass, X and Y. Given what has been said thus far, how might our preference for choosing X (over Y) be shaped? Part of the answer seems clear:

Ceteris Paribus (Everything else between X and Y held constant):

a. $>PC_1(X/Y) >U(X/Y)|p >U^*(X/Y)|p >P(X/Y)$
b. $>PC_2(X/Y) <U(X/Y)|p <U^*(X/Y)|p <P(X/Y)$
c. $>OC(X/Y) <U(X/Y)|p <U^*(X/Y)|p <P(X/Y)$

Assuming X/Y equivalence on all other dimensions, a. states that increased levels of value/disvalue for X's traits (vs. Y's) increase X's Utility over Y's on a Pass; this in turn increases processor's expected utility (U^*) for X over Y on a Pass; and, consequently, the relative chances of X (vs. Y) receiving a Pass (P) are increased. Again assuming equivalence on other factors, b. states that higher processing costs for X (vs. Y) will lower X's Utility on a Pass, X's consequent expected utility to processor, and, in the end, X's relative chances of being passed. Finally, given equivalence otherwise, c. states that higher opportunity costs (OC) for passing X (vs. Y) will lower X's relative Utility, consequent expected utility to processor, and, therefore, relative chances for a Pass.

Modeling P': the Chances of Case Success

Discussion thus far has focused on the possible Utility returned to processors for their decisions. It is clear, however, that this return is largely conditional — that it depends on other major factors. Figure 3 indicates two such factors. One of these, P'', involves processor's estimate of personally receiving positive or negative payoffs for particular processing outcomes. The other, P', is more basic, for it involves processor's estimate of how likely it is — in the first place — for a particular processing outcome to occur.

By illustration, our imaginary scout wonders if BW will play as well in the pros as in college. Or our imaginary D.A. wonders if RS' case will look as good on trial as it does at the point of arraignment. Both examples illustrate the question of P': given a Pass, will the case Show the trait(s)? But our scout also wonders how much credit will be returned him if BW is hired by the scout's team; if BW succeeds, will the team recognize the critical role the scout played? Alternatively, if BW fails, will the team (hopefully) forget that critical role? Analagously, if RS' trial is successfully prosecuted, will the public recognize the D.A.'s critical role? Alternatively, if the prosecution fails, will the public (hopefully) forget the D.A.'s critical role? In both these examples, the clear reference is to P'': given the outcome of a Pass (S or $\bar{S}$), will the processor receive gains or costs?

Of the two factors, P'' is the simpler to model, and we shall return to it in the next section. For the moment, the logically prior question of the other major conditional, P', is before us. How likely is a passed case to Show the trait(s) in question?

Earlier we said that several unorthodox conceptual features mark the decision model. One of these, of course, is the distinction between P'' and P'. The others involve the modeling of P' or processor's estimate of the chances that a case will (S)how the desired outcome. In thinking about P', we will be trying to think in two perspectives simultaneously: (1) processor's, and (2) the demands of rationality. In so doing, we will continue to build a model which is theoretically sensible but which, increasingly, will seem empirically unrealistic.

Even in highly differentiated societies with elaborate rules and protocols for status processing decisions, there remains an important but somewhat elusive distinction between "kosher" and "unkosher" rules for judging peoples' capacities for Master Statuses. To a great extent, this problem revolves around the differences between past documented (or "actual") performance and future probable performance. In modern society, criteria for documenting and judging "actual" performance abound: an honors degree in math, absenteeism at school or work, achievement statistics in sports, keeping a clean home, number of prior times arrested or imprisoned, years of work experience, percentage of return on clients' investments, years in remission from mental illness, number of children who have completed college, proportion of cases successfully prosecuted, and so on. These criteria are often paralleled by a broad range of officially identified rules for status incumbency — such as the minimum age for the Presidency or for being processed in a particular kind of court, minimum SAT scores for a graduate admissions program, passing the Bar exam, rules of evidence in a trial, legal constraints on sentencing, and the like.

In all, these criteria and rules are commonly regarded as kosher in assessing past performance. More important, they are commonly regarded as kosher in predicting future performance. But, as we all know, they are not enough. Additional bases for estimating future performance exist which are slightly less public, somewhat more idiosyncratic, substantially more inferential, less kosher in the culture of universalism, and — needless to say — in thoroughly common use. For present purposes we identify the most important of these in a way related to the old-fashioned concept of "will power" — Attributed Motive. Although the role of more "objective" performance profiles will be incorporated in modeling P' — or case's estimated chances of Show — that role will not be of major interest here, Rather, we shall be interested in the more subtle question asked by processor: "I know s/he can do it, but . . . will s/he?" This question is important, because it helps see the peculiarly self-referential features of SPDs.

In elaborating these points, it might be useful to have some examples in mind:

Ex.1: It is the mid 1940's. BR, the owner of a baseball team, has seen a young black athlete, JR, play ball in the minor leagues. JR plays superbly. BR would like to hire JR, but is concerned that the open racism in pro ball will affect JR's performance. Given the extraordinary abuse JR has already received in the minor leagues, and his continued high level of performance, BR concludes that JR has got what it takes for the first black to make it in the majors — superb ability and "tremendous desire."

Q.: Observing JR's ability to perform is relatively easy. How does BR conclude that JR has got "tremendous desire"?

Ex.2: It is the mid 1960's. JH, the president of a bank, has watched a middle aged spinster, KM, perform her duties as loan officer for many years. KM has an obviously good head for figures and banking in general. JH would like to promote KM, but is concered that this would create resentment among males with equal seniority, and consequently affect their and KM's performance. Given the extraordinary difficulty facing women executives in banking, JH concludes that KM need not be promoted in order to keep her performance at the same high level — for she "loves her work."

Q.: Observing KM's ability to perform is relatively easy. How does JH conclude that KM "loves her work"?

Ex.3: It is the mid 1980's. EP, a higher court judge, has heard the check forging case against ST, an accountant with no prior record. ST has two children in college and an umblemished employment record for 20 years. EP has discretionary latitude in sentencing ST, but is concerned about the ensuing costs to the state and to ST's family. Given the extraordinary circumstances of the case, EP decides that $5000 fine and six months probation are sufficient to keep ST from committing crime again — for he has been "punished enough."

Q.: Establishing that ST committed the crime was relatively easy. How does EP conclude that ST has been "punished enough"?

Figure 5 shows a simplified view of the modeling problem. P' is shown as a function of two factors, Probable Capacity (ProbC) and Attributed Motivation (AM). Probable Capacity should be thought of as processor's estimate that the case is capable of showing the MS-relevant trait(s). ProbC, in turn, is shown as dependent upon two broad exogenous factors, C or Case Characteristics, and PC ro Process Characteristics. Attributed Motivation, the factor of greater theoretical interest, should be thought of as processor's estimate of the overall "motive force" behind a case's willingness to show the MS-relevant trait(s). Attributed Motivation is shown as dependent upon the same exogenous factors as ProbC and, in addition, upon ProbC itself.

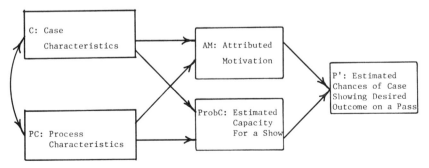

FIGURE 5.   Simplified model of P'.

Before we consider its antecedents, however, we need to spell out in more detail what we mean by Attributed Motivation and the concept's potential usefulness in modeling the decision problem.

Consider the idea that we attribute motives to others, conceive of reasons "behind" others' actions. Consider also that this is a largely inferential process (cf. Hamilton, 1978; Jones and Davis, 1965; Myers, 1980) which results in two basic kinds of (essentially modern) answers: (1) "it is in X's interest to do it," and (2) "it would not seem to be in X's interest to do it . . . so, I guess X is just . . . weird/ strange/ masochistic/ dumb/ driven/ forced to do it/ compulsive/ that kind of personality/ irrational." The first kind of answer, (1), attributes rational motives to people. A distinguishing feature of rational motives is that "everyone" understands them. Why? Because they almost inevitably entail a self-interest calculus based on payoffs with very high social communality — money, material goods, prestige, power. The second answer, (2), attributes irrational (or nonrational) motives to people. A distinguishing feature of irrational motives is that only psychiatrists "understand" them, not even X. Why? Because if they entail a self-interest calculus, the payoffs involved are so highly individualistic, so obscure, that there is little or no social communality around them.

In the notion of Attributed Motivation, we incorporate both kinds of motive attributions. A critical feature of Rational Attributed Motivation is that processor assumes it to be governed by "objective" rewards and costs outside of case's psychological idiosyncrasy — i.e., by external payoffs with a common utility calculus. Cases attributed high levels of rational motive for showing MS-traits are not too hard to understand and, other things being equal are good bets for pass decisions. From this perspective, cases with high levels of rational AM are assumed — by processor — to be quite sensitive to the effects of pass decisions per se. That is, precisely because pass/drop decisions distribute the external conditions for S or $\bar{S}$ payoffs, and precisely because high Rational AM cases are seen as truly "rational" decision makers, processors see such cases' "willingness" to Show or Not Show the trait(s) in question as relatively process-dependent. In short, both criminals and business executives attributed high levels of rational motivation can be "counted on," in Showing or Not Showing MS-relevant traits, to be highly affected by pass/drop outcomes in SPDs. Thus, if rational motivation can be assumed to be governed by external payoffs, it can also be assumed to be governable (and manipulatable) by them.

On the other hand, a critical feature of Irrational Attributed Motivation is that processor assumes it to be governed by "subjective" personality needs fully within the idiosyncracies of the case — i.e, by internal payoffs with no common utility calculus. Cases attributed high levels of irrational motive for showing MS-traits are harder to understand, although, other things being equal, they too are good bets for pass decisions. From this perspective, cases with high levels of irrational AM are assumed — by processor — to be quite insensitive to the effects of pass decisions per se. That is, even though pass/drop decisons distribute the external conditions for S or $\overline{S}$ payoffs, and precisely because high Irrational AM cases are not seen as "rational" decision makers, processors see such cases' "willingness" to Show or Not Show the trait(s) in question as relatively process-independent. In short, both criminals and business executives (or loan officers or baseball players) attributed high levels of irrational motivation can be "counted on," in Showing or Not Showing MS-relevant traits, to be highly unaffected by pass/drop outcomes in SPDs. Thus, if irrational motivation cannot be assumed to be governed by external payoffs, it also cannot be assumed to be governable (and manipulatable) by them.

Bring these ideas into the model is not theoretically difficult. Processor's estimate that a case will Show the trait(s) if passed, or P', is seen as a direct function of the case's Probable Capacity (ProbC) and Attributed Motivation (AM). Attributed Motivation, in turn, is defined by two elements: a rational (or expected utility) component and an irrational (or internal) component.

$$P' = f(AM, ProbC) \tag{13.}$$

where

$$AM = m(IM + U^{*\prime}) \tag{14.}$$

where

$$IM = \text{Attributed Internal Motivation (Irrational)}$$
$$U^{*\prime} = \text{Attributed External Motivation (Rational)}$$

This elaboration is incorporated in Figure 6, which deliberately decomposes AM into external ($U^{*\prime}$) and internal (IM) components. $U^{*\prime}$, in turn, is shown as a rather complex product function of three terms. The first of these, U', is processor's estimate of the Utility (or Disutility) returned to case for Show. Generated by two exogenous factors — (1) processor's estimate of case's "objective" payoff for a Show (C_1), and (2) processor's estimate of case's "objective" opportunity costs for a Show (C_2) — U' represents processor's estimate of subjective value which could be returned to case if case produced a Show. What of the second product term, Prob'?

Because our rational model demands that processor — in trying to assess a case's "willpower" — must estimate expected utility for case (U*), we must also allow processor the ability to represent case's estimate of the chances of receiving personal Utility for a Show (as in, "what does s/he really think her chances are?"). In Figure 6, this is shown by Prob', or processor's estimate of case's perceived chances of a payoff for Show. But of all the demand discussed thus far, Prob' would seem to be the most difficult to meet. The reason for this is that, where in most of the estimates discussed so far processor is generally free to rely on statistical generalities to provide case specific answers, however good or bad, in trying to represent Prob' processor is asked to estimate an extremely variable phenomenon across individuals. (And the estimate is, after all, a "double" one: P(S), P(U)|S.) Putting it more directly, where most Americans could represent or estimate the "reasons why" a middle-aged man might want to become an Olympic Gold Metal pole-vaulter, understand his qualifications, and so on, most would be extremely hard pressed to represent, to themselves, (a) *his* perceived chances of making the team, and — in necessary combination with (a) — (b) *his* perceived chances of receiving Utility were he to win the medal. (These are both second order estimates of the sort mentioned on p. 21.)

Hopefully, this example helps identify a point of major empirical tension in the model. In considering the issue, note that a second probability estimate, ProbC, lies figurately below Prob'. The latter term is by no means difficult to deal with. For it simply represents a basic, explicit, and common task of most processors in formal SPDs — estimating a case's capacity for Showing the trait(s) in question. The complexity of the formal model would be significantly reduced if we could treat ProbC and Prob' as functionally equivalent. That is, if we could imagine processor using an estimate of ProbC as a perfectly good stand-in for Prob'. But we cannot, for two reasons. First, because Prob' is the product of two probabilities, the probability of S and, given S, the probability of U. Second, ProbC cannot stand-in, precisely because we would like processor to be able to distinguish his or her "objective" assesement of the chances that case can Show the trait(s) from his or her reading of what case "thinks" these chances are. No matter how complex or formal, virtually all SPDs we can think of are not "blind" to this reading of case's self-perception. All this means is that processor is often in the position of finding large discrepancies between his or her view of a case's capability and case's "own view" (i.e. processor's view of case's own view).

Although we can think of situations where there is little discrepancy of this sort, we prefer the inclusion of both terms. The inevitable conclusion, however, would seem to be that, no matter how confident the estimates of U', because estimates of Prob' are shaky much of the time,

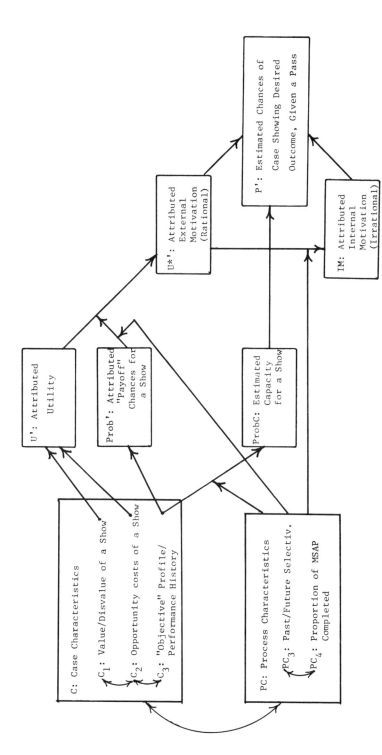

FIGURE 6. Determinants of P', or Processor's Estimated Chances of Case Showing Desired Outcome, Given a Pass.

the ensuing product term, U^{*}' (Attributed External Motivation), would therefore also seem to be shaky much of the time.

But there is a reasonable solution. Note that, in Figure 6, an arrow from the Process Characteristics block is shown leading to the effect of Prob' on U'. This is a schematic way of indicating the effects of the third product term in U^{*}', or Attributed External Motivation. The arrow means that, in estimating U^{*}', processor's uncertainty is conditioned by some assessment of the case vis-a-vis past and future steps in the entire Master Status Attainment Process. Two factors identified as critical here are "Past/Future Selectivity" (PC_3) and "Proportion of MSAP Completed by Case" (PC_4) in this context, the self-referential character of the decision problem is quite clear. Professional processors are well aware of the general "weeding out" principles which applied to the prior processing of cases they now have before them; and processors are also generally aware of future "weeding out" principles which will apply to the same set of cases, should the cases be Passed. In parallel terms, processors are generally aware of the tiered, progressive character of steps in MSAPs. It is therefore not difficult to estimate, at least in an approximate sense, "how far" a case has "come," "how far" a case "has yet to go." Information of this sort may help greatly in reducing the uncertainty attached to U^{*}', Attributed External or Rational Motivation.

It should be obvious that processors at later stages in an MSAP have a basic advantage over processors at earlier stages — considerably greater confidence in their ability to estimate or attribute various levels of External Motivation to a case. For example, it should be easier for a Senior Law Partner to estimate Lawyer X's External Motivation at t_n than for a Law School Admissions Officer to have estimated Candidate X's at t_{n-1}. (Note that this is not the same thing as saying that Lawyer X's External Motivation is perceived as higher than Candidate X's, but rather than the attribution occurs with more confidence.) It is hypothesized that the magnitude of this "proportion" effect (PC_4) increases directly with "selectivity" (PC_3) — the more selective the process, the easier it is to attribute External Motivation with confidence. Consider an example from disvalued processing: given greater "selectivity" in the production of heroin sellers than in marijuana sellers, a D.A.'s attribution of External Motivation to heroin seller X will be made with more confidence than the same attribution to marijuana seller Y. (Note again this is not the same thing as saying the level of motivation attributed X will be higher than that attributed Y.)

Figure 6 also indicates that these same two PC factors — "proportionality" and "selectivity" — play an interactive role, with C_3, in producing ProbC, the most conventional endogenous element in the model. Stress on universalism means that documented performance "records" are used to identify, and often accompany, cases to be Passed. These records play a critical, sometimes self-fulfillingly prophetic, role in estimating ProbC. As indicated, however, the role of the record (C_3), is seen as interactive with PC_3 and PC_4. At earlier points in MSAPs, it is harder to take C_3 seriously and, consequently, it will be weighted accordingly by processor. And the Darwinian quality of "selectivity" implies that the record, C_3, will be weighted more heavily in highly selective processes, whatever the stage of the process.

Finally, Figure 6 establishes a theoretically informative connection between Attributed External or Rational Motivation and Attributed Internal or Irrational Motivation. The causal flow is shown as inverse, with higher levels of Attributed Internal Motivation (IM) dependent on lower levels of Attributed External Motivation (U*'). This is an important point, for we are thus postulating that processors will have an overall tendency to attribute low levels of irrational motivation to cases they perceive as having high levels of rational motivation and high levels of irrational motivation to cases they perceive as having low levels of rational motivation. Yet, as Figure 6 also indicates, the magnitude of this inverse effect is seen as process-dependent: in the early stages of MSAPs, the effect is thought to be weak, in later stages strong; analagously, in less selective processes the effect is thought to be weak, in more selective processes, strong.

In summary form, the modeling of P' may therefore be expressed as follows:

$$P' = f(ProbC, U^*, IM) \tag{15.}$$

where

$$IM = g(-U^{*\prime} \cdot (PC_3, PC_4)) \tag{16.}$$

$$U^{*\prime} = h(U)' \cdot Prob' \cdot (PC_3, PC_4)) \tag{17.}$$

where

$$U' = i(C_1, C_2) \tag{18.}$$

$$ProbC = j(C_3 \cdot (PC_3, PC_4)) \tag{19.}$$

$$Prob' = k(C_3, PC_3, PC_4) \tag{20.}$$

(3) Modeling P'': Processor's Payoff Chances

Three final estimates enter the rational model. Two of these, U and P', have been discussed. The third, and last, is P'', or processor's estimate of receiving payoffs for a particular processing decision. For present purposes, P'' is much easier to model than P'.

Figure 7 indicates three intertwined aspects of the processor's role which affect the chances of U, or payoffs to processor. The first, "discretion" (R_1), refers to the fixedness of pass/drop criteria in the particular context of the SPD. These criteria may be codified, as in law, or simply informally understood. At certain points in processing — perhaps in sentencing for a particular crime or in certification once the Bar exam is passed — there is very little room for discretion. At these points, certain processing decisions are mandatory or near mandatory. Equally clearly, most processing decisions have varying degrees of latitude. It should be obvious that higher levels of processing discretion are associated with higher chances of receiving U (utility or disutility) for "good" or "bad" processing decisions.

Visibility (R_2) refers to the transparency of processor's role to peers and/or the public in particular processing decisions. Some processor roles, like D.A., have high public visibility. Other roles, like pro scout, have high visibility within a private organization. Given "good" processing decisions, high role visibility tends to be "money in the bank," especially when — as is often the case — no one processor has done more or less than another to facilitate a "good" decision. But, of course, highly visible roles also accrue costs when "bad" decisions are made. In either case, it is clear that higher levels of role visibility are associated with greater levels of P".

Finally, given that processor's role is embedded in an organizational setting, no matter how loosely or tightly organized, Accountability (R_3) refers to the informal and formal features of that setting which allow for the review of particular processing decisions. In this sense, most courtroom roles have high accountability, though most victims of crimes — in deciding whether or not to report a crime — do not. Similarly, though senior partners in a Law firm have high accountability in taking on a new partner, most admissions personnel at a private college — in deciding whether or not to admit an applicant — do not. Obviously, as "accountability" increases, so too do the chances of receiving payoffs (U) for "good" and "bad" decisions.

Clearly these three factors covary and interact in complex ways. But, for the moment, they are sufficiently identified. So too is our presentation of a formal model of rationality in status processing decisions. There is no question that the model is quite complex in the abstract. There is also no question that its demands on processor are quite high, so high, in fact, that it is extremely difficult to imagine the model actually simulates processing decisions, or that processors could use it if they wanted to.

As we said earlier, however, the model would be presented as an ideal-type — a representation of what subjectively rational decision-making would "require" were it actually to be accomplished in status processing

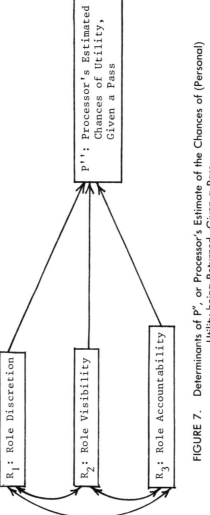

FIGURE 7. Determinants of P″, or Processor's Estimate of the Chances of (Personal) Utility being Returned, Given a Pass.

decisions. This is not to say the model is totally unfamiliar. Most of us, including the authors, have made processing decisions and should find the concepts discussed quite familiar. The empirical questions, then, would seem to involve a processor's ability to meet the total set of demands in the model, not any one demand in particular.

Hopefully, the reader will recall that this is a paper on bias, not on rationality. As it turns out, our extended discussion of the rational model has been a necessary part of a rather long argument. In what follows, we shall use the model to build what we think is a more empirically likely representation of actual status processing decisions. In working toward this end, and by introducing what we have called social heuristics, we shall find ourselves facing a vastly simplified form of the decision problem. Interestingly enough, we shall see that this simplied form does seem to meet the demands of subjective rationality. Paradoxically enough, we shall also see that the same simplified form provides a powerful basis for biased decisions.

RATIONALITY AND SOCIAL HEURISTICS: TYPE & COUNTERTYPE

Heuristics are devices which aid in discovery. Like maps, they simplify the problem of getting from A to B, especially in difficult terrain. Social heuristics may be thought of in similar terms. They provide all adult members of a culture an enormous compendium of "cookbook" knowledge and a wide variety of "tried and true" assumptions for dealing with the decision problems of everyday life. Different heuristics have varying degrees of social communality. "You better go to college!" is, in our culture, a heuristic with very high communality. It is often told young adolscents with no particular plans for the future, and regardless of their talents. Various food taboos, in our culture, have variable communality. But they all have a common outcome: restricting or narrowing down a range of possible choices.

A critical feature of high communality heuristics is that they are deeply intertwined with elemental aspects of social structure, such as particular modes of production, divisions of labor, and caste, class, and age relations. Among orthodox Jews, for example, the rules of kashruth or food heuristics are tied to seasons, group relations, and specialized roles for food handlers. More commonly, gender heuristics — perhaps the most powerful of all social heuristics — have acted throughout history to restrict the roles of males and females to broad classes of life and career choices. High communality heuristics, necessarily deeply embedded in social structure, are extraordinarily resistent to social change. There are many ways to argue why this is the case, but for our purposes they boil down to one: high communality heuristics serve many people's interests.

The kinds of social heuristics we are concerned with here are related to the attainment and occupancy of Master Statuses. Though it is changing, our culture, like others, maintains a basic "cookbook" of ingredients for the occupants of Master Statuses. These ingredients can be thought of as attributes of an abstract person who can (correctly) occupy the status. In some cases the ingredients, or attributes, are simply viewed as "probably needed." For example, being tall is "probably needed" for becoming a Pro Basketball player. Or being in debt is "probably needed" for becoming an embezzler. In other cases, the attributes are viewed as "almost certainly needed." For example, being a good talker is "almost certainly needed" for becoming a politician, or being sexually frustrated is "almost certainly needed" for becoming a rapist. Finally, the attributes seem "definitely needed." Being over 18 is requisite for being an army officer, or being a woman is (was?) requisite for being a housekeeper, or having a law degree seems requisite for being a lawyer (though it is actually not).

Though we have illustrated the idea by using categories like "probably needed" and so on, in the general case we would like to envision the attribute-MS relation as a probabilistic one. That is, we want to be theoretically free enough to imagine any conceivable attribute A as tied to any Master Status with a probability ranging from 0 (no tie) to 1 (perfect tie). Clearly, social heuristics narrow down the range of likely, possible, and impossible attributes for various Master Statuses. In doing so, these heuristics tend to establish bi-directional links between Master Statuses and human attributes. By this we mean that if a Master Status, A, implies an attribute B (with probability X), then that attribute, B, is likely to imply that Master Status, A (with probability Y). For example, the status Electrical Engineer implies the attribute Male (with probability X), and the attribute Male implies the status Electrical Engineer (with probability Y). In this case, the "front" (or MS-to-attribute) probability is pretty high in our culture, while the "back" (or attribute-to-MS) probability is much lower.

Heuristics linking Master Statuses and attributes involve images of psychological and physical features of ideal-type incumbents. These features, in turn, may be thought of as being variously, "demographable" to the population at large. In some cases, the mental graphing is easy: the mathematical attributes which are tied to Electrical Engineer are easily "demographed" onto the dimension Gender, with the ensuing image "Male". In other cases, the mental graphing is hard: the meticulous attributes tied to Electrical Engineer are not so easily "demographed" onto Gender, or other demographic dimensions. It can thus be said that MSs distribute attributes at the level of the ideal-type individual, but that these attributes have various demographic aspects to them — like gender, age, education, income, race, etc. In the following, our stress will be on these demographic aspects.

The Concepts of Type/Countertype

Contemporary psychology and social-psychology contain mountains of work on the notion of stereotyping. Much of this effort has been traditionally focused on the question: "What attributes of a personality do people perceive as going together?" For example, if I believe a person is "warm," am I then likely to think of that person as "intelligent" or "lazy"? Related work can be found in sociology proper, including Schutz's (1964) on typification. Much of this effort has focused on what we have called social heuristics: mapping rules which, by typifying features of the social landscape, simplify everyday life and create the appearance of order and regularity. In an important sense, this work, too, looks at "things which go together," or, in our terms, phenomena which are tied — As and Bs with relatively high probability relations.

The general thrust of this kind of work has clearly informed attempts to study bias in status processing. In the courts, for example, the conceptual language for observing race bias is framed inevitably in terms of "social typing," "stereotyping," and the like. The same is true for the workplace and, say, studies of gender discrimination. Yet, as we argued initially, such work is not very satisfying. Part of the reason for this, we think, lies in starting from the conventional question of what attributes "go with" what statuses. Suppose, instead, we started from a different point and asked the less obvious questions: what attributes are "not supposed to go with" what statuses?

In answer, we do not propose a list, but rather, the general idea that social regularities are as much defined by "non-tied" phenomena as by "tied" phenomena (as a forest is as much defined by spaces between trees as by the trees themselves). This basic point can be found in White et al.'s (1976) brilliant and paradagmatic breakthrough in the modeling of social networks, where the absence of ties between individuals — and not ties — are taken as the basic unit of input in model construction. Additional clarification comes from Gestalt psychology. Here a Gestalt, or whole picture, is conceived of as composed of two basic parts, figure (or foreground) and ground (or background). Though people appear to "find and name" a Gestalt on the putative basis of figure, from this holistic perspective it makes little sense to think of figure without ground or ground without figure. That is, a "good" Gestalt must have a clear background in order to have any kind of (perceived) foreground, or, more radically, to form any kind of "picture" at all.

In present terms, this means that sensible heuristics for Master Status attributes must also rely on "background" assumptions, assumptions about particular attributes which "do not go with" particular statuses. We do not, for example, expect the attribute "Ph.D." for the status Car Mechanic or the attribute "Black" for the status Embezzler. Though we might call these "non-tied" attributes "background" assumptions in the Gestalt tradition, we will not. Instead, we will call them "countertypical." The reason for doing so is that, in everyday social life, as opposed to textbook Gestalt theory, many "bad" Gestalts actually occur. That is, in modern social life, a variety of Master Statuses end up being filled by incumbents with less than ideal-type attributes. Because of our stress on the demographic aspect of these "bad" Gestalts, we will think of such social anomalies as *Countertypes*.

Coining concepts is usually not a good idea unless the concept provides a new way of of seeing previously hard-to-explain phenomena. In the case of bias in MSAPs, we think the concept of Countertype provides that kind of cutting-edge. What shall prove particularly useful is the concept's ability to (a) help portray the ways in which processors attribute motives to the cases they process, and, consequently, (b) help understand bias as a dynamic problem in status processing.

SIMPLIFYING THE MODEL: HEURISTICS & PROCESS

We have noted several times that in its complexity the rational model presented earlier seems to require a great deal from processor. On the surface this complexity appears to be a function of the sheer number of "calculations" demanded by the model. But this is only a surface view. The conclusion is misleading, and is so in a very important way. Many social scientists, sociologists in particular, are often quite resistant to what we will call a "high agency" view of human action — a view which allows the average actor the possibility of high levels of complex judgmental ability. Almost certainly a denial of self-knowledge, this resistance is in large measure a byproduct of intellectual heritage: certain ways of aggregating social phenomena seem to preclude the "high agency" view. And, to some extent, it also represents the failure of relevant theory (in, say, the area of cognitive psychology) to develop conceptual imagery which is readily portable to macro-social levels of aggregation.

There is ample evidence that people are capable of evaluating relatively complex bundles of information in decision-making (cf. Ofshe and

Ofshe, 1970; Anderson et al. 1983; Leik and Gifford, in this volume). The real question, we believe, lies not in the structure of the processing "machinery," but in the nature and source of acceptable information to put into it. In modeling any phenomenon, a strong distinction must be made between structural and input parameters. The rational model we have presented involves a series of interrelated structural parameters — a machine, as it were, for processing information. But this machine goes nowhere without that information. And that is precisely where the model's complexity lies — not in the internal capabilities of Mind, but in the supply of information to be processed. It is here, in terms of input parameters, that the heuristics of Type/Countertype come into play.

By definition, decision-making problems involve at least two choices. In our earlier discussion we had one occasion to frame this as a problem in choosing person X vs. person Y (in discussing opportunity cost, p. 21). For the most part, however, we stuck to a different way of framing the choice dilemma: as a problem to pass or drop Case X, based on whether X would Show or Not Show the trait(s) in question, and so on. As it turns out, these alternative ways of seeing the choice problem are at the heart of the question of the model's complexity. For in framing the choice problem as a problem in passing or dropping Case X — a necessary approach at the time — we posed what is surely an empirically comparative question as a theoretical absolute. That is, in real life the question tends not to be "Should I pass Case X? " but rather, "Should I pass Case X compared to Case Y?" In short, the problem needs "relativizing."

Whether one's conceptual heritage comes from cognitive psychology or from reference group theory, it is clear that people anchor or reference their judgments in comparisons. A is tall because A is taller than others. B is rich because B makes more money than C, D, E . . . Z. Steak is better than hamburger. An extra $100 would mean more to a poor than a rich person, and so on. We believe this is also the case in MSAP decisions. Rather than self-anchoring or referencing the decision problem of Case X against Case X (S vs. $\overline{S}$), it is far easier to anchor or reference Case X against Case Y, especially if social heuristics provide some short-cuts. In so doing, we shall argue, processors find a double anchor-point: (1) the reference of Type against Countertype, and (2) the reference of both against Process Stage.

Given this basic orientation, it is possible to "use" the rational model presented earlier and generate a set of expectations about the production of bias in MSAPs. Several fundamental ideas guide these expectations.

First, the notion of Type/Countertype provides processor a useful heuristic for distributing virtually all the input parameters of the model's major elements — the chances of Case Showing or Not Showing the trait(s) in question (P'), the payoff returned to processor for good (and bad) decisions (U), and the estimated chances (P'') of processor receiving that payoff. Consider the following illustrations:

Ex.1: It is the mid 1930's. Dr. S., director of admissions at a prestigious medical school, has one slot left to fill for the entering class. On paper, his two most promising candidates are about evenly matched, M, who is male, and F, who is female. It is an agonizing decision but he admits the male. He is questioned about this only by his wife. He responds: "In the end, I thought she would buckle under the strain of being the only woman in the class. Besides, it is not clear that people are ready to have a woman as their doctor; we may have done her a favor." Though some self-doubt remains, Dr. S. goes to bed "knowing" that M will bring credit to the school and that if F does succeed in medicine elsewhere, his decision not to admit her was "perfectly understandable to anyone in medicine."

Ex.2: It is mid 1950's. DR, an 8th grade music teacher, has enthusiastically supported the prospects of two flautists, W, who is White, and B, who is Black. One day, DR receives a call from a famous high school for the performing arts, where both students are applicants. Both are under serious consideration, but there is only room for one; would DR mind writing on behalf of the better candidate? The decision is difficult, but DR writes on behalf of the White. She is questioned about this only by her husband. She responds: "I thought B might buckle under the pressure of being the only Negro in the program. Besides, it is not clear the world is ready for a Negro flautist; I may have done him a favor." Though some self-doubt remains, DR goes to bed "knowing" that W will bring a credit to her and the school, and that if B were to succeed as a flautist anyway, DR's decision was "perfectly understandable to anyone who knows the world of music."

Ex.3: It is the mid 1970's. WH, bureau chief of the San Francisco office of the U.S. Secret Service and charged with security on the President's upcoming visit to the city, has read through the dossiers of 40 "possibles" presently under surveillance. That afternoon he is visited by SM, a woman and previous FBI informant. She tells him she knows the President is coming to town and that she has a gun in her pocketbook. WH tells her to take better care of herself and not worry about things. She leaves, but telephones the next day and repeats the message. WH informs an aide to keep an eye out on her if possible. The President arrives. On the street after addressing a luncheon meeting, he is shot at and missed 3 times by SM. Under harsh questioning by a Senate committee, WH responds: "Senator, she just did not fit our profile. If we had to do it again, we would probably do the same thing." Though some self-doubt remains, WH goes to bed "knowing" that the mistake will not cost him his job and that the decision not to bring SM into protective custody was "perfectly understandable to anyone who knows the risks."

A second basic idea, related to the notion of Type/Countertype and to what we earlier termed the "highly self-referential" character of status processing, will also guide the forthcoming discussion of bias. In the three illustrations just cited, we intended to portray processor as "forward looking," that is, as informed about, and comfortable with, the likely impact of present decisions on future events. But these illustrations do not really convey what is meant by the idea of highly self-referential processing. For each of the illustrations fails to identify processor's concern for the implications of processing decisions which preceded the present "receipt" of particular Types and Countertypes. And each of the illustrations fails to identify processor's assessment — at a decision point in what is known to be a process with a long past and probably longer future — of how it is possible to have "received" any Countertypes at all! To illustrate this point, we will use only two examples, one from a valuing MSAP and one from a disvaluing MSAP. But we will do something different in the examples, by taking snapshots of a single case at several steps along the way.

> Ex.1. Node 1: It is the early 1960's in JFK, a large urban Jr. High. The school's population is 12% Black, 88% White. George B., a Black male, impresses his teachers with his skills in English. TK, the guidance counselor, recommends that he enroll in a class in advanced English composition, where he will be the only Black among 15 students.
>
> Node 2: In 1965, George B. is a senior at Minuet High, one of the best public schools in the country. The school's population is 6% Black, 94% White. George is currently enrolled in a class on Shakespeare with 29 Whites, and has applied to Ivy with an expressed interest in majoring in English. RP, an admissions officer at Ivy, is troubled. He has seen only 2 similar applicants in the past 5 years, both of whom were rejected. On the one hand, George B.'s record, from a very competitive high school, is quite strong. On the other, his SATs are no higher than the national average. RP decides to save the case for last, at which point he compares it to the strongest remaining White's record. RP decides to take a chance on George B. and urges acceptance.
>
> Node 3: In 1969, Goerge B is a senior at Ivy. The school's population is 3% Black, 97% White. Of 120 graduating English majors, he is 1 of only 2 Blacks. MB, admissions director of Princeton's graduate program in English, has received George's application and is troubled. The last Black applicant to the department, 9 years ago, was Jamaican and a Rhodes scholar. MB is generally impressed with George's record at Ivy, but is somewhat concerned about his GREs and career interests in the Elizabethan period. MB leaves the case for last. After phoning a friend in the English department at Ivy, MB compares the case to the strongest remaining White. Largely based on the phone call and his intuition, MB concludes that George has

sufficient drive to complete the program and pursue a career in English, despite the apparent problems. MB argues the case for George B.

Node 4: In 1975, George B., the only Black in Princeton's graduate English program, is finishing his Ph.D. dissertation and applying for a teaching position. TW, chair of recruiting at Stanford's English department, has received George's application and is troubled. The department has never hired a Black, for lack of suitable qualifications. Yet the deparment is under strong administrative pressure to comply with Affirmative Action guidelines. TW is impressed with George's academic history, but is somewhat critical of the large amount of published work that George has submitted with his application. After a phone call to MB, TW concludes that George B. is a very highly motivated though not first-rate candidate. Warning his committee that George B. may be a bit of an opportunist and trying to capitalize on being Black, TW nonetheless makes the positive case for George and recommends hiring.

Ex.2. Node 1. It is the early 1960's in JFK, a large urban Jr. High. The school's population is 50% female, 50% male. Mary K., a White 12-year old, has been doing reasonably well in school. One day she is found beating a neighbor's child with a stick. The child is treated for neck and scalp lacerations. After much discussion with Mary and her parents, the beaten child's parents decide to keep the incident between them, assured that it was a behavioral aberration related to temporary stress.

Node 2. A year later, Mary is seen attempting to steal a radio from an unlocked car. The car's owner, LW, calls the police. They arrive and ask Mary K. where she goes to school and what her father does. After severely admonishing her, one officer ask LW if the radio "looks okay" and, after privately telling LW that "the girl may have been punished enough," asks him if he would still like to press charges. LW is troubled but concludes that he will not.

Node 3. In 1965, Mary K. is a senior at FDR High, and has been arrested for selling marijuana. The public prosecutor for juvenile court, FM, has considered 500 similar cases that past year, 450 of which were male and 50 female. After discussion with Mary's parents, FM agrees to not go forward with the case if her parents agree that they will supervise her more closely and, as a family, see a court-appointed social worker every week.

Node 4. In 1975, Mary, K., who is now married and works as a hair stylist, has been found guilty of breaking and entering and assault with a deadly weapon. The presiding judge, JS, has considered 500 or so similar cases in his career, 480 of which were male and 20 female. JW is especially troubled because he has never seen a female defendant before who has the come all the way up through plea bargaining on a "solo B & E." Considering the physical harm done the victim and Mary's "potentially irremediable" profile, she is judged by JS to be a clear and present danger to the community and sentenced to 20 years in prison, the maximum penalty under state law.

Though these examples do not effectively illustrate the usefulness of Type/Countertype as a decision heuristic, they do portray the major imagery we are after at the moment — the idea that processing decisions are highly self-referential. The choice of Countertype persona in both cases helps reinforce the point. As later and later nodes in an MSAP are reached, Countertypes become increasingly rare. The appearance of a "late node" Countertype provides a unique set of signals to processor, suggesting that precisely because prior processing is ordinarily so selective against Countertypes, any remaining ones are, so to speak, special birds requiring special treatment.

This brings us to our third and last basic point. In combination with the rational model, the Type/Countertype heuristic generates expectations about bias in MSAPs. Our "snapshot" examples focused on two imaginary Countertypes and decisions about them. In both cases, it was also our intention to imply that, at successive nodes in the MSAP, each Countertype represented a successively smaller proportion of all cases reviewed by processor. Given the dynamics of processor's perception of cases across nodes, this suggests that Countertypes will be "treated" differently at successive nodes. In itself, this idea has critically important implications for understanding bias in MSAPs.

In the early stages of processing, we should expect that, compared to the proportion of Types forwarded (Passed), the proportion of Countertypes forwarded will be relatively low. According to our definition of Process Bias — numerical inequality in the comparative transition probabilities of groups matched for "true" MS-relevant traits (p. 8) — this means that in the early stages of processing (compared to the later stages) high levels of bias will be produced. And this should be the case for both valued and disvalued MSAPs.

In the later stages of processing, however, we should expect that, compared to Types, the proportion of Countertypes forwarded (Passed) will be relatively high, and even approach parity. According to our definition of Process Bias, this means that in the later stages of processing (compared to the earlier) low levels of bias will be produced. And, again, this should be the case for both valued and disvalued MSAPs.

The net effect of the argument is clear and somewhat counter-intuitive. Once we take an observer's seat at the "next to last" node of an MSAP, we should expect to see two basic phenomena: (1) far higher proportions of Types to Countertypes than in the population of large, and, paradoxically, (2) far more equitable treatment of the (few) remaining Countertypes than at earlier nodes. Obviously this position has major implications for theory, research, and social policy. Eventually we shall draw out some of the more important ones. For the moment, however, what has been said informally needs to be said more formally. Based on the rational model and the Type/Countertype heuristic, in the following we identify the specific form of our expectations for bias in status processing decisions.

EXPECTATIONS FOR BIAS IN PROCESSING DECISIONS

MSAPs occur over a series of decision nodes. Our general expectation is that, although outcome bias accumulates across these nodes, additional ("new") bias in status processing decisions (SPDs) lessens at successive nodes in a kind of Darwinian fashion. In order to detail the argument, it will help if we can offer a substantive sense of what these nodes might generally look like. We stress that, while typological features of this identification are not terribly critical to the theory or its operational assessment, assumptions about the metric underlying the nodes are.

Five nodes (and four transitions) are identified: (1) an informal node, where processing agents (parents, teachers, victims of crimes) act to facilitate or hinder, encourage or discourage, the forwarding of cases to (2) a monitoring node, where processing agents (college admissions officers, police) act to facilitate or block the receipt of cases from (1) and their forwarding to (3) a pre-conferring node, where processing agents (college faculty, public prosecutors) act to certify cases as having the trait(s) in question to a sufficient degree to warrant further transmission to (4) a conferring node, where processing agents (graduate faculty, bar examiners, judges) act to confer or not confer (5) Master Statuses (Ph.D., LL.D., Convict).

We shall assume that an equal-interval metric underlies the nodes. (Though we do not have sound theoretical reasons for doing so, we do not have sound reasons for doing otherwise.) It will eventually be seen that because our expectations are monotonic with process, alternative assumptions about the nodal metric would not do major violence to them. At this point, theoretical development centers around the application of the Type/Countertype heuristic to the rational model in 3 related areas: (1) the estimated probability that case will Show the trait(s) in question (P'), (2) processor's expected payoffs (U, P''), and (3) the consequent production of bias.

(1) Process and P': Expectations for a "Show"

It will be recalled that processor's estimated probability that a passed case will Show the trait(s) in question was given by the function,

$$P' = f(\text{ProbC}, U^{*\prime}, \text{IM}) \tag{15.}$$

where each term indicated a processor estimate, ProbC represented probable capacity for a Show, U^*' represented External or Rational Motivation (expected utility), and IM represented Intrinsic or Irrational Motivation. Let us look at each element in turn, beginning with the conceptually pivotal element U^*'.

It was indicated (p.31, (17.)) that U^*', or Attributed External Motivation, was a joint product of 4 terms: Prob', U', PC_3 and PC_4. Figure 8. (A) suggests that Prob', or processor's estimate of case's subjective payoff chances for a Show, is a positive but decelerating function of process. Reliance on our key heuristic also suggests that, while the Prob' gap between Type and Countertype is estimated by initial processors as quite high, with successive stages of processing that gap lessens and approaches parity.

Several concepts guide these expectations. First, selectivity and proportion of MSAP completed (PC_3 and PC_4) clearly suggest that progressively smaller, more highly "selected" pools of MS incumbents at successive nodes in both valued and disvalued MSAPs are increasingly likely to receive a payoff (utility or disutility) for a Show, and actually "know" this. Expressed somewhat differently, at any node a set of cases can be seen as having an empirical mean on Prob' and, at successive nodes, this mean increases. This translates to the expectation that the first slope of Prob' on process is positive.

Second, while proportion of MSAP completed (PC_4) is likely to lead to processors at successive nodes in both valued and disvalued MSAPs attributing higher and higher levels of Prob' to the groups of cases they receive, in producing more highly "selected" incumbent pools, selectivity (PC_3) simultaneously raises the level of "competition" for those payoffs. (These payoffs involve any outcome constrained in its capacity for empirical distribution, including such highly negative outcomes as a term in prison.) Expressed somewhat differently, at any node a set of cases can be seen as having their empirical mean on Prob' set in reference to the current group of cases and, at successive nodes, this reference group sets "higher" standards. This translates to the expectation that the second slope of Prob' on process is negative.

Third, social heuristic imply and reinforce the notion that both valued and disvalued MSAPs are not simply selective, but differentially selective vis-a-vis Type and Countertype. In Figure 8. (A), we represent processor as "believing" that Types and Countertypes are, in the aggregate, "realistic" in their assessments of Prob'. As such, Countertypes in the aggregate are attributed lower subjectively perceived chances of payoffs for a Show — that is, as perceptually aligned with real-world outcomes.

It is important to note that we believe this assumption works best under the condition that the relevant Types and Countertypes "include"

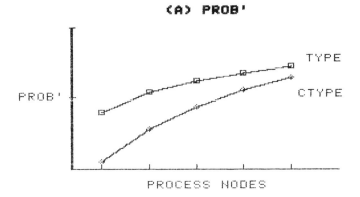

(A) PROB'

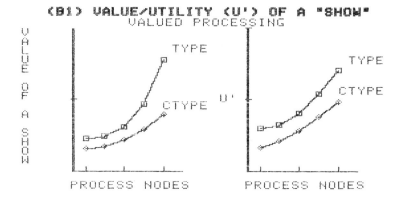

(B1) VALUE/UTILITY (U') OF A "SHOW"

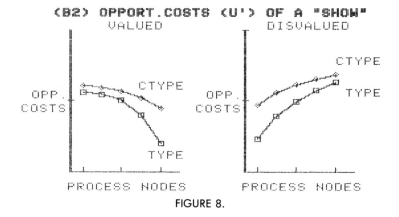

(B2) OPPORT.COSTS (U') OF A "SHOW"

FIGURE 8.

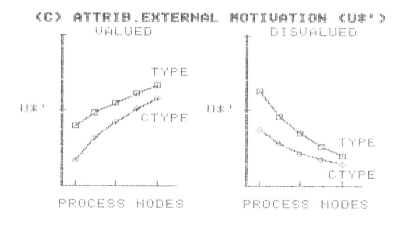

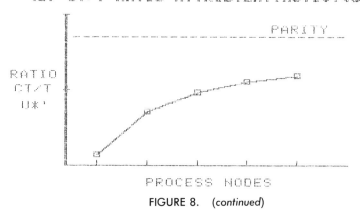

FIGURE 8. (continued)

each other as reference groups. For example, when gender is a major element distributing Type/Countertype for a Master Status, as in the case of, say, Lawyer, the assumption works easily. This is probably because of the constant integration of genders at home and in school. When a factor such as race, however, is a major element distributing Type/Countertype for an MS, like Lawyer, the assumption works less easily. Evidence from Rosenberg and Simmons (1971), for example, suggests that it is not until the 12th grade that Blacks in the aggregate come to appraise their chances of going to college "realistically." Though this is not the same thing as estimating the chances of U given the achievement of an MS (e.g., receiving gains and/or costs after becoming a lawyer), it does suggest that our assumption works best when those being processed are lead — by settings or events — to "integrate" their reference groups to include Types and Countertypes.

Figure 8.(B1), actually two figures, visually portrays cross-process expectations for processor's attribution of U', or the estimated Utility returned to case for a Show in valued processing. (We will come to the disvalued processing analogy in a moment.) The left figure establishes a guideline for the right. The left indicates the general shape of expectations for "objective value" (money/prestige) returned for a Show (C_1 in Figure 6, p. 29). It is based on recent work exploring actual dollar returns on years of education in the U.S., where the estimated power functions are for White males (here, Types) and Black males (here, Countertypes; Leik and Meeker, 1975). This figure clearly shows an increasing income difference (between "Types" and "Countertypes") as education ("process") increases, and is reasonably extrapolated to the present context.

But classical economics teaches us that value is not utility, and that utility is most likely best represented as a logarithmic function of value. The right figure, then, is no more than a simple logarithmic transform of the left figure. The major difference between the two is that the log transform tends to exaggerate differences at lower levels of value and flatten out differences at the upper levels, and therefore, to produce more extreme differences between Type and Countertype at the early stages of processing and less extreme differences at the later stages. (For valuing, though not disvaluing processes. Affirmative Action policies tend to flatten out these upper-end differences too, while leaving lower-end differences alone; cf. Wilson, 1978).

What of the estimate of U' in disvalued processing? Here the going gets a bit tougher. If we were to limit disvalued processing solely to MSAPs which had clear economically productive components for their incumbents, such as Thief or Bank Robber, we might be reasonably satisfied with Figure 8. (B1) as a guideline for U' in disvalued processing. (Suggesting perhaps the career trajectories of Type vs. Countertype in the Mafia, e.g., men vs. women). But his would be misleading for several reasons. First, we are referring to legitimate, institutionalized Master Status processing. In the case of disvalued processing, this means that when use the term "Show the trait(s) in question," we are not referring to a display of criminal or mentally ill behavior for an appreciative audience, but, rather, an audience (perhaps as small as one) predisposed to treating the display in a manner ranging from indifferent to strongly hostile. Second, by not limiting MSAPs — notably disvalued ones — to Masters Statuses with economically productive elements, we have tried to allow our conceptual framework as much scope as possible. At the moment, the cost of doing so would seem to lie in our ability to go past the economically based rationality of Figure

8. (B1), and find alternative grounds for our expectations, or different expectations altogether.

Or so it would seem. As it turns out, we have merely looked at the "upside"of economically based rationality, not the "downside." Earlier (p. 28), we indicated that U' is both a function of the estimated value of a Show (C_1) and its opportunity cost to case (C_2). Figure 8. (B2), again actually two figures, shows our expectations for processor's attribution of these costs across process.

The left figure, for valued processing, is no more than a conceptual isomorph of the left figure in 8. (B1). It suggests that, as the value (V) of a Show increases across the MSAP, the value of bypasssed alternatives — as a proportion of V — decreases. Since the proposition here involves simply inverting V, the figure shows estimated case opportunity costs (again, as a proportion of V) negatively accelerating with process, and as higher for Countertypes than Type, (Note that if we construed the U' problem as U' "net of" gains (B1) and costs (B2), the effect of conjoining the left figures in (B1) and (B2) would be to produce "net value" curves which were more pronounced than, but in the same family of power curves as, those in (B1).)

In the case of valued processing, the inclusion of opportunity costs does not add a great deal to the argument. But their inclusion is important for disvalued processing. To make this clear, however, we first need to make clear a major assymetry between the two kinds of processing: in the case of valued processing, both the gains and costs referred to accrue to what from the case's perspective is the "successful" display of the trait(s) in question, but, in the case of disvalued processing, we have deliberately limited ourselves to the costs which accrue to what from case's perspective is the "unsuccessful" display of the trait(s) in question — that is, the costs of "being caught."

This discrepancy implies that, because of shared definitions of "success," it far is easier for valued MSAP processors than disvalued MSAP processors to project "into the minds" of their cases. Be this as it may, the punitive/rehabilitative interests of disvalued processors — we argue — establish a focus on the analagous elements in case, the "downside" fear of getting wrapped up in disvalued processing. Though less likely continuous with case's perceptions than in valued processing, the perceptions of processor in disvalued processing still govern the situation. This boils down to the proposition that, in disvalued MSAPs, processors will base U' primarily on the "downside" logic of case's getting caught. As such, and despite the fact that getting caught is not necessarily the only cost in town (a thief could be a failure without ever getting caught), we also expect processors in disvalued MSAPs to estimate Prob' from this perspective. (This does not suggest a change in Figure 8. (A)'s expectations for disvalued processing, merely a refinement of their conceptual grounds.)

Having clarified this major asymmetry, a glance at the right figure in 8. (B2) seems to produce a new one. But actually it is not. The figure portrays our expectations for the process-wide attribution of opportunity costs to cases in disvalued MSAPs. It suggests that such costs, like Prob', are a positive but decelerating function of process. Our key heuristic also suggests that, while the U' (cost) gap is estimated by initial processors as high, with successive levels of disvalued processing the gap lessens.

Quite possibly, this figure best illustrates the usefulness of the Type/Countertype heuristic. The key concept here lies in the recognition of "disvalued processing" as exactly that, an MSAP which lowers the value of its incumbents (much as valued processing raises that value). Allowing proportion of MSAP completed (PC_4) into the picture means the receipt, at successive nodes, of cases who have in the aggregate received higher levels of disvaluation than those at previous nodes. Framed in terms of opportunity costs, and following a major irony in labeling theory (cf. Schur, 1971), this translates to the assumption that movement across successive disvalued MSAP nodes decreases the value of a case's alternatives to the presumed trait(s) which got him or her there in the first place.

The additional overlay of Type/Countertype heuristic suggests that successive processing (Passing) increases Type costs at a faster rate than those for Countertype, but that Countertype costs are uniformly higher than those for Type. Since "stopping" cases from displaying the disvalued trait(s) in question is the putative goal of disvalued MSAPs, this idea had very important implications for SPDs in disvalued processing. For it suggests that a "little bit" of punishment will go "a longer way" for Countertype than Type and, in disvaluing processes, simply being in process (for example, having been arrested) should be construed as punishment in its own right. Expressed somewhat differently, given total discretion, the assumption that such processing is intrinsically (and increasingly) punishing, and a genuine interest in "stopping" repeat displays, we should expect processors in disvalued processing to find functional and "just" equivalence in dropping Countertypes at early nodes, and Types at later ones. Given these implications, the actual receipt of Countertypes at the tail-end of processing — that is, receipt of the very small number who have remained in process — must be taken as a signal to processors in disvalued MSAPs that they have been handed some very "hard" cases to deal with.

The product of U' and Prob' yields a near approximation of U*', or Attributed External (Rational) Motivation. Figure 8. (C) shows consequent expectations for U*' across both valued and disvalued processing. (The right hand figure is an inversion of the corresponding figure in 8. (B2).)

It should be clear that, in both cases, Type is atrributed more "rational" motivation than Countertype, but that, with additional processing, Countertype approaches Type. Though not shown, this approach toward parity might be thought of as having a confidence band around it (established by PC_3 and PC_4). At successive nodes, this band should be expected to narrow, implying greater and greater certainty that the relevant estimates are reasonable. Taking a ratio of Countertype to Type expectations for U*' yields Figure 8. (D). It makes a relatively long story short by suggesting that, at successive nodes in processing, received groups of Types and Countertypes tend to look more and more similar in terms of the level of "rational" motivation they are attributed. The heuristic may therefore be said to become less and less "useful" to processors at successive nodes. (The greater the ratio's distance from parity, the more "useful" it is and, consequently, the more bias it is capable of producing.)

But still, the figure deliberately implies that parity on U*' is difficult to reach within the bounds of conventional processing. The present theory, however, says that another major element enters the picture here: Attributed Internal (or Irrational) Motivation. Statement (16.) on p.31 indicates that this element, IM, is an inverse function of U*' and conditioned by nodal characteristics (PC_3 and PC_4).

Though the precise functional form of our expectations are dependent, in the end, on assumed weights, the basic form our expectation for IM is shown in Figure 9. (A). The figure portrays IM as rising for both Type and Countertypes across nodes, but as only slightly so for Types and radically so for Countertypes. Both curves indicate the increase as accelerating, though the rate of acceleration is shown as much higher for Countertypes. Consistent with prior reasoning, we show attributed motivation to Type as higher than to Countertype. Here, though we admit to an equilibration problem (i.e. relative intercepts on the Y-axis), our justification lies essentially in the idea that it is generally extraordinarily difficult for processors to take Countertypes seriously at the early stages of processing, even in terms of attributing them irrational motivation for "being there." (The preference being for "random" or "accidental" cause.)

Combining IM with U*' across process leads to an expectation for overall attributed motivation, shown in 9.(B). Compared to Figure 8.(A), the net effect is some linearization but retained signs on slopes. Again, the expectation is for positive but decelerating levels of attribution across process, with overall attribution of "motive force" to Type consistently higher than to Countertype. From the perspective of bias production, the important thing to note, once more, is the hypothesized convergence of the curves. This is summarized in Figure 9.(C) as a trace of the ratio of the curves in 9.(B). We have deliberately implied that this ratio, which

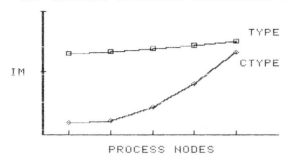

(A) ATTRIB. INTERNAL MOTIVATION (IM)

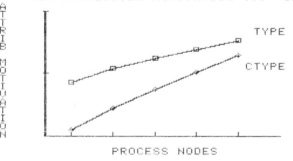

(B) ATTRIBUTED MOTIVATION (U*'+IM)

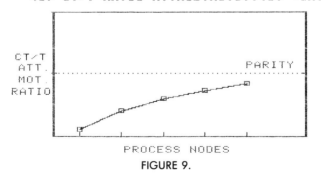

(C) CT/T RATIO ATTRIB.MOTIV.(U*'+IM)

FIGURE 9.

now includes both motivational elements, comes closer to parity than the ratio for U*' alone (Figure 8.(D)).

We are thus ready to infer to the final element in the chain of argument, P' or processor's estimate that a case will Show the trait(s) in question. Since we assume that ProbC (Figure 6) — or case's capacity for Show — has the same contours and justification as Prob' (see the discussion on pp. 28–31 and pp. 44–47), the final combination of U*', IM, and ProbC, leads to the expectation indicated in Figure 10.

The figure indicates that we expect an important process-wide change in the relative balance of P' estimates favoring the Passing of Types over Countertypes. In the early stages of MSAPs, processors will be inclined overall to estimate substantially higher chances of a Show to Types than to Countertypes. Processors will thus have a major preference for Passing Types forward in much higher proportion to their population rates than comparable groups of Countertypes. At later stages of MSAPs, however, processors will be inclined overall to estimate more nearly equal chances of a Show to Type and Countertype. This implies that, at these nodes, processors will have a preference for Passing Types and Countertypes forward in equal or near proportion to their relative frequencies at "point of receipt." Rather than indicate a precise relation between P' parity and process — which, we stress, is not important for the theory — Figure 10 indicates that this trend should be construed as continuous, upward, and decelerating toward parity within a band. The figure also suggests that this band may actually cross the parity threshold and that, therefore, at late nodes of processing, Countertypes may be attributed higher levels of P' than Types.

Two major ironies mark these observations. The first concerns process bias and involves Figure 10's expectation of ever-increasing P' parity between Types and Countertypes across process nodes. Though the implication here is for ever-increasing equity, there is just so much equity a processor at the final node of an MSAP can hand out across Types and Countertypes if he or she has "received" cases at a ratio of the magnitude 20:1, Types to Countertypes. The second irony involves the basis for the implied bias expectation in Figure 10, and goes back to the very beginning of our argument. For it was there that we reasoned that bias should not be seen as the outcome of an abitrary or malicious quirk of personality, or as the capricious application of a double-standard. At this point, there is enough development in our thesis to see that once the Type/Countertype heuristic is in place, Status Processing Decisions can both meet the demands of careful and rational subjective accounting *and* produce biased outcomes at the same time.

Narrative in this section concerned P', or only one of several major elements in the rational model. Again relying on Type/Countertype, in

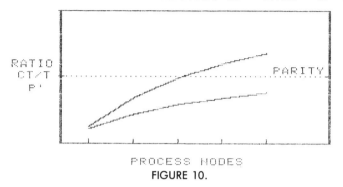

CT/T RATIO EST.CHANCES OF "SHOW" (P')

RATIO
CT/T
P'

PARITY

PROCESS MODES
FIGURE 10.

the next section we will discuss the remaining ones, U or utility returned to processor good and bad decisions, and P'' or the perceived chances of receiving U. Before proceeding, there is some concern that the reader may over-interpret the graphic form of the expectations generated in this section. The theory behind these expectations is essentially a theory of changing ratios, such as the CT/T ratio of Attributed External Motivation, and not a theory at the level of intercepts or precise structural parameters. This means that the most appropriate form of our expectations is not a graphic one, but is, instead, a set of comparative statements about slopes and their rates of change. For readers comfortable with this approach, the following set of differential inequalities provides the more appropriate expression. (Readers uncomfortable with this approach may skip to the next section, but are forewarned not to confuse the general theory with a visual representation.)

It will be recalled that:

$$P' = f(ProbC, U^{*'}, IM) \qquad (15.)$$

where

$$IM = g(-U^{*'} \cdot (PC_3, PC_4)) \qquad (16.)$$

$$U^{*'} = h(U' \cdot Prob'(PC_3, PC_4)) \qquad (17.)$$

where

$$U' = i(C_1, C_2) \qquad (18.)$$

$$ProbC = j(C_3 \cdot (PC_3, PC_4)) \qquad (19.)$$

$$\text{Prob}' = k(C_3, PC_3, PC_4) \tag{20.}$$

Denoting Process as P, Countertype as CT, and Type as T, for $U^{*\prime}$ it is argued that:

$$\text{Prob}'_T > \text{Prob}'_{CT} > 0.00 \tag{21.}$$

$$d\text{Prob}'_{CT}/dP > d\text{Prob}'_T/dP > 0.00 > \\ d''\text{Prob}'_T/dP'' > d''\text{Prob}'_{CT}/dP'' \tag{22.}$$

and

$$U'_T > U'_{CT} > 0.00 \tag{23.}$$

where for valued processes

$$dU'_T/dP > dU'_{CT}/dP > 0.00 \tag{24.}$$

and

$$d''U_T/dP'' > d''U'_{CT}/dP'' > 0.00 \tag{25.}$$

but for disvalued processes

$$0.00 > dU'_T/dP > dU'_{CT}/dP \tag{26.}$$

and

$$d''U'_T/dP'' > d''U'_{CT}/dP'' > 0.00 \tag{27.}$$

thus

$$d(U^{*\prime}_{CT}/U^{*\prime}_T)/dP > 0.00 > d''(U^{*\prime}_{CT}/U^{*\prime}_T) \mid dp \tag{28.}$$

Using the same notation, for IM and ProbC:

$$IM_T > IM_{CT} > 0.00 \tag{29.}$$

$$d'IM_{CT}/dP > d'IM_T/dP > 0.00 \tag{30.}$$

and

$$d''IM_{CT}/dP'' > d''IM_T/dP'' > 0.00 \tag{31.}$$

thus

$$d(IM_{CT}/IM_T)dP, d''(IM_{CT}/IM_T)/dP'' > 0.00 \tag{32.}$$

and

$$ProbC_T > ProbC_{CT} > 0.00 \tag{33.}$$

$$dProbC_{CT}/dP > dProbC_T/dP > 0.00 >$$
$$d''ProbC_T/dP'' > d''ProbC_{CT}/dP'' \tag{34.}$$

Therefore, for the final ratio P'_{CT}/P'_T:

$$d(P'_{CT}/P'_T)/dP > 0.00 > d''(P'_{CT}/P'_T)dP'' \tag{35.}$$

Process and U, P'': Expectations for Processor's Payoffs

What of the expected returns to processor for "good" and "bad" processing decisions? And how might we expect these returns, or payoffs, to vary across MSAP nodes? Hypothesized answers involve two basic variables, U or the possible rewards/costs returned to processor for case "Shows," and P'' or the chances of U given case "Shows." We turn first to the question of U.

Clear parallels exist between U, an element in payoffs to processor, and U', an element in (attributed payoffs to case. In establishing process-wide expectations for U, we initially looked at the question of value, or "objective" returns for a Show (the diagram on the left in Figure 8.(B1)). Here we generated an empirically grounded expectation based on recent data showing the dollar returns on years of education, where for both Type and Countertype value was shown as a power function of process. Though this general expectation holds for U, and though U and U' are structurally homologous, there are some reasons to expect a difference.

Consider the issue initially in terms of valued processes. On the one hand, features of social organization strongly tend to support the unequal return of value to Type and Countertype for displays of MS-relevant traits. From the perspective of Type's or Countertype's interests, this is one thing. On the other hand, from the perspective of organizational interests. Type and Countertype displaying MS-relevant traits return value at a more nearly equal rate. (Expressed more directly, features of social organization tend to "use" people differentially.)

This translates to the expectations indicated in Figure 11. As in the

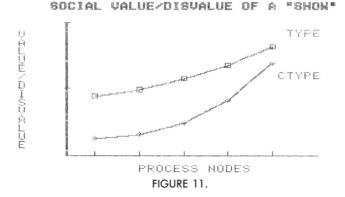

FIGURE 11.

case of U', successive processing nodes imply increased levels of social value returned for a Show, with Types returning more than Countertypes. And, as in the case of U', the increase is shown as positively accelerating for both Types and Countertypes. But, because we are now taking the interests of MS-relevant social organization as paramount, we now expect the rate of acceleration (on organizational returns) to be greater for Countertype than Type. Considerations of P'' aside, this implies a process-wide movement toward Type/Countertype parity or convergence on U (as opposed to some growing divergence on U').

The analogy appears to hold up for disvalued processing. At successive nodes, in this case, displays of (negative) MS-relevant traits produce social costs or disvalue. It is argued that the same features of social order which produce and support the Type/Countertype heuristic filter, or meliorate, the perceived disvalue of MS-relevant trait displays by Countertype, but that, with successive processing, this perceived difference becomes "harder" to sustain. For example, at the early, informal stages of identification, the perceived social costs produced by a potential female delinquent are considerably outstripped by those perceived for a potential male delinquent. But, at later, more formal stages of processing, the perceived difference attenuates.

Other factors enter into U. In Figure 12.(A), we portray the expectation that the dollar costs of a Pass increase as a decaying function of process, with Countertype costs exceeding Type Costs, but with the ratio of the two decreasing across successive nodes. The critical assumption here, that the ratio decreases across process, is based on the reasoning that: (a) at successive processing nodes, the differential "need" for special Countertype vs. Type training, handling, housing, etc. decreases, and (b) at successive processing nodes, the differential "difficulty" in documenting Countertype vs. Type claims to legitimate, final MS incumbency decreases.

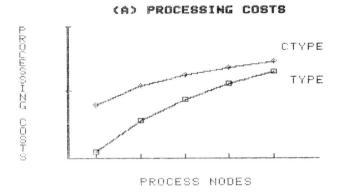

(A) PROCESSING COSTS

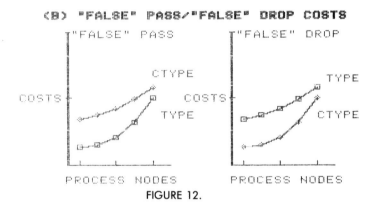

(B) "FALSE" PASS/"FALSE" DROP COSTS

FIGURE 12.

Earlier, we suggested that the decision problem facing processors was set into sharp relief by the twin prospects of the "false" pass and the "false" drop. Again from the perspective of "organizational interests," Figure 12.(B) portrays our expectations for the costs of such mistakes. Note that both the left and right hand figures are in the same family of curves as shown in Figure 11. The reasons for these expectations are as follows.

The case of "false" drops, the right figure in 12.(B), is relatively straightforward. Within Type and within Countertype, the costs of a "false" drop can be seen as functionally equivalent to the value/disvalue of a Show (Figure 11) — in this situation, cases have been dropped and then go on to display the MS-relevant trait(s) in question. Thus, in this "mistake at work," lost opportunities (or opportunity costs) created by "false" drops are construed as self-referencing within Type and within Countertype — i.e., Type costs are tied to Type value/disvalue, and Countertype costs are tied to Countertype value/disvalue.

The problem is different and more complex in the case of the "false" pass, the left figure in 12.(B). The reason for this involves the question of how opportunity costs are anchored, and ultimately goes back to the concept of the "good" Gestalt. The easiest way for processor to frame the costs of the "false" pass (the "figure") is against the opportunity costs, or bypassed expected value, of the "true" pass (the "ground") — that is, the "true" pass which might have occured had the "false" pass not filled a vacancy. But, without some conception of the worth of a "true" pass, estimates of the worth of a "false" pass are difficult and un-anchored. There is no "ground." The Type/Contertype heuristic provides that "ground". The (bypassed) value of Type (Figure 11) is, in effect, the "false" pass cost of Countertype. In itself, this is not a problem.

By analogy, the (bypassed) value of Countertype (also Figure 11) would, therefore, seem to be "false" pass cost of Type. Strictly speaking, however, this cannot be the case. Because of their higher relative frequency, Types and not Countertypes are the "background" in the heuristic's Gestalt. This means that "other" Types (and not Countertypes) should provide the frame of opportunity costs or bypassed value in "falsely" passing Types. Consequently we might thus be lead to conclude that — since the costs of a "false" pass for both Type and Countertype are grounded on Type — we cannot differentiate "false" pass expectations by Type/Countertype. But this is unreasonable.

The costs of falsely passing Countertypes vs. Types are not simply material or materially-based. The heuristic also structures "mistakes at work" by structuring embarrassment as well. The figure portraying "false" pass costs thus suggests that mistakes in prediction, combined with more materially-based costs, lead to the overall expectation of positively accelerating organizational costs by process, and the overall expectation of higher costs for falsely passing Countertypes than Types. But, as in the case of the "false" drop, the key expectation is that, across process, the cost ratio of falsely passing Countertypes relative to Types decreases; in short, (returns on) mistaken decisions about Countertypes look increasingly like mistakes about Types.

So far we have talked about the "cost" element in opportunity costs. But note that opportunity costs were defined (p. 21) as possible rather than certain, that is, as a product of value/disvalue, just discussed, and P^*, or the probability that case Y — or X's "nearest competitor" — would be dropped if X were passed. It was also indicated that P' — which we finished discussing a while ago — might properly be an element in considering opportunity costs. To simplify matters, let us treat the final product, costs $\times P' \times P^*$, as a problem involving the successive product of two T/CT cost ratios: (1.) costs $\times P'$ and (2.) $P^* \times$ (1).

Figures 12.(A) and 12.(B) indicate expectations for costs. It should be clear that the process-wide T/CT cost ratios which can be extrapolated from these expectations have a positive slope and move toward parity. Given already stated expectations for P' (Figure 10.), in both valued and disvalued MSAPs we should thus expect the Type/Countertype ratio of the first product — costs × P' — to decrease significantly across process nodes. That is, to a point where (first product) opportunity costs for Passing Types have increased to near-parity with opportunity costs for Passing Countertypes (in a form analogous to that shown in 9.(C)).

What of P*? Though we do not visually show expectations for P*, they are essentially the same as those for "false pass" costs in Figure 12.(B). Given increasing selectivity/decreasing vacancies, as successive nodes are crossed, Passing X implies ever-increased chances for dropping or "bumping" X's nearest competitor. Given differential selectivity/vacancy for Countertype (more selectivity, fewer vacancies than for Type), there are two additional implications. One is that a Passed Countertype's nearest competitor will be more likely to be dropped from further processing than a Passed Type's, and that therefore P* for Countertype will consistently exceed P* for Type. The other is that — because surviving Countertypes at any node have faced a continually more selective process than Types — at successive nodes Passed Types "bump" other cases at a progressively faster rate than Countertypes. Thus, at successive nodes, the T/CT P* ratio will also move positively toward parity and, the final opportunity cost product — P* (costs × P') — will necessarily follow suit.

In short, across nodes in both valued and disvalued MSAPs, the expected opportunity costs of Passing Types relative to Passing Countertypes should increase markedly and approach parity. This means that, as successive nodes are reached, the Type/Countertype heuristic — in losing its "power" to simplify the calculation of opportunity costs — also loses "power" in guiding (and biasing) status processing decisions.

Combining considerations of value/disvalue with processing, "false" decision costs, and P', produces an approximation of process-wide organizational returns for a Show, by Type and Countertype. If we assume that processor's returns are a linear transform of organizational returns, and log the result as we did for U', we are led to the overall estimate of Utility/Disutility returned to processor for a Show indicated in Figure 13. Part (A) shows these expectations by Type and Countertype. Part (B), quite similar to 9.(C), expresses (A) in ratio form. Once more the implication is that, because it becomes increasingly rational for processor to do so, across process (the few remaining) Countertypes will be passed in increasingly near-equal proportions to Types.

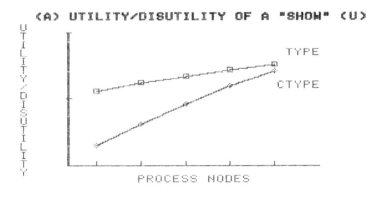

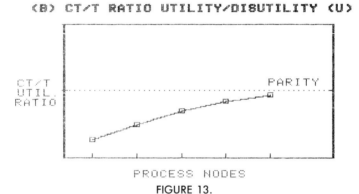

FIGURE 13.

Hypotheses for P'', or the chances of processor receiving payoffs (or U), lead to a similar bottom line. A series of assumptions structures this bottom line. In MSAPs process nodes distribute two broad phenomena related to P'': discretion and visibility/accountability. Based ultimately on the idea of increasing selectivity across nodes, with concomitantly increasing "stakes," Figure 14 suggest that the two phenomena are virtual reflections of each other, with visibility/accountabilty a waning function of process and discretion the waxing inverse.

In the general case, then, we expect discretion to be a negative, decelerating function of process. Since it is reasonable to assume that higher levels of discretion are tied to higher chances of personally receiving payoffs and lower levels of discretion to lower chances of receiving pay-offs, when considered by itself, discretion consequently provides the basis for process-wide expectation of negative, decelerating levels of P''. More critically, as Figure 15.(A) suggests, discretion provides the basis for looking toward increasing Type/Countertype convergence on P''.

DISCRETION, VISIBILITY, ACCOUNTABILITY

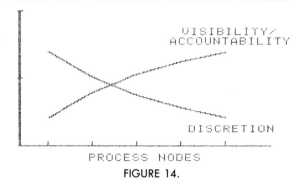

FIGURE 14.

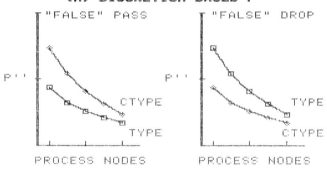

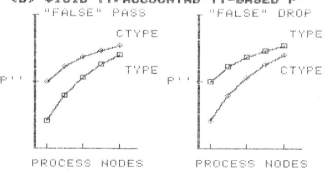

FIGURE 15.

The left portion of 15.(A) indicates that, although "false" passes entail ever-lowered levels of P" (because of ever-lowered levels of discretion), we expect that throughout valued and disvalued MSAPs, processors are consistently more likely to "pay" for falsely passing Countertypes than Types, but that at successive stages of processing the difference attenuates. The right portion of 15.(A), for "false" drops, portrays the "shadow" analogy. Here the chances of "paying" for a bad decision based on discretion are also seen as abating across process, though in this case processors are consistently more likely to pay for falsely dropping Types than Countertypes. Again, as in the case of "false" passes, the relevant CT/T ratio (on P") converges toward parity.

If we restricted the argument to the discretion dimension, we might be left with the implication that, at successive nodes in MSAPs, processors look at ever-lower chances of gains or costs for good, or bad, decisions. But that is not our intention. As noted, Figure 14 carries the inverse expectation based on visibility/accountability: at successive MSAP nodes, visibility and accountability increase and, as a consequence, so does P". This translates to the "net" position that (a) discretion, and (b) visibility/accountability are, as it were, countervailing elements in a final vector. But it does not translate to the "net" position that the two wash each other out. (The latter question involves the relative calibration of (a) and (b) along the Y-axis. Though by implication Figure 14 calibrates a "washout" on P", we do not intend it, preferring, instead, to leave the theory sufficiently general to incorporate alternative positioning of (a) and (b) along Y.)

Figure 15.(B) shows parallel expectations for P" based on the Type/Countertype heuristic and visibility/accountability. Based on the assumption that the latter increases with process, both left and right segments indicate that P" is also expected to increase. In the case of the left figure, the "false" pass, the suggestion is that, across MSAPs, processors are again consistently more likely to "pay" for falsely passing Countertypes than Types. On the other hand, the right figure, for "false" drops, suggests that, across MSAPs, processors are again more likely to pay for falsely dropping Types than Countertypes. (The right figure also serves as a graphic indication of expectations for the P" of processor gains, or positive U, returned for "true" passes.)

Finally, considering the building blocks, Figure 16 portrays the critical overall expectation for P": as successive processing nodes are reached, the chances of receiving payoffs (negative and positive U) for passing or dropping "true" or "false" Countertypes increasingly approaches parity with the analogous chances for Types.

This completes discussion of the third and last major element in the decision problem, P". We once again stress that the most appropriate

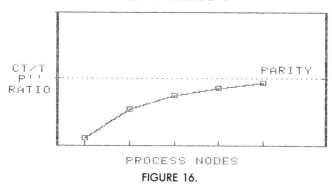

PROCESS NODES

FIGURE 16.

way of presenting our expectations is in the form of comparative slopes and their rates of change. We therefore close this section with the arguments for U and P'' expressed in the form of differential inequalities. In the next section we come to a final and general summary statement of our expectations for Process and Outcome Bias in MSAPs.

It will be recalled that:

$$U = f(PC_1, PC_2, OC) \qquad (8.)$$

Recall that the term OC represents opportunity costs for a Pass, and that while we have spoken of the opportunity costs of a Drop, we have not found it necessary to model this related issue formally (as the two are variants of the same problem). Again denoting Process as P, Countertypes as CT, and Type as T, for U it is argued that:

$$PC_1T > PC_1CT > 0.00 \qquad (36.)$$

$$dPC_1CT/dP > dPC_1T/dP > 0.00 \qquad (37.)$$

$$d''PC_1CT/dP'' > d''PC_1T/dP'' > 0.00 \qquad (38.)$$

and

$$PC_2CT > PC_2T > 0.00 \qquad (39.)$$

$$dPC_2T/dP > dPC_2CT/dP > 0.00 \qquad (40.)$$

$$d''PC_2CT/dP'' < d''PC_2T/dP'' < 0.00 \qquad (41.)$$

and

$$OC_{CT} > OC_T > 0.00 \qquad (42.)$$

$$dOC_T/dP > dOC_{CT}/dP > 0.00 \qquad (43.)$$

$$d''OC_T/dP'' > d''OC_{CT}/dP'' > 0.00 \qquad (44.)$$

therefore, and given (35.),

$$d(U_{CT}/U_T)/dP > 0.00 > d''(U_{CT}/U_T) / dP'' \qquad (45.)$$

Using the same notation, and adding the terms D for Discretion, VA for Visibility/Accountability, and Prob for P'', for P'' (Prob) it is argued that:

$$dProb/dVA > 0.00 > dProb/dD \qquad (46.)$$

where

$$dVA/dP > 0.00 > d''VA/dP'', \; dD/dP, \; d''D/dP'' \qquad (47.)$$

and where, for D-based Prob, (a) on "false" passes

$$Prob_{CT} > Prob_T > 0.00 \qquad (48.)$$

$$dProb_{CT}/dP > dProb_T/dP < 0.00 \qquad (49.)$$

$$d''Prob_{CT}/dP'' > d''Prob_T/dP'' < 0.00 \qquad (50.)$$

and (b) on "false" drops

$$Prob_T > Prob_{CT} > 0.00 \qquad (51.)$$

$$dProb_T/dP > dProb_{CT}/dP < 0.00 \qquad (52.)$$

$$d''Prob_T/dP'' > d''Prob_{CT}/dP'' < 0.00 \qquad (53.)$$

but where, for VA-based Prob, (a) on "false" passes

$$Prob_{CT} > Prob_T > 0.00 \qquad (54.)$$

$$dProb_T/dP > dProb_{CT}/dP > 0.00 \qquad (55.)$$

$$d''Prob_{CT}/dP'' > d''Prob_T/dP'' < 0.00 \qquad (56.)$$

and (b) on "false" drops

$$Prob_T > Prob_{CT} > 0.00 \qquad (57.)$$

$$dProb_{CT}/dP > dProb_T/dP > 0.00 \qquad (58.)$$

$$d''Prob_T/dP'' > d''Prob_{CT} < 0.00 \qquad (59.)$$

therefore

$$d(Prob_{CT}/Prob_T)/dP > 0.00 > d''(Prob_{CT}/Prob_T)/dP'' \qquad (60.)$$

Process and Outcome Bias

Our major thesis has been that the Type/Countertype heuristic simplifies the rational demands of processing decisions while simultaneously producing biased outcomes in Master Status Attainment Processes. But our analysis of the problem across processing nodes also suggested that bias was dynamic in character. Process-wide expectations for each of the 3 major elements in the rational model — P', U, and P'' — pointed to a common theme: at successive nodes in processing, the rational conditions for forwarding higher ratios of Countertypes to Types improve. The broad resulting expectation — a product of the 3 major components — is shown in Figure 17.

The theoretical grounds for the expectation are fully in place. Across nodes in both valued and disvalued MSAPs, we expect that, of the "can-

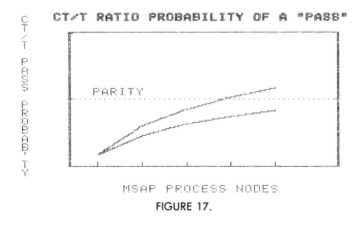

FIGURE 17.

didates" received, the ratio of the probability of "Passing" Countertypes to Types will increase (at a decreasing rate) toward parity, and perhaps even exceed it. This is not the same thing as saying that, at successive nodes, the probability of passing any candidate or group will increase or decrease. At successive nodes, such probabilities may well change, but that is not relevant; what counts is the Countertype to Type ratio of these probabilities. Nor does it matter, in Figure 17, what the absolute numbers of Countertypes and Types are at any given node. What counts is whether the ratio of Countertypes to Types forwarded or Passed from node n to node $n + 1$ is higher or, as we propose, lower than that transition ratio from node $n + 1$ to $n + 2$. (The reader is encouraged to re-examine Figures 1 and 2 and the related discussion).

What, then, of bias? Earlier we distinguished two ways of using the term, Process Bias and Outcome Bias. Hopefully some of the advantages of this distinction now emerge. We defined Process Bias as "numerical inequality in the comparative transition probabilities of groups 'matched' for 'true' MS-relevant traits" (p.8). And we defined Outcome Bias as "numerical departures from the Equity Baseline," where one definition of Equity Baseline was "comparative group rates of MS-relevant traits at the first node of an MSAP" (also p.8).

Theory underpinning Figure 17 involves both kinds of bias, because, in effect, they are closely related. For example, a processor at a "late" node, say"conferring" (p. 43), receives 200 Type candidates and only 10 Countertype candidates. The processor knows that, in the population at large, their ratios are more like 8:1 or even 1:1. But the Outcome Bias at present (based on the receipt of 20:1) becomes the ground for a relatively even-handed treatment of the two groups in the future; i.e., little or no additional Process Bias is added to change Outcome Bias.

Graphically, this translates, first, to the simple expectation that Process Bias is no more than a mirrored inverse of the CT/T ratio of the probability of a Pass (Figure 17). At successive nodes in MSAPs, we should therefore expect Process Bias to decrease (though decreasingly) and approach parity. The notion of successive movement toward parity in processing decisions is rather important, for it implies very clearly that such end-game activities as courtroom watching and governmental checks on the Affirmative Action policies of law school admissions are likely to come up empty handed. Figure 18 portrays this expectation for Process Bias.

Coming up empty handed on Process Bias in this example does not mean that our imaginary courtroom watcher or H.E.W. official does not see bias at all. On the contrary and quite paradoxically, the relative absence of Process Bias may well signal the pre-existence of high levels of Outcome Bias, distributively irreversible and fully in place. This means that while, yes, 50% of group CT was forwarded along with 50% of group T — so

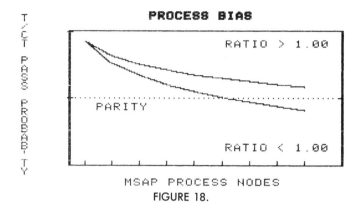

FIGURE 18.

no Process Bias was observed — the population-based rate of group T was still 10 or 20 times the population-based rate of group CT!

Mathematically, Outcome Bias is the process-wide sum of the Equity Baseline parameter multiplied by successive Process Bias transition ratios in the MSAP chain. Whatever we initialize the Equity Baseline at, and since we have shown Process Bias as a log function, this means that the summated function of Outcome Bias is an "S" Curve or 3rd order polynomial in the family of linear logistic or Gompertz curves.

Figure 19 portrays this expectation graphically and does so in two slightly different ways. The right hand segment shows the hypothesis for disvalued processes, and the left for valued ones. Though the graphs are very similar, the left is more exaggerated. The reason for this has to do with a major difference between valued and disvalued processing which

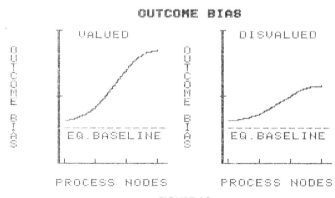

FIGURE 19.

we have not discussed, namely, that the volitional self-attrition of cases is much more likely in valued than in disvalued processes.

Though cases in both kinds of processes might prefer to drop out of the MSAP, and almost certainly a far greater proportion has this preference in disvalued processes, the freedom to make this choice is highly asymmetrical across the two. Proportionally far more cases in valued MSAPs can follow through on the wish to drop out. We would therefore like to think of Outcome Bias (as opposed to Process Bias) as joint function of decisions by processor and decisions by case, that is, as a joint function of processor's bias and cases' self-attrition. As such, we are free to let the latter term weigh heavily in considering Outcome Bias for valued processes, and drop to near $-$ O in considering Outcome Bias for disvalued processes.

Though we have developed a theory of bias in MSAPs from the perspective of processor, from the very same perspective we have pointed to processor's need for a thoroughgoing reading of case and process. But what makes sense from this perspective also makes sense from case's perspective. Case, too, "reads" processors and process. By extension, at the early stages of processing (and relative to Type), high proportions of Countertypes will self-attrite, followed by smaller proportions (of the fewer remaining ones) who are "still in the game" at successive nodes. The simplest process-wide approximation of the CT/T self-attrition function is thus identical to the Process Bias function. Though based on a reading of MSAP-related costs, gains, and chances which may be thoroughly realistic and quite rational, the decision to self-attrite may therefore be seen as producing additional or "shadow" bias in its own right, and as structural homology to Process Bias. Whatever the relative magnitude of CT/T self-attrition "bias" compared to Process Bias in disvalued MSAPs, it should thus be clear that CT/T self-attrition "bias" will act in valued processes to exaggerate the basic contours of the "S" curve shown for disvalued processes. The left and right segments of Figure 19 reflect this conclusion.

Relying on earlier notation, and substituting the term Pass for the Probability of a Pass, the expectations behind Figure 17 thru 19 may be expressed as follows:

$$d'(\text{CT/T Pass})/dP > 0.00 > d''(\text{CT/T Pass})/dP'' \tag{61.}$$

therefore

$$d'(\text{CT/T Process Bias})/dP, d'' (\text{CT/Process Bias})/dP'' < 0.00 \tag{62.}$$

and, given the transition ratio (or Process Bias) product rule,

$$d'(\text{CT/T Outcome Bias})/dP > 0.00 \tag{63.}$$

$$\text{and where } d'(\text{CT/T Outcome Bias}) = f(P, -P^2) \tag{64.}$$

Let us stress what is hopefully by now an obvious bottom line. These arguments mean that *the more Outcome Bias has accumulated, the less the reason to look for, and to find, new levels of bias introduced into the system.* This conclusion is based largely on our starting point, Kanter's insightful admonition to the effect that our "neglect" of the relative frequencies or "proportions of interacting social types . . . has sometimes led to inappropriate or misleading conclusions" (cited on p.1). We feel that nowhere could the value of this point be clearer than in the study of bias.

Having fully closed the theoretical circle, in the following section we examine a small set of findings which lends some plausibility to our theoretical framework. The findings are confinded to processing in the area of criminal justice. Though this area is just one example of disvalued processing, let alone one example of processing more generally, in all the modern attempts to study social bias there is possibly no area showing a more fruitless accumulation of effort. After looking at these findings, we conclude with a brief discussion of some of the implications of our theory.

ILLUSTRATIONS FROM CRIMINAL JUSTICE

The influence of the defendant's sex could not be measured because there were too few females in the sample. (Clarke and Koch, 1976:57)

Females are easier to intimidate . . . I guarantee her jail if she is not clean. Females are impressed with this more than males. (Probation Officer, Springfield, Ma., cited in Daly, 1983:20)

Liberal and theoretical beliefs to the contrary, available data on criminal justice processing show no clearcut evidence of bias against particular social groups (cf. Hagan, 1974; Bernstein et al., 1977; Harris and Hill, 1982). Paradoxically, it is well known among criminologists that demographic differences between offenders are far more pronounced in arrest data than in "true" rate estimates based on self and victim reports. As we have argued in detail, however, there are very good reasons for expecting these observations to emerge simultaneously.

Disvalued processing is most opaque to the outside observer at its early stages, precisely the points at which we should expect the most Process Bias to occur; and it is least opaque at the tail-end stages, precisely where we should expect the least Process Bias to occur. But, unfortunately, this observation implies that the most appropriate form of a sample on which to test the present theoretical framework (or an alternative framework) would be an extraordinarily large, extraordinarily cooperative panel. In that panel's absence, however, it is still possible to look for evidence where one can find it. The following small set of findings does not represent a random sample of all relevant findings. Because of this, the prospect of "disconfirmation" is not relevant. Rather, the findings are presented as illustrations in two senses. First, they do offer the present theoretical framework some empirical plausibility. And second, they suggest that even though this framework has heavy operational demands as a whole, it is potentially useful in interpreting otherwise anomolous and uninterpretable data.

SES and Sentencing

(a) Chiricos and Waldo's (1975) work on the effects of Socioeconomic Status (SES) on courtroom sentencing created quite a stir. Based on a very large number of cases (over 10,000), the authors presented strong evidence this status characteristic did not act in the way conflict (and/or labeling) theorists thought it would: higher levels of SES were not associated with less severe sentencing outcomes. Subsequent responses to this work argue that the analysis is flawed because the distribution of cases on the SES variable is so highly skewed toward lower SES.

It is informative to reexamine these data briefly from the present perspective. For each of 3 states, 13 crimes were examined for the SES-sentence length relationship. Conflict theory predicts a negative relation. Since the present theory demands at least two MSAP transitions (and here there is only one), it makes no explicit prediction. But because the data are taken at the last node of an MSAP chain, the present theory sensitizes one to the likelihood that — if SES distributes a Type/Countertype heuristic on the status Criminal — then the observed relation between SES and sentencing will not be robust and may even invert.

Of the 37 reported correlation coefficients in the Chiricos and Waldo data (Table 1), 22 are positive or, from the conflict perspective, in the wrong direction. In addition, the only significant coefficients are positive. If there is any pattern here, it is one indicating that, relative to the nodal distribution, the status "higher SES" (Countertype) is associated with a more severe processing outcome. Interpretable by the present framework, these data from the tail-end of an MSAP reflect a common pattern in most such datasets: (1) the unexpected and seemingly unaccountable absence of Process Bias (or its unexpected and unaccountable "reversed" presence), and (2) simultaneously enormously skewed distributions of, as

TABLE 1.   Simple coefficients (r's) between SES and Sentence Length, for 3 States and 17 Crimes. (Adapted from Chiricos and Waldo, 1975)

Crime	Florida	South Carolina	North Carolina
2nd Degree Murder	.14	. . .	. . .
Voluntary Manslaughter	−.01	.05	.03
Involuntary Manslaughter	. . .	. . .	−.09
Forcible Rape	−.12	.19	.19*
Statutory Rape	. . .	. . .	.04
Aggravated Assault	−.05	.10	.12*
Armed Robbery	−.04	−.05	.12*
Unarmed Robbery	−.03	.17	−.01
Burglary	.09*	−.03	.04
Larceny	.09	.01	−.06
Auto Theft	.03	. . .	.04
Receiving Stolen Property	−.08	. . .	.09
Embezzlement	. . .	. . .	.08
Forgery	−.02	−.07	.03
Drug Offenses	−.05	−.13	.01
Escape	.10	. . .	. . .
Arson	. . .	. . .	.17

* $p \leq .05$

Kanter calls them, "social types." (We believe that, when this occurs, most researchers are so intent on supporting or challenging a particular — and inadequate — theory they cannot see the forest for the trees.)

(b) Bernstein et al. (1977) improve on the Chiricos and Waldo design in several ways, including the use of a panel observed across several criminal justice processing nodes, appropriate controls for prior record, and multiple regression techniques. They, too, find little or no support for the conflict or labeling perspective.

Bernstein and her associates use two measures of processing decisions, magnitude of charge severity and charge reduction. Observations on each are taken at two close points in final processing. Table 2 shows the partial regression slopes of the severity measures on 5 statuses (Type = 0, Countertype = 1). From the conflict/labeling perspective, we should expect to see disadvantaged and stereotypically "criminal types" more severely sanctioned than those referred to here as Countertypes. In terms of Table 2 this means that, according to conflict/labeling: (1) for the charge severity columns we should expect negative (−) coefficients, indicating that discretion in the system (and present offense) leads to less severe charges against Countertypes than Types, and (2) for the charge reduction

TABLE 2.   Partial slopes (b's) of Sanction Severity on Countertype Statuses (Adapted from Bernstein et al., 1977)

Countertype Status	Charge Severity			Magnitude of Charge Reduction		
	Expected[a] Sign	t_1[b]	t_2[b]	Expected[a] Sign	t_1[b]	t_2[b]
White	$(-)$	n.s.[c]	$-.10$	$(+)$	n.s.	n.s.
Older	$(-)$	$-.20$	n.s.	$(+)$	.16	n.s.
Female	$(-)$	n.s.	.10	$(+)$	n.s.	n.s.
Few Arrests	$(-)$	.12	.14	$(+)$	$-.12$	$-.15$
No Record	$(-)$	.12	.15	$(+)$	$-.14$	$-.13$

[a] Expected sign according to conflict/labeling theory.
[b] At two successive points in criminal court proceedings.
[c] (n.s. = not significant; all other coefficients are significant.)

columns we should expect positive $(+)$ coefficients, indicating that discretion in the system (and present offense) leads to a greater willingness to "bend" justice for Countertypes than Types. In all, there are 20 relevant outcomes in the table. In 17 of these, the conflict/labeling expectation is not upheld, the relation being either insignificant (8 cases) or "reversed" (9 cases). Again interpretable by the present framework, these findings are unexpected and unaccountable by conventional theories and, once more, occur in the context of highly skewed population marginals.

Motives Attributed to Offenders

Phillips and DeFleur (1977) use a vignette design to study differences in the public's perception of male and female offenders. Each respondent rated hypothetical offenders for the likely role of 7 possible motives in committing 4 different offenses. In some vignettes the offender is male, in others female. Apart from this one difference, the vignettes ascribed common characteristics to the imaginary offender — including being 25 years old, White, employed, convicted of the offense, and a first offender. The 4 offenses used were shoplifting, embezzlement, second degree murder, and selling narcotics. It is instructive to recast the findings in a different form than Phillips and DeFleur use. Their offenses may be rank ordered on the basis of how highly sex-typed they are. According to national arrest figures at about the time of the Phillips study, and based on rates adjusted for population size, Male:Female arrest ratios stood at 2.19 for "shoplifting" (larceny), 2.98 for embezzlement, 6.21 for manslaughter,

TABLE 3.   Ratios of Motive Levels Attributed to Female Offenders vs. Male Offenders, by Type of Motive and Type of Offense[a] (Adapted from Phillips and DeFleur, 1977, and Hill and Harris, 1981)

Motive	(Low ← Male Typing → High)				$\bar{X}$ Motive Level[b]
	Shoplifting	Embezzling	Manslaughter	Narcotics	
Please Spouse/ Lover	1.08	.86	1.09	1.26	1.97
Please Peers	.88	.97	1.06	1.08	2.04
Thrill	.97	1.08	1.06	1.14	2.06
Did Not Think it Wrong	.98	1.05	.93	1.04	2.29
Mental Illness	1.03	1.04	1.11	1.16	2.42
Drunk or on Drugs	.98	1.04	.95	1.05	2.53
Expected to Gain Something	.97	.99	1.17	1.01	3.45
Col. $\bar{X}$ F:M Motive Ratio:	.98	1.00	1.06	1.10	
No. of Times in Column the F:M Ratio Exceeds 1.00:	2/7	4/7	5/7	7/7	

[a] Equivalent Uniform Crime Report categories are larceny, embezzlement, manslaughter, and drug offenses.

[b] $\bar{X}$ Motive Level is aggregated across motives attributed to male and female offenders.

and 6.40 for "narcotics" or drug offenses (Hill and Harris, 1981). Needless to say, the more "typed" a behavior or trait is, the more "countertyped" it also is. More highly sex-typed crimes, like murder, are usually male-typed, and imply that the rare Countertype females who do exist are unusually "tough" or "sick" or "doing it for some male." Based on the present framework, we would therefore predict that levels of motivation attributed by the public to female offenders relative to male offenders would vary directly (and not, as common sense might have it, inversely) with the degree an offense is male-typed.

The offense columns in Table 3 are arrayed from left to right according to increasing degree of male-typing (as noted). The motive rows are arrayed from top to bottom according to the increasing importance the sample attached to each of the 7 motives as a factor in producing the offense (as indicated by the sample means in the rightmost column). Cell entries derive from the original work, which shows sex × offense × motive level means, and indicate the female/male ratio of attributed motivation levels.

Despite the fact that each respondent did not rate both males and females, the prediction is upheld quite firmly. Looking first to large effects, column means of CT/T ratios show an orderly increase in the expected direction. Since shoplifting is almost certainly a female-typed offense (not adequately reflected in the UCR estimate, which is aggregated across other forms of larceny as well), it is reasonable to assume that the male to female offense rate ratio for shoplifting is actually less than 1.00. For this particular offense, the sample mean CT/T "motive" ratio is .98. Moving right, in the direction of increased male-typing, comparable column ratios shift to 1.00, 1.06, and, for narcotics, the most highly male-typed crime, the ratio shifts to 1.10. Thus, at aggregated sample level, motivation attributed to Countertype females increases according to degree of "Countertypical-ness," and, for manslaughter and narcotics sales, actually exceeds the levels of motivation attributed males. A somewhat stronger test of the prediction is offered in a column-by-column comparison of the number of times the CT/T motive ratio exceeds 1.00. The expectation is that, moving rightwards in the direction of male-typing, the frequency of ratios greater than 1.00 should increase. As Table 3 indicates, the relevant frequency moves from 2/7, to 4/7, to 5/7, to 7/7.

Bias in Process

Hill's work on juvenile justice processing (1980) provides one of the very few attempts to approach bias as a dynamic, not static problem. Based on a representative sample of over 3,000 juveniles in Illinois in the 1970's, the work provides what might be called a "near-panel" analysis of a single sample's processing experience across several successive nodes in a dis-valued MSAP. Four basic nodes (and three transitions) are represented: (1) self-reported criminal behavior, (2) being brought to a police station, (3) unofficial court contact, and (4) official court contact. Regression tech-niques, which allow for the necessary control of potentially confounding case characteristics, are used to examine the question of Process Bias. The demography of offenders and offenses parallels other recent findings and comparable UCR data, suggesting that sex and race are the major covariates of getting into trouble with the law. (Age is also important, but not highly relevant for this particular sample.) As important correlates of delinquency, and as eminently visible features of cases, sex and race pro-vide some of the most basic of all Type/Countertype heuristics.

Table 4 reveals the effect of sex and race on transitions net of offense seriousness and SES. Rows 1 and 2 display the effects of sex within race, with females coded 0 and males coded 1. The entry in the upper left cell,

TABLE 4. Standardized Partial Slopes (betas) of Node Transitions on Sex (within Race) and Race (within Sex), Net of SES and Offense Seriousness (Adapted from Hill, 1980)

	Delinquent Behavior (N_1) to Police Station (N_2)	Police Station (N_2) to Unofficial Court (N_3)	Unofficial Court (N_3) to Official Court (N_4)
Sex Effects[a]			
Among Whites:	.141*	−.019	−.179*
Among Blacks:	.106*	.000	−.090
Race Effects[b]			
Among Males:	.072*	.060	−.082
Among Females:	.117*	.035	−.101

[a] Coded Female = 0, Male = 1.
[b] Coded White = 0, Black = 1.
* $p \le .05$

for example, shows that, among Whites and net of "true" delinquent behavior, males are significantly more likely to be brought to a police station than females (beta = .141). This means a higher "Pass" rate for Type than Countertype. Of the Whites having police station contact, however, and again net of "true" behavior, the middle entry in the top row suggests that being male or female makes no significant difference in Whites' transition to unofficial court contact (beta = −.019). Moving one more step to the right, and again net of other major factors, we now see that among Whites with unofficial court contact, females are significantly more likely than males to have official court contact (beta = −.179). This means that in the final transition observed Countertypes are more likely to be "Passed" than Types.

Though not quite as strong, the same pattern across nodes can be observed for Blacks — a pattern which seems to "favor" Countertype at the early stage of the disvalued MSAP and Type at later. Similarly, net of SES and "true" delinquent behavior, this shift of "favor" can be seen in the lower two rows by race (Whites = 0, Blacks = 1). Among males, being White has a small but significant "advantage" over being Black in the transition from delinquent behavior to being brought to a police station (.072). But, by the final transition, "advantage" has shifted to Blacks (Types), with the relevant coefficient at −.082. Among females, the shift by race seems even more marked. The main hypothesis generated by the present theory does not demand that "advantage" actually shifts to Countertype, but rather that, in a table such as this, the trend from left to right be a trend toward ever decreasing (less positive or more negative) coefficients. In the present case there are 12 such comparisons to be made ($N_{1-2} > N_{2-3}$ and N_{3-4}, and $N_{2-3} > N_{3-4} \times 4$ rows). In each of the 12, the hypothesis is supported.

CONCLUSIONS AND IMPLICATIONS

In this essay, we have developed a new, and we hope useful, way of conceptualizing and studying bias in status attainment. We do not think that operationalizing the theoretical framework as whole would be easy. Far from it. Rather, we think that parts of the framework could be used in more modest research tasks involving only a few transitions, or in, say, vignette studies of attributed motivation or mock pass/drop decisions. A more general use of the framework is as a sensitizing or interpretive device. Though we would hope for a more rigorous test than this, given the present "static" orientation we think the framework's orienting qualities are useful in their own right. For regardless of whether or not an approach to bias in MSAPs is based on a theory of attributed rationality or irrationality, Types and Countertypes, we strongly believe that a process approach is the only one capable of demystifying bias's subtle accomplishment.

Any such gains ought not be seen as limited to theory, but, at least, as illuminating with respect to the difficulties of social change and the policies attempting to promote it. In the United States and other post-industrial societies, public awareness of inequities in status attainment has increased dramatically during the last several decades. So too have government sponsored attempts to regulate the breakdown of these inequities. Yet, from the theoretical perspective generated here, such attempts run the risk of being more than expensive, highly visible palliatives.

Once adjusted for population baselines, Type-to-Countertype ratios at the final nodes of both valued and disvalued MSAPs can easily run in the range of 20:1 or 30:1. While the pressures of Affirmative Action policies can bring about some changes in population transitions at the tail-end of processing, it is not clear that such gains are very meaningful. For one thing, as we have argued, at this point in processing, transition equality or near-equality is likely — there is probably not much to improve on. For another, in considering valued processing one must recognize that the free market of decisions cuts across both processor and case. The self-attrition of cases in the valued Master Status market is likely to be overwhelmingly Countertype. Insofar as self-attrition is based on a perfectly reasonable reading of the expected returns of "staying on course," then the intrinsic problem here cannot be remedied by simply easing the problem of access to final certification. One must deal with the question of post-process returns at the same time.

But, if the approach taken here is correct, then the strong tendency for employers is to assume that the few Countertypes who are in the system are obviously so sufficiently motivated by intrinsic rewards they require less in the way of extrinsic rewards. Still more paradoxically, if Affirmative Action policies are sufficiently robust to increase the market value of Countertypes to parity with, or in excess of, the market value of Types, then a reciprocal risk is run: the perception of Countertypes as motivated predominantly by the "opportunism" of expected gain, and not intrinsic commitment.

From the present perspective, it seems rather clear that the most effective policy in reducing bias in status attainment must necessarily focus on the early stages of bias production. This is as important for disvalued processes, where self-attrition is likely to be foreclosed after entry into official processing, as it is for valued processes, where the "shadow" bias of self-attrition is likely to increase with process once incumbents more carefully assess the marginal returns of additional processing. Although it is probably far more difficult to break down bias in the early stages of status attainment than in later ones, it is also probably far more cost-effective in the long run. Regulated equity at the tail-end of bias production requires a great many generational iterations before any major distributional change in Type/Countertype occurs, and it does so regardless of maximally optimistic assumptions about the generational transmission of status. Thus, from our perspective, unless the "early" strategy is attempted, high levels of bias are likely to remain in the system for the very long run. Such pessimism aside, our hope is that — if not actually provided by it — the present analysis will prompt more effective approaches to the study of bias in the future than the very ineffective ones of the past.

REFERENCES

Anderson, Andy B., Anthony R. Harris, and JoAnn Miller
    1983   "Models of deterrence theory." Social Science Research 12:236–262.
Arnold, William R.
    1971   "Race and ethnicity relative to other factors in juvenile court dispositions." American Journal of Sociology 77:211–227.
Berk, Richard A, and Subhash C. Ray
    1982   "Selection biases in sociological data." Social Science Research 11:352–398.
Bernstein, Ilene N., William R. Kelly, Patricia A. Doyle
    1977   "Societal reaction to deviants: the case of criminal defendants." American Sociological Review 42:743–755.
Blau, Peter, and Otis D. Duncan
    1967   The American Occupational Structure. New York: Wiley.

Chiricos, Theodore G., and Gordon P. Waldo
   1975   "Socioeconomic status and criminal sentencing: an empirical assessement of a conflict proposition." American Sociological Review 40:753–772.
Clarke, Stevens H., and Gary G. Koch
   1976   "The influence of income and other factors on whether criminal defendents go to prison." Law and Society Review 11:57–92.
Daly, Kathleen
   1983   "Order in the Courts: Gender and Justice." Unpublished PhD dissertation, Amherst, MA: University of Massachusetts.
Dohrenwend, Bruce P. and Barbara S. Dohrenwend
   1976   "Sex differences and psychiatric disorders." American Journal of Sociology 81:1447–1454.
Duncan, Otis D., David L. Featherman, and Beverley Duncan
   1972   Socioeconomic Background and Achievement. New York: Seminar Press.
Elliot, Delbert S., and Suzanne S. Ageton
   1980   "Reconciling race and class differences in self-reported and official estimates of delinquency." American Sociological Review 45:95–110.
Featherman, David L., and Robert M. Hauser
   1976   "Changes in the socioeconomic stratification of the races, 1962–73." American Journal of Sociology 82:621–651.
Featherman, David L., Robert M. Hauser, and Gary D. Sandefur
   1981   "Opportunity and change." Social Forces 59:867–886.
Hagan, John
   1974   "Extra-legal attributes and criminal sentencing: an assessment of a sociological viewpoint." Law and Society Review 8:357–383.
Hamilton, V. Lee
   1978   "Who is responsible? Toward a social psychology of responsibility attribution." Social Psychology 41:316–328.
Harris, Anthony R., and Gary D. Hill
   1982   "The social psychology of deviance: toward a reconciliation with social structure." Annual Review of Sociology 8:161–186.
Hauser, Robert M., and David L. Featherman
   1976   "Equality of schooling: trends and prospects." Sociology of Education 49:99–120.
Hauser, Robert M., and Thomas N. Daymont
   1977   "Schooling, ability, and earnings: cross-sectional findings 8 to 14 years after high school graduation." Sociology of Education 50:182–206.
Hill, Gary D.
   1980   "The Production of Bias in Deviant Status Attainment Processes." Unpublished PhD dissertation, Amherst, MA: University of Massachusetts.
Hill, Gary D., and Anthony R. Harris
   1982   "Changes in the gender-patterning of crime, 1953–1977: opportunity vs. identity." Social Science Quarterly 62:658–671.
Hindelang, Michael J., Travis Hirschi, and Joseph G. Weis
   1979   "Correlates of delinquency: the illusion of discrepancy between self-report and official measures." American Sociological Review 44:995–1014.
Hirschi, Travis, and Michael J. Hindelang
   1977   "Intelligence and delinquency: a revisionist review." American Sociological Review 42:571–586.
Hofstadter, Douglas R.
   1980   Gödel, Escher, Bach: An Eternal Golden Braid. New York: Basic Books.

Hughes, Everett C.
1945 "Dilemmas and contradictions of status." American Journal of Sociology 50:353–359.
Jensen, Gary F.
1976 "Race, achievement,and delinquency: a further look at delinquency in a birth cohort." American Journal of Sociology 82:379–87.
Jones, Edward E., and Keith E. Davis
1965 "From acts to dispositions: the attribution process in person perception." Pp. 219–266 in Leonard Berkowitz (ed.), Advances in Experimental Social Psychology, Vol. 2. New York: Academic Press.
Kahneman, Daniel, and Amos Tversky
1982 "The psychology of preferences." Scientific American 246:160–173.
Kanter, Rosabeth M.
1977 "Some effects of proportions on group life: skewed sex ratios and responses to token women." American Journal of Sociology 82:965–990.
Kessler, Ronald C., and Paul D. Cleary
1980 "Social class and psychological distress." American Sociological Review 45:463–478.
Kessler, Ronald C., and James A. McCrae
1981 "Trends in the relationship between sex and psychological distress." American Sociological Review 46:443–452.
Leik, Robert K., and Barbara F. Meeker
1975 Mathematical Sociology. Englewood Cliffs, NJ: Prentice-Hall.
Myers, Martha A.
1980 "Social contexts and attributions of criminal responsibility." Social Psychology Quarterly 43:405–419.
Ofshe, Lynne, and Richard Ofshe
1970 Utility and Choice in Social Interaction. Englewood Cliffs, NJ: Prentice-Hall.
Phillips, Doretha M., and Lois B. DeFleur
1977 "The 'masculinization' of female offenders and its impact on recommended dispositions of offenders." Unpublished manuscript, Pullman, WA: Washington State University.
Rosenberg, Morris, and Roberta Simmons
1971 Black and White Self-Esteem: the Urban School Child. Rose Monograph, Washington, D.C.: American Sociological Association.
Schur, Edwin M.
1971 Labeling Deviant Behavior; Its Sociological Implications. NY: Harper and Row.
Schutz, Alfred
1964–73 Collected Papers. Ed. Maurice Natanson, The Hague: M. Nijhoff.
Slovic, Paul, Baruch Fishoff, and Sarah Lichtenstein
1977 "Behavioral decision theory." Annual Review of Psychology 28:1–39.
Tudor, William, Jeannette Tudor, and Walter R. Gove
1979 "The effect of sex role differences on the societal reaction to mental retardation." Social Forces 57:871–886.
Weber, Max
1930 The Protestant Ethic and the Spirit of Capitalism. Trans. Talcott Parsons, NY: Scribner's.
White, Harrison, C., Scott A Boorman, and Ronald L. Breiger
1976 "Social structure from multiple networks. I. Block-models of roles and positions." American Journal of Sociology 81:730–780.

Wilson, William J.
  1978   The Declining Significance of Race: Blacks and Changing American Institutions. Chicago, IL: University of Chicago.
Wright, Erik O.
  1979   Class Structure and Income. NY: Academic Press.

Two

Searching For Structure In Beliefs

Robert F. Saltz
Pacific Institute for Research and Evaluation
Berkeley, CA

INTRODUCTION

Developments within the various social sciences have given rise, in the last twenty years or so, to schools of thought that challenge some of the most fundamental assumptions of their parent disciplines. So-called "Chomskian" linguistics, "cognitive" psychology, the "new ethnography" in anthropology, and "ethnomethodology" in sociology have each proposed new directions for their fields to take, alternative criteria for evaluating their models and theories, and invented methods for meeting the problems generated by their conceptions of their subjects.

Although the great differences in their traditions and terminology make any generalization risky, I would say that these schools share a conviction that the "mechanistic" image of human behavior has proved ineffectual, however valuable it has been in generating coherent research strategies. The social sciences now have to confront those phenomena that the behaviorists of an earlier day had proudly ignored—cognition, language, knowledge, meaning—what we could refer to as the "creative" aspects of human behavior. Cognition, the exercise of knowledge in practical affairs, has moved from the periphery of our attention to the center.

In our discipline, this development has brought with it a renewed interest in an interpretive sociology, in that the latter has traditionally maintained that the social world depends upon the active engagement of its members with one another through the creation of an understanding between them. Such a relationship between actors is said to preclude the success of any "behavioral" analysis of social interaction. Instead, we must, as sociologists, discover and describe the *sense* that people recognize in each other's actions, and in the various scenes encompassing them.

But this requirement has been most difficult to meet. For, as persuasive as its critique of scientism may be, the interpretive approach has not offered an attractive alternative program for research. This paper seeks to address that deficiency by developing a method for discovering and representing what people "know" about their world, so as to facilitate further research into how that knowledge becomes effective in any system of action.

Following a line of reasoning that can be traced to Max Weber, I want to argue that any sociological analysis must include an explication of a relevant "scheme of interpretation" that provides organization to a course of action. Such schemes are interrelated sets of beliefs that connect types of acts with types of actors, social settings with typical motives, and various purposes with the best means by which they can be met. Because any set of such beliefs is never wholly articulated, it is up to the sociologist to devise some way to uncover it and demonstrate the systemic properties that it must have in order to be salient for any organized social relationship. This task, in its general form, is the one I shall pursue here.

A social relationship depends on its members having some basis on which to anticipate a meaningful course of action. These expectations are possible because members are provided with normatively-warranted schemes of interpretation in terms of which human action is predicted and accounted for.[1] In a formulation particularly well-suited for our purposes, Kaufman summarized the argument thus:

> To say that a society of a particular kind exists at a certain place and time means that there exists a field of application for a scheme of interpretation. (1958: 161)

A game of cards, then, is identified as a social relationship, with its rules providing a scheme of interpretation by which players can understand and predict each other's actions. That the predictions may be wrong in no way weakens the necessity for having the scheme.[2] It provides the sense of rationality without which organized action would be impossible.[3] One cannot *relate* to arational behavior.[4]

---

[1] To say that such schemes are unnecessary because people learn to behave through inductive learning begs the question. How, for instance, can one learn to recognize an "act" when it can be accomplished through many different means?

[2] Indeed, were predictions 100% correct there would not be the sense of a "game," and perhaps no sense either of a *social* interaction.

[3] Here one may see the tie to Weber's analysis of "rationalization"—which describes how schemes of interpretation become increasingly complex, coherent, and consistent.

[4] Rationality is not inherent in behavior in the "abstract."

Unfortunately for sociologists, the task of discovering such schemes of interpretation in the world at large is much more difficult than in the card game. Their existence is only dimly perceptible and partially accessible to the members involved. Thus, sociologists are faced with the problem of how to discover, describe, and explicate these schemes.

Although I have used Weber's terms as a starting point, a "scheme of interpretation" should be a familiar concept to anyone who acknowledges the existence of some system of presupposed beliefs. With some reservation, one can say that equivalent notions underlie references to a frame of reference, definition of the situation, ideology, Weltanschauung, emic classification, collective representation, and belief system. Whatever "it" is, our methodological problem remains the same: How can we render it accessible to empirical research?

Because "belief system" is the most generic, familiar, and neutral of the terms listed above, it would be to our advantage to substitute it for "scheme of interpretation" in order to facilitate a more general discussion. But, because we are not interested in just any collection of beliefs, I want to restrict our attention to systems of beliefs with the following characteristics:

1. *Content.* By definition, belief systems contain propositions, any one of which is said to be "true." While we cannot be certain of what specific kinds of propositions we might find relevant for a given social relationship, we are especially interested in those that:

a. name the acts people are capable of (e.g., witchcraft; insults)
b. give reasons for why people do those acts (a vocabulary of motives)
c. identify who does what (a role system)
d. link specific situations to resulting actions (causal theories).

The belief system (like rules for a game) contains statements that relate social positions, actions, motives and situations in particular ways (e.g., "Judges don't let criminals go free unless they've been threatened or bribed").

2. *Structure.* It is redundant to say so, but we must stress that a belief system is a *structured* set of beliefs. So much attention has been given to the content and evaluation of beliefs that this more theoretically important aspect of beliefs has been overlooked. If beliefs were not structured in some way, it would be necessary to subject all *possible* propositions to rote memorization, as any statement heard for the first time could elicit no judgement, true or false, in response. Likewise, the observation that some beliefs are changed easily, while others are not, tells us that beliefs are differentially valued, and this is most likely the result of their having different statuses relative to other beliefs. That one can

amend his or her own beliefs on force of cogitation poses problems for the "hammered in" theory of belief acquisition. In that propositions express relations between objects, any newly-admitted proposition will have consequential effects throughout the system. Sudden "gestalt shifts" are dependent on our having extensive and interrelated expectations relative to one frame of reference, which are then thrown aside for those of another.

In sum, we can effectively describe a belief system as an inferential "net" of relations between culturally-defined objects that generates criteria for evaluating the truth of any proposition.

3. *Function.* To say that belief systems (as interpretive schemes) are functional is to say that they have a *utility* in the world and that they are a *social,* and not a psychological, phenomenon.

The first point follows directly from Weber's argument. The assertions contained within the belief system *enable* us to understand and anticipate each other's actions. "Friends don't lie" enables us to "see" who our friends are, and also gives us reason to believe what our friends tell us; it aids in pulling our friends "into line," but also leads us to see that our telling lies must mean we no longer feel friendly towards the recipient. The belief that "friends don't lie" tells us little about whether, in fact, friends do or do not lie. It does not even allow us to say that noticed lies between friends will be cause for sanction or remark. It does tell us that it is available as a resource for multiple purposes as they arise in day-to-day life. We do not "internalize" these beliefs and then act in accordance with them; many if not most of them are not prescriptive or proscriptive in the crude sense that that model suggests. Rather, again like the rules for a game, they provide a sense of organization—they are *constitutive* beliefs.

Our second point, that the belief systems we are interested in are necessarily social, is a bit more difficult to convey.[5] Let us assume for the moment that they are not—that belief systems, frames of reference, or whatever, are properly understood as individual-level phenomena, that each person has his "own" interpretive scheme. It is necessary to appreciate that, in the social world, such individual schemes would be specifically useless, like card players announcing "I'll play my game, you play yours, and we'll see who wins." Coordinate social action depends on the possibility of recognizing correct and incorrect action, a possibility

---

[5] We should not be taken to be arguing against the existence of beliefs that individuals hold. It is just that we are interested here in those that are "sanctionable," especially those that a society labels as "knowledge."

eliminated in the solipsist's world. In the same way that conventional systems of measurement allow coordinated constructions, so does a conventional belief system allow for a constructed reality.[6]

The function of a belief system for action is thus closely analogous to the function of a grammar for speaking. Notice in particular that the "rules" of grammar enable us to understand one another, that it makes little sense to say that we each have our own "grammar." More interestingly, note that often a rule of grammar is purposely "disobeyed" (as when an informal address is substituted for the proper formal) in order to achieve some result (e.g., an insult) that could only be planned within the context of that set of rules. Rules, that is, enable even their violation to be meaningful.

The analogy to grammar also lets us more clearly understand the long-range research strategy for the student of belief systems, for representing and explicating the system, an enormous task in itself, is only the preliminary step towards a full understanding of social action. Action "on the scene" is, as we have suggested, action which is informed but not "predicted" by interpretive schemes. In fact, we must allow for the possibility that some social relationships will involve negotiations over which of several competing (but conventional) schemes will be applied. A variety of contingent events, both planned and fortuitous, lead the social actor to adopt various strategies as the occasions arise, a process the symbolic interactionists have long been concerned with, but strategies that can only be recognized relative to the frame of reference. While the prospects of such a full and detailed undersanding of social action seem remote, any progress in that direction should bring some intermediate satisfaction.

We now have some understanding of the nature of our query. Functional belief systems are the lay person's equivalent of Weber's Ideal Types. They are not simply records of what people know, but are what allow the "recognition" of culturally-significant situations, actors, and intentions.

We must develop, for any social domain, some procedure that will permit us to represent a functional system of beliefs that may not be consciously available as such to any member. We want to be able to supply an "ethnography of belief".

---

[6] There is much that can be said here about alternative forms of interpretive sociology, from symbolic interaction to ethnomethodology. Such a discussion would take us far away from the central concerns of this paper, however, so we must make more general remarks that are less specifically applicable to one particular school.

II

An understanding of any social relationship requires an analysis of a relevant "scheme of interpretation" by which actors organize their course of action. This scheme constitutes a logically-related set of beliefs that links action with actors, causes with results, motives with reasons, ends with means. It incorporates folk theories of attribution, motivation, rationality, and order. It is through the organization of these concepts and their application that a belief system gives meaning to social action. The methods I am going to describe here are intended to recover and represent that organization.

The unit of analysis for these methods is the *domain*. The concept of a domain is used variously by researchers (primarily anthropologists and linguists) to describe a relatively coherent body of concepts and relations that a culture provides for its members to apply in specified social settings. In most cases, the domain is understood to be a *categorization* of cultural phenomena. Its coherence derives frm the member's ability to see the relations within a domain as relevant to the cultural objects it describes and defines. Criminals may be more easily categorized by how "dangerous" they are than restaurant cooks could be, for whom a different set of relations might be seen as relevant.

In so-called primitive societies, cultural domains may be relatively few, with each one applying to a large segment of social life, while we expect large, heterogeneous societies to include a complex system of domains with relatively specific applications.[7] Even in the smallest societies, however, the discovery and identification of cultural domains presents a formidible challenge to the ethnographer, as these domains provide a *context* for communication, and are rarely in themselves the subject of discussion.

Sociologists, to the extent that they are students of their own culture, are in the enviable position of having most cultural domains charted out in advance. One could say, in fact, that the modern discipline of sociology has divided its labor along corresponding cultural domains, as when we have a "sociology of work" or a "sociology of religion."

I have chosen the domain of "crime and criminality" to illustrate how one might analyze a system of beliefs. Though this choice was somewhat arbitrary, it has several virtues.

First, "crime and criminality" is an area within sociology that has developed a rich theoretical tradition. It should be correspondingly easier

---

[7] Of course, this distinction may be an artifact of an inability to appreciate complexity in the primitive societies.

to identify the implications that a belief system might have for related action. A second feature of the chosen domain is that it is at once fairly broad and yet relatively well-circumscribed within the culture. This is really a guess, but one might suppose that the more general domain of "deviance," for example, may have boundaries less easily distinguished by members of the culture. The area of crime and criminality has the advantage of its association with a relatively public set of codifications (i.e., laws) that constrain the variability in cultural definition and decision-making. Finally, the institutionalization of the culture's beliefs in the area of criminality allows us to more easily investigate the implications that may be identified from work on the belief structure. The "arena" of action related to these beliefs is much more open to us than is the case with many other domains. Decisions are more often made in public, with reasons given for the disposition. One can, in other words, more easily assess the "outcome" of actions related to specific beliefs.

The procedures I shall describe draw most heavily from Roy D'Andrade's article entitled "A propositional analysis of U.S. American beliefs about illness" (1976).[8] They are employed to (1) systematically elicit statements of belief in propositional form, and (2) analyze underlying relationships among the beliefs that may not be consciously available to members of the culture. The limited length of this paper permits me to give only the briefest possible report of the design, leaving many intermediate steps out altogether. The reader interested in a full description (with suggestions for modifying the procedures) should consult Saltz (1981).

First Stage: Eliciting Beliefs about Crime and Criminality

In gathering statements of belief, one might attempt to overhear conversations in hopes of recording such statements as they occur. Ignoring the question of its efficiency, such a procedure would be sure to miss many important beliefs and emphasize those that are in dispute. A more efficient strategy would be to create a large collection of "candidate" statements of belief, and then ask informants to tell which of them are "true" and which are "false."

This is what I have done by adapting the "substitution-frame" technique introduced by Metzger and Williams (1963, 1966). Through questionnaires, interviews, and my own judgement, I collected nearly 100 statements about crimes and criminal behavior, each one constructed

---

[8] See D'Andrade (1976) and Saltz (1981) for a more detailed discussion of these techniques and of how they can be generalized to other applications.

TABLE 1.   Fifty Crimes Used in The Analysis

1. Kill someone.
2. Sell heroin.
3. Hijack an airplane.
4. Hold up a bank or store.
5. Assault someone with a gun.
6. Kidnap someone.
7. Assassinate a public official.
8. Make sexual advances to children.
9. Kill a spouse.
10. Use heroin.
11. Mug someone.
12. Start a fire in a building.
13. Desert to the enemy in time of war.
14. Exceed the speed limit.
15. Seduce a minor.
16. Sell marijuana.
17. Commit incest.
18. Break into and enter a store.
19. Cash stolen checks.
20. Blackmail someone.
21. Neglect to care for own children.
22. Beat someone up
23. Drive while drunk.
24. Burglarize a home.
25. Take bribes.
26. Refuse to obey a police officer.
27. Steal a car.
28. Loot goods in a riot.
29. Pass counterfeit money.
30. Beat up their spouse.
31. Buy stolen goods.
32. Refuse to serve when drafted.
33. Resist arrest.
34. Use false identification.
35. Lie on an income tax return.
36. Drive while their license is suspended.
37. Shoplifts.
38. Smuggle goods.
39. Refuse to make essential repairs to rental property.
40. Engage in homosexual acts.
41. Fix prices of a consumer product.
42. Sell pornographic magazines.
43. Falsely advertise.
44. Disturb the peace.
45. Be drunk in public.
46. Use marijuana.
47. Forcibly rape someone.
48. Vandalize someone's property.
49. Engage in prostitution.
50. Embezzle from an employer.

TABLE 2.   Final Set of Fifty Frames Used in The Analysis

1. —— is a violent act.
2. —— is morally wrong.
3. —— is done for material benefit.
4. —— involves use of force.
5. —— is an irrational act.
6. —— is only technically wrong.
7. —— is an everyday crime.
8. —— can happen accidently.
9. —— is a serious crime.
10. —— is an impulsive act.
11. —— is a sex crime.
12. —— requires having a weapon.
13. —— requires planning.
26. —— is hard for authorities to detect when it happens.
27. A person caught for —— will receive a severe penalty.
28. People could be prevented from ——.
29. A person could have justifiable reasons for ——.
30. Whatever is done, —— will always occur.
31. One could —— without knowing it.
32. Drunkenness can lead a person to ——.
33. If they thought they could get away with it, most people would ——.

TABLE 2. *(continued)*

14. ———— requires learning how to do it first.
15. ———— is a street crime.
16. ———— happens in a public setting.
17. If ———— were not outlawed, everyone would do it.
18. ———— is a victimless crime.
19. ———— is done to gain power over others.
20. ———— is done out of an urge or compulsion to do so.
21. People expect to be a victim of ———— at some time.
22. Everyone will be a victim of ———— at some time.
23. ———— does little harm to anyone.
24. One can make a living from ————.
25. ———— causes personal injury.

34. Insanity could cause a person to ————, even if they didn't want to do it.
35. A person who has ———— has only affected him or herself.
36. A person who has ———— will get away with it.
37. A person who has ———— is mentally ill.
38. A person who has ———— is irresponsible.
39. A person who has ———— is highly emotional.
40. A person who has ———— could commit other crimes as well.
41. A person who has ———— is just the same as anyone else.
42. A person who has ———— will see him or herself as a criminal.
43. A person who has ———— has attitudes similar to everyone else's.
44. A person who has ———— is generally hostile toward others.
45. When a person has ————, the victim is a stranger to the criminal.
46. When a person has ————, the victim is responsible for the harm done.
47. When a person has ————, the victim will report the crime.
48. A person who has ———— is a misfit.
49. A person would have ———— to make money.
50. A person could have ———— for no particular reason.

so as to include reference to a specific act (e.g., "Killing someone is a violent act"; "A person who has raped someone is a misfit"). I then selected a set of 50 crimes, each of which could be substituted for another in the statements obtained (e.g., "Smoking marijuana is a violent act"; "Stealing a car is a violent act"). With the set of sentence "frames" (e.g., "————is a violent act") and the 50 acts (e.g., "stealing a car"), I constructed nearly 5000 statements. This set of statements was broken into questionnaires of 100 statements each that respondents were asked to judge as being true or false.[9]

Preliminary analysis determined that many of these frames were not salient. If a frame makes no distinction between crimes, that is, if it takes the same truth-value no matter which crime is substituted into it, it is of little use to the belief system in making further inferences. Such a frame shows up in the data as having a low variance in respondent's judgements across all the crimes substituted into it. A low variance would also result from respondents' uncertainty regarding a statement, or from its having no consensus. In any of these cases, the frame would not be considered crucial to the domain. For these reasons, only 50 frames with the highest variances were retained for analysis.

The analysis of the belief system is thus based on the pattern of judgements given when the crimes listed in Table 1 were substituted into the frames listed in Table 2.

Second Stage: Finding Structure in Beliefs

Table 3 presents the Frame-by-Crime binary matrix (50 Frames by 50 Crimes) produced by respondent judgements, where a "1" indicates that the sentence formed by the intersecting row (frame) and column (crime) was "true," and "0" indicates "false". In this table we can find, for example, that Frame #23 ("———does little harm to anyone") is "true" for only three crimes—#34, #40, and #46 ("using false identification," "engaging in homosexual acts," and "using marijuana").

Perhaps the best way to view Table 3 is by regarding each frame as a *category* relevant to crime and criminality. "——— is a violent act" represents the class of violent acts, with the "1"s in that row identifying the acts that fall into that category. We are interested in the organization of these categories, specifically that which would allow a member of the culture to make inferences from one category to another.

Patterns arising out of data such as we have here (in Table 3) may be sought out in a variety of ways. Typical strategies involve some sort of clustering algorithm (see Stefflre et al. (1971) for an example). I have chosen D'Andrade's (1976) approach instead, since, as we will see, it permits a much more detailed analysis than does clustering.

We can begin by constructing, from the data in Table 3, a four-cell contingency table for each pair of frames (pairs of rows in the data matrix). Take, for example, frames (rows) #1 ("——— is a violent act") and #9

---

[9] Pretest experience found that a larger number of statements greatly increased respondent fatigue, and decreased the rate of response.

TABLE 3. Aggregated Judgements of Propositions Regarding Criminality

DISPLAY TRUTH

		1	2	3	4	5	6	7	8	9	10	11	12	13	14	15	16	17	18	19	20	21	22	23	24	25	26	27	28	29	30	31	32	33	34	35	36	37	38	39	40	41	42	43	44	45	46	47	48	49	50
VIOLENT	1	1	0	1	1	1	1	1	1	1	0	1	1	1	0	1	0	1	1	0	0	1	1	1	0	1	1	1	0	1	0	0	0	0	0	0	0	0	0	0	0	0	0	1	1	0	0
MORALLY	2	1	1	1	1	1	1	1	1	1	1	0	1	0	1	0	1	1	1	1	1	1	1	1	1	1	1	1	0	1	1	1	0	1	1	1	0	0	0	1	1	1
MATERIAL	3	0	1	1	1	1	1	0	0	0	0	1	1	0	0	0	1	0	1	0	1	0	0	0	1	1	0	1	1	0	1	0	0	1	1	0	1	1	0	1	1	0	0	0	0	0	1	1
FORCE	4	1	0	1	1	1	1	1	1	0	1	0	0	0	0	0	0	1	0	0	0	1	0	1	0	0	0	0	1	0	1	0	0	0	1	0	0	0	0	0	0	0	0	0	0	1	1	0	0
IRRATIONAL	5	1	0	1	1	1	1	1	1	1	1	0	1	0	1	0	0	0	0	0	1	1	1	0	0	1	1	1	0	0	0	0	0	0	1	0	0	1	0	1	0	1	0	0	0	1	0	0
TECHNICALLY	6	0	0	0	0	0	0	0	0	0	0	1	1	0	1	0	0	0	0	0	0	0	0	0	0	1	1	0	1	0	0	0	1	0	0	0	1	0	0	0	1	0	0	0	0	0	1	1
EVERYDAY	7	0	1	0	1	0	0	0	1	0	1	1	1	0	1	1	0	0	1	0	1	0	1	1	1	1	1	0	0	0	1	0	0	1	0	1	1	0	1	1	0	1	1	0	0	1	1	1
ACCIDENTALLY	8	1	0	0	0	0	0	0	0	0	1	0	1	0	0	0	0	0	0	1	0	0	1	0	0	1	0	1	0	0	1	0	0	0	0	0	0	1	1	1	0	0	0	0	0
SERIOUS	9	1	1	1	1	1	1	1	1	1	0	1	1	1	0	1	0	1	1	1	1	1	1	1	1	1	1	1	0	0	0	1	0	0	1	1	0	0	1	0	1	0	0	0	0	1	1	0	1
IMPULSIVE	10	1	0	0	0	1	0	1	0	0	0	0	0	1	1	0	0	0	0	0	0	1	1	0	0	1	0	1	0	1	0	0	1	0	1	1	0	0	0	0	0	1	0	0	0	0	1	0	1	0
SEX	11	0	0	0	0	0	0	0	0	1	0	0	0	0	0	1	0	1	0	0	0	0	0	0	0	0	0	0	0	0	0	0	0	1	0	0	0	0	0	0	1	0	0	0	0	0	1	0	0
WEAPON	12	1	0	1	1	1	1	1	0	1	0	1	0	0	0	0	0	0	0	0	0	0	0	0	0	0	0	1	0	1	0	0	1	1	1	0	1	0	1	1	1	0	0	0	0	1	0	1
PLANNING	13	0	1	1	1	1	1	0	0	1	1	1	1	0	0	1	0	1	0	1	1	1	0	0	0	1	0	0	0	1	0	1	0	1	0	0	0	0	1	1	1	0	0	0	1	0	0	0
LEARNING	14	0	0	0	0	1	0	0	1	0	0	1	0	0	0	0	0	0	0	1	0	0	1	0	1	0	0	0	0	1	1	1	0	1	0	0	1	1	0	0	0	1	1	0	1	1	1	0
STREET	15	1	1	0	1	0	0	1	0	1	1	0	0	1	0	1	0	1	0	0	0	0	1	1	1	1	1	1	1	0	1	1	1	1	1	0	1	1	1	0	0	0	1	1	1	0	1	1	0
PUBLIC	16	1	1	1	0	0	1	0	0	1	1	1	0	1	0	1	0	0	1	1	0	0	1	0	1	0	1	0	1	0	0	1	1	0	1	1	0	1	1	0
EVERYONE WLD	17	0	0	0	1	0	0	0	0	0	0	0	0	1	0	0	0	1	0	0	0	1	0	0	0	0	1	0	0	1	1	1	0	1	1	0	1	1	0	1	1	1	0	0	0	1	0	0	0	1
VICTIMLESS	18	0	0	0	0	0	0	0	0	0	0	0	0	0	1	0	0	0	1	0	0	0	0	0	0	0	0	0	0	1	0	0	1	0	0	0	0	0	1	0	0	1	1	0	0	0	0
POWER	19	1	0	1	0	0	1	0	0	0	1	1	0	0	0	0	0	1	0	1	0	0	1	0	0	1	0	1	0	0	1	0	0	0	0	1	0	0	0	1	0	0
COMPULSION	20	1	0	1	0	0	0	1	1	0	0	1	1	0	1	0	1	0	1	0	1	0	1	0	1	0	1	0	1	1	0	1	0	1	0	1	1	0	0	1	1	0	1	1	1	0	0
EXPECT BE VIC	21	0	0	0	0	0	0	0	0	0	0	1	0	1	0	0	0	0	0	0	0	0	1	0	0	0	0	1	0	1	0	1	0	1	0	1	0	1	0	0
WILL BE	22	0	0	0	0	0	0	0	0	0	1	0	0	0	0	0	0	0	0	0	0	0-0	0	0	0	0	0	1	0	1	0	0	1	0	0	0	1	1	0	0	0	0
LITTLE HARM	23	0	0	0	0	0	0	0	0	0	0	0	0	0	0	0	0	0	0	0	0	0	0	0	0	0	0	1	0	0	0	0	1	0	0	0	0	1	0	0	0
MAKE LIVING	24	1	1	0	1	1	0	0	0	0	1	0	1	0	0	1	0	0	0	0	1	0	1	0	1	0	1	0	0	1	1	0	1	0	0	0	0	0	1	0	0	1	1	0	0	0
PERSONAL INJ	25	1	0	1	0	1	1	1	1	1	1	1	1	0	0	0	1	0	0	1	1	1	1	0	0	0	0	1	0	0	1	1	1	1	0	1	1	0	0	0	0	1	0	0	1
DETECT	26	0	1	0	0	0	0	0	1	0	0	0	1	1	1	0	1	1	0	1	1	0	1	0	1	0	0	0	0	0	1	1	1	0	0	0	0	0	0	0	1	0	0	0
SEV PENALTY	27	1	1	1	1	1	1	0	1	0	1	0	1	0	0	0	0	0	0	1	0	1	1	1	0	0	1	0	1	0	1	1	0	1	1	1	1	0	0	1	0	1
PREVENTED	28	1	0	1	1	0	1	1	0	0	1	0	1	0	0	1	0	1	0	1	0	1	1	0	0	1	1	1	0	0	0	1	0	1	0	1	1	1	0	1	0	1	0
REASONS	29	0	0	0	1	0	1	0	0	1	1	0	1	0	1	0	1	0	0	0	1	0	0	0	1	0	0	1	0	1	0	1	1	0	1	0	1	1	1	1	1	0
ALWAYS	30	1	1	1	1	1	1	1	0	1	1	1	1	1	0	1	1	0	1	1	0	1	1	0	1	0	1	0	1	1	1	1	0	1	1	0	1	0	0	1	0	0
NOT KNOW	31	0	0	0	0	0	0	1	0	1	0	0	0	1	0	0	0	1	0	0	0	0	1	0	0	1	0	0	0	1	0	0	0	0	1	1	1	0	0	1	0	0
DRUNKENESS	32	0	0	0	1	0	0	1	0	0	1	0	0	1	0	1	0	1	1	0	0	1	1	0	1	0	1	0	1	0	0	0	0	0	1	1	0	1	0	1
WOULD DO	33	0	0	0	0	0	1	0	0	0	1	0	0	0	0	0	1	0	1	0	1	1	0	1	0	1	1	1	0	1	0	1	0	1	1	0	0	0	1
INSANITY	34	1	0	0	1	1	1	1	1	1	0	1	1	0	0	0	0	0	1	1	1	1	0	1	0	1	0	1	0	0	1	1	0	0	1	1	1	1	1	0	0
ONLY HSELF	35	0	0	0	0	0	0	0	0	0	0	0	0	0	0	1	0	0	0	0	1	0	0	0	0	0	0	0	0	1	0	0	0	0	0	0	0	0	1	0	0
GET AWAY	36	0	1	0	1	1	0	1	1	1	0	1	1	0	1	1	1	0	1	1	1	1	0	1	1	0	1	1	0	0	1	1	1	1	1	1	0	1	1	1	1	1	1	1
MENTALLY ILL	37	0	0	0	0	0	1	1	1	0	0	1	0	0	1	0	1	0	0	0	0	0	0	0	0	0	0	0	1	0	1	0	1	0	0	0	0	1	0
IRRESPONSIBLE	38	0	0	1	0	1	1	1	0	0	1	1	1	0	0	0	1	0	0	1	0	0	1	0	1	0	0	1	0	0	0	1	1	0	0	0	1	0	1	1	1	0	0	0
EMOTIONAL	39	1	1	1	0	0	1	0	0	1	0	1	0	1	0	1	0	1	0	0	0	0	0	0	0	0	1	1	0	0	0	1	0	0	0	1	1	1	1
OTHER CRIMES	40	1	1	1	1	1	1	0	1	1	1	0	0	0	0	1	1	0	1	0	1	1	0	0	0	0	0	0	1	1	1	1	1	1	0	1	1	0	0	0
SAME	41	0	0	0	0	0	0	0	1	0	0	1	0	1	0	0	0	0	0	1	0	0	1	0	1	0	1	1	0	1	0	1	0	0	0	0	0	0	0	0	1	0
SEE HSELF	42	1	1	1	1	1	0	0	1	0	0	0	1	0	0	1	0	0	0	1	0	0	0	0	0	0	1	0	0	0	0	0	0	0	0	0	1	0
ATT SIM	43	0	1	0	0	0	0	0	0	0	0	1	0	1	1	0	1	0	0	0	1	1	1	0	0	0	1	0	1	1	1	0	0	0	1	1	1	1	1	1	1	0	0	1	0
HOSTILE	44	1	0	1	0	1	1	0	1	0	0	0	1	0	0	0	0	1	0	0	0	0	0	0	1	0	1	0	1	0	1	0	1	0	0	0	0	1	0	0
VIC STRANGER	45	0	0	1	1	0	1	0	0	0	1	1	1	0	0	0	1	0	0	1	1	0	0	1	0	1	0	1	1	0	0	1	1	0	0	1	1	1	1	0	0	0	1	1
RESPONSIBLE	46	0	0	1	0	0	0	0	0	1	0	0	0	1	0	0	0	0	0	0	0	0	0	0	0	0	0	0	1	1	0	0	0	1	0	0	0	1	0	0	1	1
REPORT	47	0	0	1	1	1	1	1	0	0	1	1	0	0	0	1	1	0	0	1	0	1	0	1	0	0	1	1	1	0	0	0	0	1	0	0	1	0	1	1	0	0	0
MISFIT	48	1	1	0	0	0	0	1	1	0	0	1	0	0	1	0	1	0	0	0	0	0	0	0	0	1	0	1	0	0	0	0	0	0	1	1	0	0	0	1	0	0
MONEY	49	1	1	0	0	0	1	1	0	0	1	1	0	0	0	1	0	1	1	1	0	0	0	1	1	1	1	0	1	0	0	0	1	1	0	1	1	0	1	0	0	0	0	1	1
NO REASON	50	0	0	0	0	1	0	0	0	0	1	0	0	1	1	1	0	1	0	0	0	1	1	1	0	1	0	1	0	1	1	1	1	1	1	0	0	0	1	1	1	1	0	1	0	0

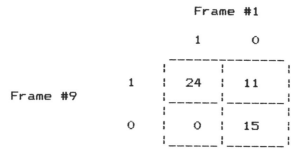

FIGURE 1.   Contingency Table for Frames #1 and #9.

("——— is a serious crime"). For Crime (column) #1 ("killing someone"), both frames are "true," so Crime #1 would be placed in the 1-1 quadrant of the four-cell table. Crime #2 ("selling heroin") is false for Frame #1 and true for Frame #9, so it would be placed in the 0–1 quadrant for the same four-cell table. After assigning all 50 crimes in a similar manner, we are given the completed contingency table in Figure 1.

What can a table like this tell us? The table in Figure 1 reveals that there is no crime out of the 50 that is true for Frame #1 and false for Frame #9. This means that, in the belief system, all crimes that are "violent acts" are also "serious crimes" without exception. There are, on the other hand, eleven crimes that are "serious" without being "violent." Also, we can see that 15 crimes out of the 50 are considered neither "serious" nor "violent." According to the belief system, then, if an act is "violent," it follows that the crime is "serious."

The empty or "zero" cell in Figure 1 allowed us to identify the superset-subset relation between the two frames in our example. The *location* of the zero-cell is what informs us of the *type* of relation between the frames. If, for example, the top-right cell in the figure were the empty one, we would conclude that "all serious crimes are violent acts," that serious crimes form a subset of violent acts.

Besides the subset relation, the presence of one or two zero-cells may identify several other relationships between pairs of frames, as is shown in Figure 2. Note, for example, that an empty cell in the "true-true" (upper-left) quadrant identifies an "exclusive" relation between two frames. In this case, knowing that an object falls into one category also tells us that it cannot be a member of the other category. In our data, for instance, we will find that there is no crime that is both "victimless" and "violent." As in the case of the subset relation, the exclusive relation permits a logical conclusion to be drawn from one category to another.

Figure 2 lists other substantively-meaningful relations that one might

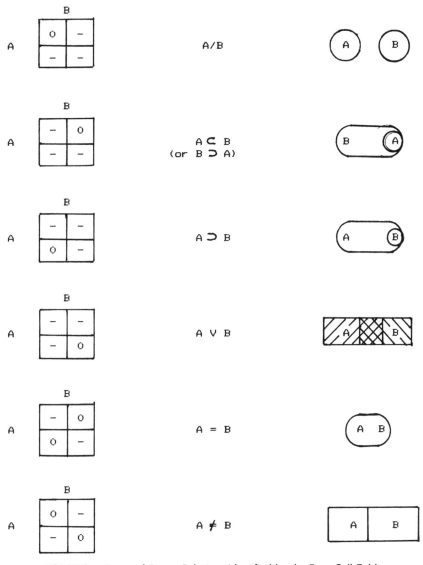

FIGURE 2.   Types of Frame Relations Identified by the Four-Cell Table.

find with any data. Accompanying each relation listed in Figure 2 is a Venn diagram that illustrates the same relation in a way perhaps more familiar to some.

Of the types of relations listed, I will, in this paper, confine my discussion to the subset–superset relation (A ⊂ B and its complement B ⊃ A). My interest in this relationship comes from the fact that it is unique

TABLE 4. Frame Relations with No Exceptions

DISPLAYC MAT0

	1	2	3	4	5	6	7	8	9	10	11	12	13	14	15	16	17	18	19	20	21	22	23	24	25	26	27	28	29	30	31	32	33	34	35	36	37	38	39	40	41	42	43	44	45	46	47	48	49	50
VIOLENT	1																																																	
MORALLY	2	c																																																
MATERIAL	3		c																																															
FORCE	4	c																																																
IRRATIONAL	5																																																	
TECHNICALLY	6																																																	
EVERYDAY	7																																																	
ACCIDENTALLY	8																																																	
SERIOUS	9	c																																																
IMPULSIVE	10																																																	
SEX	11	c																																																
WEAPON	12	c																																																
PLANNING	13																																																	
LEARNING	14																																																	
STREET	15																																																	
PUBLIC	16																																																	
EVERYONE WLD	17																																																	
VICTIMLESS	18																																																	
POWER	19	c																																																
COMPULSION	20																																																	
EXPECT BE VIC	21																																																	
WILL BE	22																																																	
LITTLE HARM	23																																																	
MAKE LIVING	24																																																	
PERSONAL INJ	25																																																	
DETECT	26																																																	
SEV PENALTY	27																																																	
PREVENTED	28																																																	
REASONS	29																																																	
ALWAYS	30	v																																																
NOT KNOW	31																																																	
DRUNKENESS	32																																																	
WOULD DO	33																																																	
INSANITY	34																																																	
ONLY HSELF	35																																																	
GET AWAY	36																																																	
MENTALLY ILL	37	c																																																
IRRESPONSIBLE	38																																																	
EMOTIONAL	39																																																	
OTHER CRIMES	40																																																	
SAME	41	v																																																
SEE HSELF	42																																																	
ATT SIM	43																																																	
HOSTILE	44	c																																																
VIC STRANGER	45																																																	
RESPONSIBLE	46																																																	
REPORT	47																																																	
MISFIT	48	c																																																
MONEY	49																																																	
NO REASON	50																																																	

94

by virtue of its being both *asymmetric* (i.e., A⊂B is not the same as B⊂A) and *transitive* (i.e., if A⊂B and B⊃C, then A⊂C). These properties allow us to construct an *ordering* of the frames, from the most inclusive to the most included (assuming that the belief system contains such subset relations). This ordering may be thought of as the "skeleton" of the belief system. It is the most significant feature of the system in that it represents the primary tool people have for *generating* beliefs by tracing through the "logical" implications of any crime's assignment to a category. Once this ordering is described, other relations may be used to give a more refined or accurate interpretation of the structure as a whole, putting flesh on the skeleton, so to speak.

With 50 frames, our data requires inspecting 1,225 pair-wise contingency tables for those containing a zero-cell. Fortunately, a computer can do this rather handily, and Table 4 identifies all of the relations that obtain. From this table we can discover, for instance, that Frame #1 ("———— is a violent act") is a subset of Frames #2 and #9 ("———— is morally wrong" and "———— is a serious crime"), is a superset of Frame #37 ("A person who has ———— is mentally ill"), and that it contrasts with Frames #18, #22, and #23 ("———— is a victimless crime," "Everyone will be a victim of ———— at some time," and "———— does little harm to anyone"). Schematically, we could show the relationships to Frame #1 ("violent acts") as in Figure 3.

Figure 3 tells us that violent acts are serious crimes and morally wrong, but also that those crimes for which mental illness is attributed are all violent acts. Finally, there are no crimes that are violent acts and that are also either victimless, do little harm to anyone, or of which everyone will be a victim.

Figure 4 shows the subset-superset relations from Table 4 with selected "contrast" relations. The diagram has been simplified to make it easier to read. First, where A⊂B, B⊂C, and A⊂C, the line between A and C has been left out (e.g., the direct line from 2 to 37). Secondly, where two frames, one a subset of the other, contrast with a third, the contrast

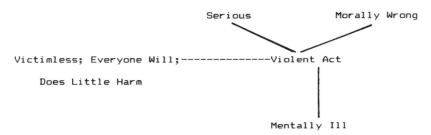

FIGURE 3.   Zero-Cell Relations for Selected Frames.

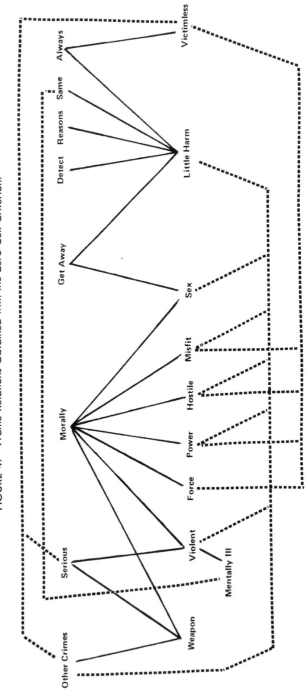

FIGURE 4.　Frame Relations Obtained with the Zero-Cell Criterion.

(dashed) line is drawn only for the superset, as the subset would contrast through transitivity. Thirdly, where several frames contrast with another frame, one dashed line is shown leading to the frame they contrast with (e.g., 4, 19, 44, and 48 all contrast with 18). Finally, frames which relate to others only by contrast have been left out of the diagram, as they would adversely affect its readability (e.g., frames 6 and 22).

What can be said about the beliefs represented in Figure 4? First, the overall structure seems to divide into two substructures: (1) those crimes which are "morally wrong" (Frame #2), and (2) those categories of crime that contain crimes which "do little harm to anyone" (Frame #23). The sense of this split is strengthened by the number of frames in each substructure that contrast with frames in the other.

Interestingly, the two substructures differ in shape—the frames on the left are all included in a single frame ("morally wrong") while the frames on the right bear a weaker relationship to each other by virtue of sharing a common subset ("does little harm to anyone"). The significance of this difference lies in the result that a crime which falls into any of the categories or frames on the left-hand substructure is thereupon known to be morally wrong as well (crimes to which mental illness is attributed are, in fact, know to be violent, serious, *and* morally wrong). For the majority of the frames on the right-hand substructure, however, such determinations cannot be made. Only for crimes that "do little harm to anyone" can we then say are also contained in frames 36, 26, 29, 41, and 30. Knowing that a crime is contained in any of these latter frames will *not* enable us to identify another membership.

Isolating these two substructures brings our attention to the elements they have in common, the frames that "link" them. The set of crimes people "will get away with" (36) contains a subset from each of the two major substructures, namely, "sex crimes" (11) and "those that do little harm to anyone" (23). Thus, while these two frames have no crimes in common, they do share the attribute of being things people will get away with. If either "sex crimes" or those people "will get away with" were left out of the diagram in Figure 4, the two substructures would be completely isolated from each other.

There are, finally, a few miscellaneous observations to be made concerning Figure 4. Crimes with a weapon, violent acts, and those attributable to mental illness (i.e., numbers 12, 1, and 37) are distinct from other morally wrong crimes by being serious crimes as well. Those crimes that require having a weapon are, in addition, crimes committed by people who "would commit other crimes as well" (Frame #40). Having committed a crime that required a weapon, in other words, is a *sufficient* criterion of one's potential to commit other crimes as well.

On a more substantive level, I am intrigued by the distinctions made between "victimless crimes" (18) and those that do "little harm to anyone" (23). The basic reason for the distinction is that the class of victimless crimes is larger than those that do little harm, and, in fact, the two share only one crime, "using marijuana" (refer to Table 3). Otherwise, "homosexual acts" and "using false identification" do little harm but are not victimless crimes, while selling marijuana, refusing to serve when drafted, lying on income tax returns, driving with suspended license, selling pornographic magazines, and being drunk in public are all victimless crimes but are not those that do little harm to anyone. This closer look at the crimes that distinguish victimless crimes from harmless crimes suggests that victimless crime is not, in the belief system, so much a category of harmless crime as it is crime for which the "victim" is ambiguous or unknown, especially for crimes against the state or "public good."

There are, undoubtedly, several other details that one could look at in the belief system of Figure 4, including an investigation into the frames located through the contrast relation. Instead of doing so, I would rather shift our attention to how the analytic strategy just described for the "zero" cell analysis may be generalized for less than "perfect" frame relationships.

QUALIFIED FRAME RELATIONS—"SMALLEST-CELL ANALYSIS"

The relationships depicted in Figure 4 are based strictly on the existence of a so-called "zero-cell" in a given pairwise contingency table. The diagram lets us say that where a line connects one frame to another, there are absolutely *no* exceptions to the relationship. The chief advantage to keeping this strict criterion for frame relations is that transitivity is held throughout the belief system as it is represented, i.e., we know that if A is a subset of B, and B contrasts with C, then, without exception, A contrasts with C.

There are, however, many reasons to relax this criterion for frame relations so as to identify *implicit* relationships that may admit of "exceptions." The simplest reason for relaxing the empty cell criterion is methodological. When the identification of a relation is made or broken on the assignment of a single crime to one of the cells, we make a demand for rigor that cannot be met by the methods used in collecting the data. This is reason enough to allow a range of "tolerance" (e.g., one or two exceptions to an empty cell) for mistaken assignments of truth values. This allowance is especially reasonable in that we are concerned more with *frame* relationships than with the more specific relationships of crimes to frames.

There are, as well, extrinsic or substantive reasons for looking at imperfect frame relations. First, there exist many classification systems that admit exceptions and are nevertheless considered useful. Thus, "birds can fly," but not ostrich nor penguin. Moreover, the number of exceptions can be relatively large when the exceptions form a sub-category of their own, e.g., sea mammals relative to mammals taken together.

We may also wish to consider frame relations that are considered to hold "in general" and which may be violated in certain circumstances for uncertain reasons. Social action is often directed by such "probabilisitc" relations and inferences others might make, as when one takes pains to guard against misinterpretations that may not be likely, but merely possible. That a person who is an X is *sometimes* a Y is often sufficient reason for X's to be defensive (e.g., used-car salespeople). A full understanding of social action would depend on having information about "possible" as well as necessary relations within belief systems.

Finally, the rationale of last resort for consideration of these "qualified" frame relations would be so that our curiosity may be satisfied. There would seem little harm in "pushing" the analysis to its logical extension, as long as we are conscious of the limitations of the analysis. Again, my interest in the analysis of beliefs is so that it may inform social research, to lend the latter more coherence than it currently manifests. Weak or questionable results are thus not as damaging as they would be in standard hypothesis-testing.

These considerations lead me to propose an analysis of frame relations based on the cell with the *smallest* number of crimes (in the four-cell table) instead of the cell with *no* crimes. This strategy allows us to include frames that "intersect," so that if *most* of the crimes in one frame were found in another, the first would be, to a measurable extent, a subset of the second. Figure 5 shows the types of frame relations analogous to those in Figure 2. Note that the degree of intersection or "overlap" determines whether one frame is a subset of the other, whether they contrast, or whether they are equivalent. Also, unlike the zero-cell criterion, the use of the smallest cell opens the possibility that two cells in the same row or column, or even any three cells, turn out to be the smallest. This situation arises, for example, when one frame is exactly half-included in another (i.e., half the crimes true for one frame are true for the other). For convenience, I will call such four-cell tables "degenerate," and consider them a finding that the two frames are unrelated.[10]

Admittedly, relaxing the criterion of association in this way "forces" the data, and caution in interpreting the results is required. At the same

---

[10] The frames are unrelated, in that knowing that a crime is true for one frame tells one nothing about its truth in the other, unlike frames in either the subset or contrast relations.

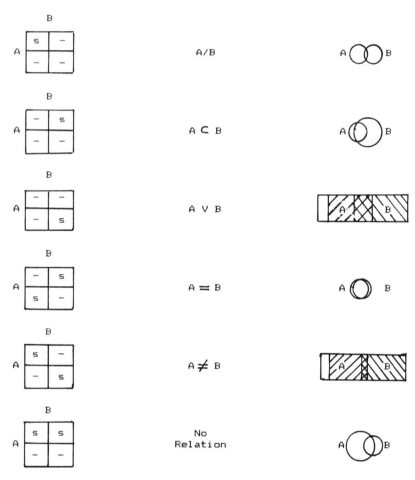

FIGURE 5.   Types of Frame Relations Identified by the Smallest-Cell Analysis.

time, a finding of no relationship is possible, and the data allow us to know how much stock to put into a particular pairwise relation, as we can recover the number of exceptions for any given contingency table.

I want to emphasize once more that I do not regard the analysis of belief systems as an end-in-itself. To study beliefs in isolation of what people actually do would be as seriously mistaken as the converse. In a complete course of research, an investigator would be as interested in suggested or implied relationships within beliefs, so that he or she could look for other empirical manifestations of the suspected connection in social interaction.

Having made my prefatory remarks, we can look at Table 5, which

TABLE 5. All Possible Frame Relations

DISPLAYC BIGMAT

1	VIOLENT
2	MORALLY
3	MATERIAL
4	FORCE
5	IRRATIONAL
6	TECHNICALLY
7	EVERYDAY
8	ACCIDENTALLY
9	SERIOUS
10	IMPULSIVE
11	SEX
12	WEAPON
13	PLANNING
14	LEARNING
15	STREET
16	PUBLIC
17	EVERYONE WLD
18	VICTIMLESS
19	POWER
20	COMPULSION
21	EXPECT BE VIC
22	WILL BE
23	LITTLE HARM
24	MAKE LIVING
25	PERSONAL INJ
26	DETECT
27	SEV PENALTY
28	PREVENTED
29	REASONS
30	ALWAYS
31	NOT KNOW
32	DRUNKENESS
33	WOULD DO
34	INSANITY
35	ONLY HSELF
36	GET AWAY
37	MENTALLY ILL
38	IRRESPONSIBLE
39	EMOTIONAL
40	OTHER CRIMES
41	SAME
42	SEE HSELF
43	ATT SIM
44	HOSTILE
45	VIC STRANGER
46	RESPONSIBLE
47	REPORT
48	MISFIT
49	MONEY
50	NO REASON

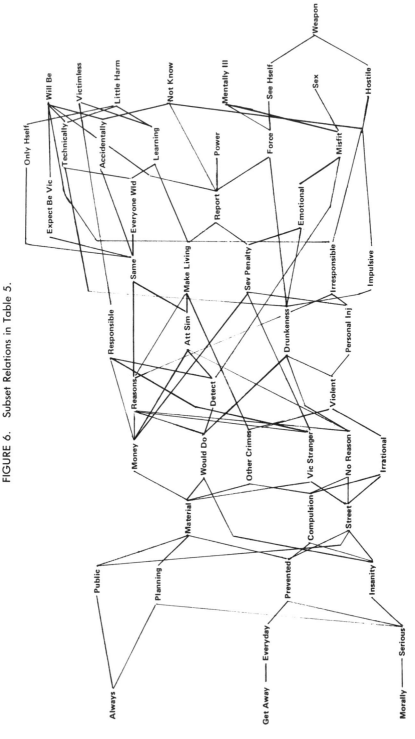

FIGURE 6. Subset Relations in Table 5.

shows, for each pair of frames, the type of relation, if any, that obtains when using the smallest cell to identify it. Figure 6 represents the simplified graph of the superset-subset relations contained in Table 5 (where two frames are connected by a line, the frame to the right is a subset of the one to the left). The task now is to decide what we can make of them.

INTERPRETING THE STRUCTURE OF BELIEFS

Before we consider specific aspects of the belief system represented by Table 5, a couple of points need to be made about the relations in general. First, as I previously mentioned, allowing exceptions means that transitivity of frame relations is not necessarily maintained. Figure 7 illustrates a hypothetical case in which A is a subset of B, which is a subset of C (each with some exceptions), and yet A contrasts with C. This possibility is greater in the case of frames that vary greatly in size (i.e., the number of crimes "true" for them).

Secondly, since the total number of crimes is 50, for each four-cell table, the greatest that the number of "exceptions" can be (the "weakest" relationship) is 12 in any given cell. Moreover, if the "smallest" cell does have 12 crimes, there must be two of the four cells with 12 crimes, and the other two must have 13 each, or there would be a cell with less than 12 somewhere. A four-cell table with this distribution is obviously the weakest relationship possible—we would hesitate to call it a relationship at all.

For these reasons we will have to consider many aspects of the pairwise relations when interpreting Figure 6. Let us first take the diagram as a whole, and then consider its elements in more detail.

Figure 6 is perhaps easiest to interpret if we consider the frames as "dimensions" or "factors" of criminality. The diagram tells us that a given frame is a subset of another if it is joined to the *right* of the other. Thus, all serious crimes are morally wrong: if a crime causes personal injury, it is a violent act, and if the crime requires a weapon, then the person who commits it will see himself or herself as a criminal *and* will be generally hostile towards others; or, if a person commits a crime for which mental illness is attributable, it will make use of force and the person is a misfit.

FIGURE 7.   Non-Transitive Property in Qualified Subset Relation.

TABLE 6. The Number of Exceptions, if any, for Relations in Table 5

DISPLAY EEE (THE NUMBER OF EXCEPTIONS, IF ANY, FOR RELATIONS IN TABLE

1	VIOLENT
2	MORALLY
3	MATERIAL
4	FORCE
5	IRRATIONAL
6	TECHNICALLY
7	EVERYDAY
8	ACCIDENTALLY
9	SERIOUS
10	IMPULSIVE
11	SEX
12	WEAPON
13	PLANNING
14	LEARNING
15	STREET
16	PUBLIC
17	EVERYONE WLD
18	VICTIMLESS
19	POWER
20	COMPULSION
21	EXPECT BE VIC
22	WILL BE
23	LITTLE HARM
24	MAKE LIVING
25	PERSONAL INJ
26	DETECT
27	SEV PENALTY
28	PREVENTED
29	REASONS
30	ALWAYS
31	NOT KNOW
32	DRUNKENESS
33	WOULD DO
34	INSANITY
35	ONLY HSELF
36	GET AWAY
37	MENTALLY ILL
38	IRRESPONSIBLE
39	EMOTIONAL
40	OTHER CRIMES
41	SAME
42	SEE HSELF
43	ART SIM
44	HOSTILE
45	VIC STRANGER
46	RESPONSIBLE
47	REPORT
48	MISFIT
49	MONEY
50	NO REASON

Another way to see Figure 6 is that elements or aspects on the right are sufficient to establish elements to their left. Thus, the fact that a crime requires the use of a weapon is *sufficient* (in the system of belief) to establish, among other things, that the person would commit other crimes as well, and that the crime was serious and morally wrong. Committing a crime that requires use of a weapon, in other words, has many implications, where knowing only that the crime is "everyday" only lets us expect that the criminal will get away with it.

Because the lines in the diagram represent varying degrees of strength (as measured by the number of exceptions to them), one needs to know how many exceptions there are to each relation depicted or implied. Table 6 provides that information, which would be vital for anyone wishing to study the belief system on a more refined level than this.[11]

The frames in Figure 6 were placed on the page so as to keep frames on the same path as close together as possible. Thus, if there were a "global" aspect to the set of beliefs as a whole, we might be able to spot it in the manner that the frames are distributed in the diagram. Such an aspect is suggested in Figure 6 when we notice that the structure seems to divide into two "streams"—one at the top and one at the bottom of the diagram. This tendency is magnified if we take the diagram and eliminate all but the "strongest" path for every pair of points, as I have done in Figure 8.[12]

It seems clear that this break follows the "rational" vs. "irrational" aspects of crime and criminality. Reading the diagram from left to right, the distinction first becomes visible at the level that identifies crimes done for material benefit, street crimes, and those done out of an urge or compulsion to do so. From this point on to the right side of the structure, there is a clear separation of the two branches (with a couple of crossing paths). The irrational (bottom stream) includes the violent, the specifically irrational, sex crimes, crimes committed by highly emotional people, and those that could be caused by drunkenness, while the more rational (top stream) includes those crimes that do little harm, that everyone would do if not outlawed, that are committed by people who are the same as anyone else, or that someone could have justifiable reasons for committing.

These two streams would suggest that the culture has two distinctive "packages" of expectations that combine types of persons (e.g., the

---

[11] If A/B, the number of exceptions is the number of crimes true for both; if A⊂B, it is the number true for A but not for B.

[12] The "strongest" paths were computed by taking the number true for both frames, and dividing that by the sum of the number true for each frame. In some cases, there were two paths of equal strength, or where the strongest path *from* one frame was not the same as the strongest path *to* a frame in the next level. In either case, both lines were left in.

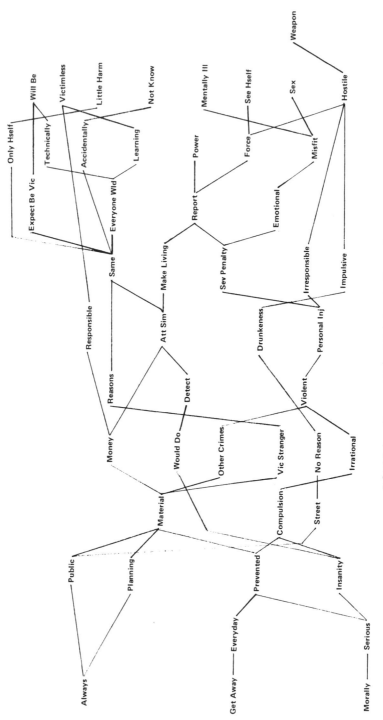

FIGURE 8.   Strongest Subset Relations in Figure 6.

"same") with types of crimes (the technically wrong) and a motive (to make money). Conversely, the hostile are connected with violent acts possibly done for no reason at all.

If we look within each of the two components of the belief structure, we come upon an intriguing difference in that the rational component takes types of *crimes* (e.g., technically wrong, victimless, ones everyone would do if not outlawed, etc.) and *from* them ascribes to the criminal the property of being the "same as anyone else," whereas in the irrational component, it is the type of *person* (e.g., hostile, mentally ill, misfits) that determines the type of *crime* (force, impulsive, personal injury, etc.). The suggestion of this difference calls for research that might see, for instance, if defense lawyers emphasize the type of person being tried. Does the possible distinction have consequences for the "labeling" theory? It does if it means that an attribution of some "character" to a person is more efficacious for the irrational class of crimes.

As we become more specific in our concerns with the structure represented in Figure 6, we must pay specific attention to the problem of transitivity that was brought up earlier. If we want to look at the belief structure in the context of a particular frame, we must use the information in Table 5 that was not included in the graph of the subset relations (Figure 6). This is made necessary by the fact that many possible paths may connect a frame to others in Figure 6, and yet respondents may have declared it in contrast to one that can be traced from it in some way. Note, for example, that a path can be found between crimes that are morally wrong and those that do little harm to anyone, yet Table 5 shows them to be in contrast. While the latter are an *implied* subset of the former (by transitivity), they are found to be, *directly,* in contrast with them.

As we turn our attention to *frames,* I will therefore highlight, in diagrams, the paths that are specifically relevant to each. This can be done by tracing all the paths for that frame that connect it to frames that are either its superset or subset, as determined by Table 5. Figure 9 shows, for example, the paths relevant to "street crimes." One can see, by comparing the implied paths to the "empirical" paths for street crime, that crimes receiving a severe penalty are implied subsets of street crime by virtue of their being a subset of crimes with victims who are strangers to the criminals, but respondents nevertheless put these two factors (severe penalty/street crime) in contrast (in Table 5).

Being able to isolate specific pathways in this manner allows us to compare different elements within the belief structure to see if anything of interest might be found. Take, for instance, Figure 10, in which the paths just highlighted for street crime are compared with the paths for crimes for which criminals would commit other crimes as well. These two categories of crime are distinguished by the fact that street crimes comprise

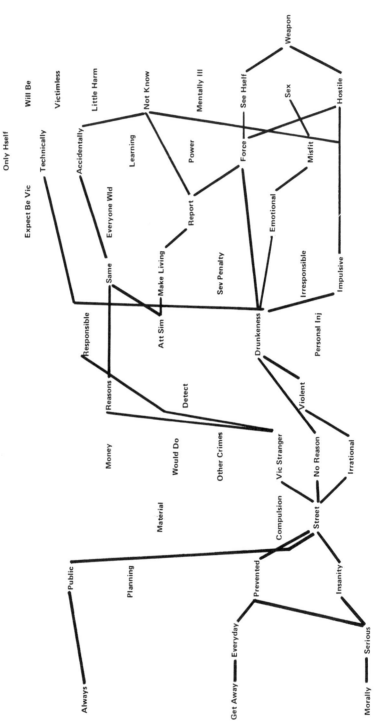

FIGURE 9. Graph of Paths Specific to "Street Crime."

108

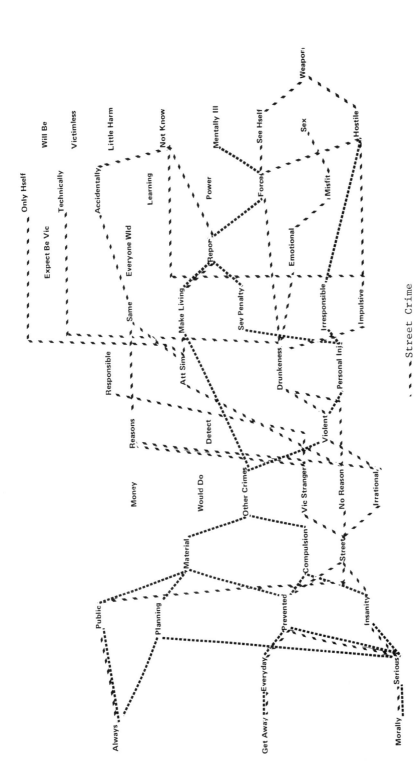

FIGURE 10. Graph of "Street Crime" vs. "Would Commit Other Crimes."

Street Crime

Other Crimes

109

those that could be done without knowing it, or that could be done accidently or impulsively. Also, if the crime was one of those committed by one who is just the same as anyone else, or for which one could have justifiable reasons, then he or she would have committed a street crime, but would not be a person who would commit other crimes as well. Interestingly, having a stranger for a victim implies a street crime, but is not strongly associated with one who would commit other crimes, either (Table 5 does indicate a weak equivalence).

The person *would* commit other crimes if the crime was one that carried a severe penalty, if he or she is mentally ill or irresponsible, or if the crime caused personal injury. If the person is the sort who would commit other crimes, his or her crime was done for material benefit and was one that required planning.

The classes of crime that are *both* street crimes *and* those for which the criminal would commit other crimes include those that require a weapon, that are violent, or that make use of force. Both classes of crime are considered preventable, everyday but serious crimes.

It would seem, from this comparison, that street crime is the larger category, in that it can include elements associated with "people who are the same as everyone else" and various elements of caprice that are not part of the picture for those who would commit other crimes as well.

Remembering that there are well over a thousand such pairs of frames, we have no hope or reason to be exhaustive in comparing them. Instead, I want to construct just a few of these comparisons, in order to give a sense of what the data are capable of revealing and how they could inform a broader programme of research.

Figure 11 compares crimes that are morally wrong with those that are serious. From their positions in the overall belief system, we would expect them to be quite similar, and their specific comparison here confirms that expectation. What *does* distinguish the two categories is that the morally wrong includes criminals whose act only affects themselves, things people would do if those acts were not outlawed, and crimes for which the victim is responsible for the harm done, none of which are seen as serious crimes. Crimes done to make money are sufficient to establish their wrongfulness, but they are not necessarily serious. Perhaps most interesting in this comparison is the finding that drunkenness is capable of leading to serious crime but not to those that are morally wrong. Would this imply that drunkenness is a weak excuse for one but not the other? Can the finding help us to predict *when* someone's having been drunk will be considered in his or her defense? Further research could pursue these questions.

Figure 12 compares the paths associated with three frames: crimes that require the use of a weapon, those to which mental illness is attrib-

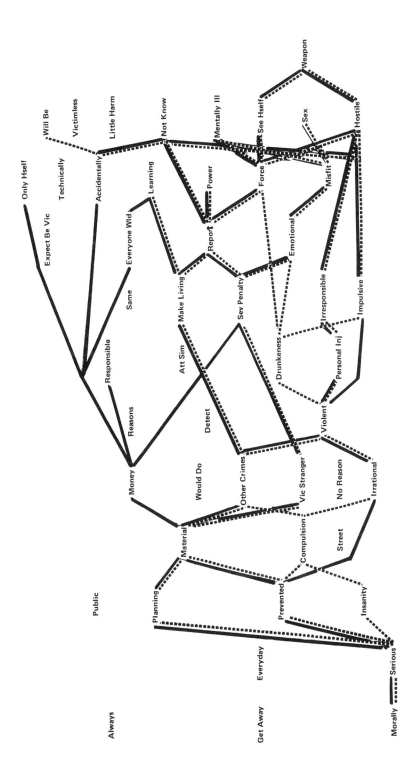

FIGURE 11. Graph of "Morally Wrong" vs. "Serious Crime."

Morally Wrong ———

Serious Crime ▬▬▬▬

111

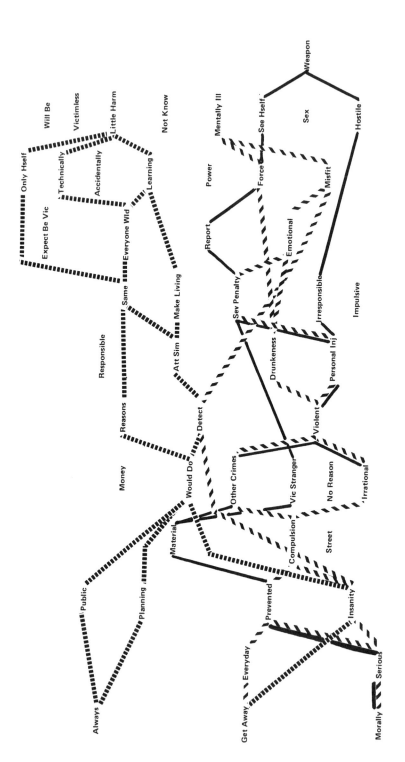

FIGURE 12. Graph of "Weapon," "Mentally Ill," and "Little Harm."

112

utable, and those that do little harm to anyone. Here, the rational and irrational branches of the belief system are reproduced in the pattern of these specific paths. Note that crimes that do little harm to anyone are those that people would do if they thought they could get away with it, but *not* if they were done for material benefit.

The interesting comparison to make in Figure 12 is that of the crimes requiring use of a weapon with those attributable to mental illness. Let us imagine a defense attorney whose client has committed a crime that involved the use of a weapon, and the defense strategy is to plead innocent by reason of "insanity." Figure 12 might be thought of as a blueprint for such a defense, in that it shows which elements of criminality distinguish between these two aspects of the crime in question. The argument for the defense would thus seek to emphasize the elements congruent with the insanity defense and de-emphasize the elements congruent with crimes that require weapons.

What elements would those be? The diagram would lead us to predict that such a defense would try to establish the defendant's being a misfit, and that he or she was highly emotional. Likewise, the defense is in a good position to make the distinction if the crime was *not* done for material benefit, if the victim was *not* a stranger to the criminal, or if the defendant did *not* think of himself or herself as a criminal. Thus, we would expect a trial of this sort to concentrate on: (1) a *motive* for the crime, and (2) the *type* of person up for trial.

Research into crime is often concerned with what crimes people fear or expect to be victimized by, so I have included Figure 13 to look at crimes that the belief system says everyone *will* be a victim of, that they *expect* to be a victim of, and, since "street crime" is often linked with people's fears, the paths associated with that class of crime. Any distinction between the first two frames is interesting insofar as it shows that the system distinguishes reality from beliefs *about* reality.

The diagram shows, unsurprisingly, that the crimes that people *will* be victims of *are* ones they expect to be victims of. But the crimes they will be victims of also belong to classes of crime they do not expect to be victims of, including those that can happen accidently, those committed by irresponsible people, those that require planning, and serious crimes. People do not expect to be victims of crimes one can make a living from (is that what allows criminals to make a living at it?).

Street crime includes crimes that the belief system holds *not* to be within people's expectations or their experience. These, for the most part, include crimes from the lower-right, "irrational" region of the diagram (those that make use of force, sex crimes, those requiring the use of a weapon, violent acts, and the like). It is not that these serious crimes do not overlap to some degree with people's expectations (i.e., *some* violent

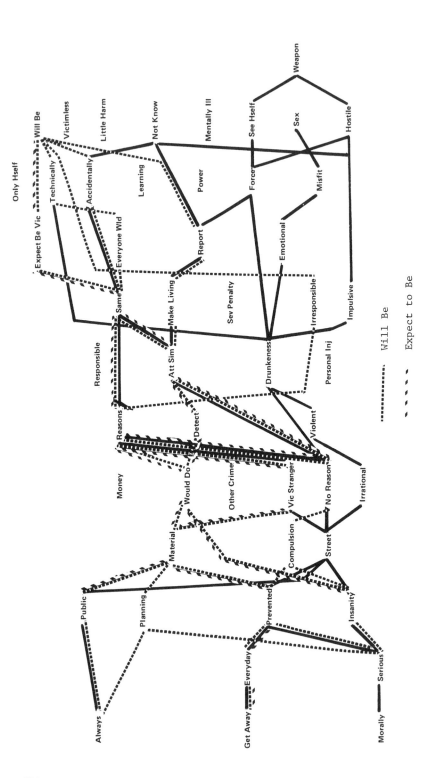

FIGURE 13. Graph of "Expect to be," "Will be," and "Street Crime."

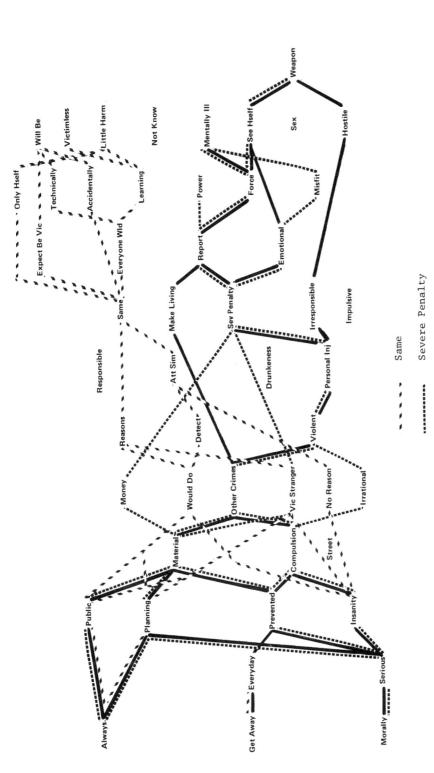

FIGURE 14. Graph of "Same," "Severe Penalty," "Other Crimes."

115

crimes may be expected), but rather that the class of serious crimes does not, on the whole, comprise people's expectations.

As a formal example of the kind of comparisons made possible by Table 5 and its associated graphs, Figure 14 compares crimes committed by people who are the same as anyone else, those that receive a severe penalty, and those committed by people who would commit other crimes as well. Note how dissimilar the paths are for crimes committed by people who are the "same" from the the other two categories of crime. If we know that a crime is committed by someone who is the same as everyone else, *and* that it carries a severe penalty, then we know that the belief system expects that the crime was committed against someone who was a stranger to the criminal, that it happened in public, required planning, and "will always occur." Otherwise, these two categories of crime are very distinct. This emphasizes, perhaps, the value many lawyers place on the client's being easily identified with, or alternatively, the possible disadvantages for a defendant who is already "different" in some way.

I hope these examples give an impression of how the techniques and the data they produce can be of value to social research. I believe that the data are extremely rich in the possible relationships they suggest for this culture's beliefs with regard to criminality. Research into any aspect of crime or criminality should be enhanced by incorporating this analysis. It strikes me as inconceivable that we will ever understand social interaction without being fully aware of what different social ascriptions imply for the members of a culture. Such implications, which may never be overt, must have salience for what people do.

TOWARD A QUANTITATIVE ANALYSIS

Before closing this section, I would like to discuss, if briefly, how a complementary analysis of the belief structure might be pursued. In addition to the substantively-oriented interpretation that I followed above, we can also look for features brought out by a more "quantitative" analysis of the belief structure.

Here I have in mind the possibility that one may invent various measures relevant to the data that might be used to describe the "shape" of the belief system (its complexity or coherence, for instance) or some quantitative measure of the relative significance of a given frame.

These considerations are actually premature, though, in that much more experience with this kind of data is required before new measures can suggest themselves. Nevertheless, I want to make just a few remarks about what these measures might look like.

If we wanted to compare one belief system to another, especially when they concern different cultural domains, we would have to find some way of talking about the *shape* of the belief structure independently of the substantive *content* of the beliefs. How might this be accomplished?

One of the first things we might want to know about the belief structure concerns its "complexity," the degree to which and the way in which the frames are inter-related. The simplest and most crude measure would be to take the average number of frames to which any frame is related in some fashion. Table 5 contains 2,298 relations of all kinds; hence, each frame has some relation to an average of 45.96 other frames. Of course, if each relationship was of the same type (subset, contrast, etc.) the structure would be less "complex," so some account would need to be taken of the "mix" of relations. One could use, perhaps, the ratio of the contrast relations to the subset relations, the idea being that a ratio of "1" would reflect the maximum "complexity" of any system. The ratio for Table 5 is 1014 divided by 1064, equaling 0.953, but again,, these numbers have little meaning without our having some experience with different systems.

The number of "levels" in the system could be a basis of comparison. Figure 6 shows that the shortest path connecting the widest points in the system is of length 7 (from "morally wrong" to "requires a weapon"). The number of levels would be an indirect measure of how "consequential" any element of the system could be—how many other frames are implied by membership in it.

Given the possibility that frames that we expect to be subsets of others by transitivity may not be judged to be subsets in the actual data, we could take any difference (of the expected and observed subsets) as a measure of the degree of "consistency" within the belief system. If all paths implied by transitivity from Table 5 were counted, there would be 810 such paths. Of these possible or implied subsets, 178 are explicitly contradicted by respondents, who judged them to be in contrast (an example, again, is that of the frames "morally wrong" with "does little harm to anyone"). The proportion of these two numbers could then be an index of belief consistency (here, 0.22). An index of this sort could compare belief systems with entirely different contents.

There is the question of how one might detect any general "components" or "streams," like the rational/irrational groups we earlier identified, in a substantive way. One strategy, which I have tried, is to take from Table 5 a sub-table that marks which frames are either a subset or a superset of others (i.e., a binary matrix that has a "1" wherever a "⊂" or a "⊃" appears in Table 5). This binary matrix can then be put into a blockmodel algorithm (I used Breiger, Boorman, and Arabie's CONCOR algorithm (1975) to see if any components (blocks) are found. Figure 15

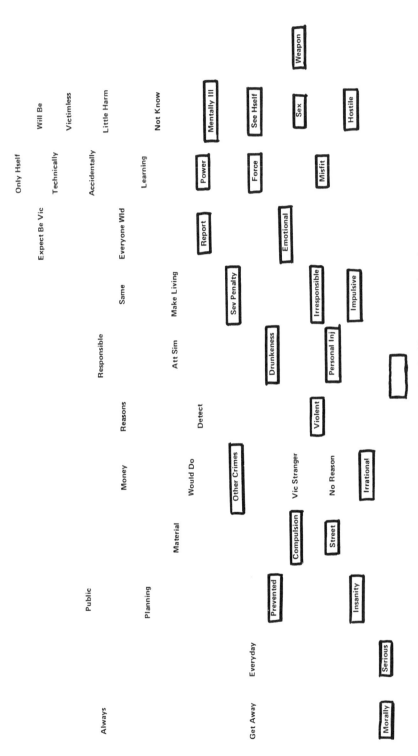

FIGURE 15. Components Identified by Concor Algorithm.

shows the result—the algorithm divides the beliefs in a manner nearly identical to what we had intuitively described. Having a "mechanical" way of identifying components would be especially helpful when analyzing non-standard or otherwise unfamiliar beliefs, or whenever one might have reasons to doubt his or her interpretive impressions.

Another class of measures may be constructed that would compare the frames themselves. It is fairly easy to spot the most general and most specific frames in the system (e.g., "morally wrong" and "ue of a weapon"), but we could also look for more interesting features of the frames.

We can, for example, look more specifically at the "contradictions" discussed above to see how much each frame contributes to the total number of contradictions. Table 7 represents these contradictions and where they occur. A "1" in the table indicates that the column frame is a "logically" *implied* subset of the row, but respondents *explicitly* related them as contrasting. A substantive interpretation of these "contradictions" is a little hard to provide without further investigation, but the least we can say is that they could point to "problematical" categories of crime. "Done for material benefit" has sixteen other frames as implied subsets that nevertheless contrast directly with it, having the largest number in the group. Does this mean that this category requires greatest "qualification" when making attributions from it (as when a politician is accused of making money from some scheme)? Staying with the same table (#7), we note that "does little harm to anyone" is the most "problematic" category for its supersets (when the columns are compared). Does this make it the most "atypical" of the set of categories? It does seem to align with that intuition.

We might, finally, try to find some way to compare how "consequential" a frame (or "dimension") is for the belief system as a whole. Some measure of this is given in the frames' variance (described earlier), but we should be able to make use of the data in Table 5 as well.

A frame may be either too general or too specific to have great "utility" relative to other frames. I suspect that the "morally wrong" is a category too broad to be of much discriminatory power for day-to-day use. In fact, Table 5 shows that knowing a crime to be morally wrong only implies that it is not a victimless crime, that it is not one that "does little harm to anyone" (i.e. , it does harm to someone) and that it is not a crime that everyone will be a victim of.

One intuition into finding a way to distinguish between frames on these terms is to see which frames have a large number of *both* subset and contrasts. The idea here would be that a frame is salient or consequential if it not only comprises a "large" number of frames, but also distinguishes a "large" number from itself. A frame with a large number

TABLE 7. Contradictions Between Implied and Actual Subsets

DISPLAY CONTR	1	2	3	4	5	6	7	8	9	10	11	12	13	14	15	16	17	18	19	20	21	22	23	24	25	26	27	28	29	30	31	32	33	34	35	36	37	38	39	40	41	42	43	44	45	46	47	48	49	50
VIOLENT 1					1	1																1																							1					
MORALLY 2																						1																											
MATERIAL 3			1		1				1	1												1													1															
FORCE 4										1																														1										
IRRATIONAL 5																																					1													
TECHNICALLY 6			1															1	1																															
EVERYDAY 7					1					1									1			1																												
ACCIDENTALLY 8																				1																			1											
SERIOUS 9																				1																														
IMPULSIVE 10																																																		
SEX 11																																																		
WEAPON 12																		1																	1															1
PLANNING 13							1	1																																										
LEARNING 14							1																										1				1	1											1	
STREET 15					1								1		1	1	1		1					1																											
PUBLIC 16																																																		
EVERYONE WLD 17																																																		
VICTIMLESS 18																																								1			1							
POWER 19																																												1						
COMPULSION 20					1								1		1	1	1					1																												
EXPECT BE VIC 21																									1	1	1													1			1						
WILL BE 22																																								1			1						
LITTLE HARM 23			1							1						1		1		1																							1							
MAKE LIVING 24			1							1						1		1				1													1								1	1						
PERSONAL INJ 25			1													1				1										1	1												1							
DETECT 26									1				1																	1	1												1							
SEX PENALTY 27					1																														1															
PREVENTED 28																		1																									1							
REASONS 29																																														1				
ALWAYS 30				1																													1																	
NOT KNOW 31																																																		
DRUNKENESS 32											1				1					1		1																		1			1							
WOULD DO 33				1						1	1									1																								1						
INSANITY 34																																																		
ONLY HSELF 35																																																		
GET AWAY 36																																																		
MENTALLY ILL 37																																			1															
IRRESPONSIBLE 38																																							1					1						
EMOTIONAL 39																																			1		1													
OTHER CRIMES 40							1	1								1		1		1		1																							1					
SAME 41																														1	1																			
SEE HSELF 42					1																																													
ATT SIM 43				1																																														
HOSTILE 44																																						1	1					1						
VIC STRANGER 45			1		1													1		1	1												1						1			1		1						
RESPONSIBLE 46																																														1				
REPORT 47																																			1		1	1	1					1	1					
MISFIT 48																																						1												
MONEY 49																					1	1	1																											
NO REASON 50			1							1	1											1																	1	1					1					

120

TABLE 8.   Results of Suggested Measure of Frame "Consequence"

Frame No.	Value	Frame No.	Value
1	.48	26	.44
2	.15	27	.35
3	.45	28	.30
4	.17	29	.37
5	.40	30	.00
6	.10	31	.00
7	.29	32	.38
8	.09	33	.39
9	.24	34	.24
10	.10	35	.05
11	.00	36	.00
12	.00	37	.00
13	.29	38	.17
14	.09	39	.16
15	.35	40	.36
16	.24	41	.36
17	.20	42	.05
18	.00	43	.39
19	.00	44	.04
20	.37	45	.33
21	.00	46	.04
22	.00	47	.25
23	.00	48	.10
24	.19	49	.37
25	.42	50	.33

of subsets only will be too general, while one with all contrasts is essentially isolated from the system.

With this in mind, I calculated, for each frame, the number of its subsets times the number of its contrasts all divided by 600, i.e., $((\#C) \times (\#I))$ divided by 600). The denominator equals 600 because this is the maximum for the numerator in our case (25×24). Table 8 gives the results of this calculation, where we find the highest values for "violent acts," "material benefit," "is hard to detect," and irrational act." Apart from "hard to detect," these frames do seem congruent with our substantive impressions *and* the place where the two large components of the belief system begin to divide. One could adopt such a measure to locate frames close to the "heart" of the belief system that may require special attention.

In summary, on the narrow question of how useful are the data collected by the procedures under our consideration, I think we have established three major points.

The first, and perhaps the most fundamental point, is that the data do reveal some organization. There was, after all, no guarantee that we would find anything that could be called a "structure" at all, or that if some "lines" *could* be drawn, that they would make any sense. I think it fair to say that the structural relations uncovered are both complex and sensible enough to have what some researchers refer to as "face validity."

Which brings me to the second point—that these data hold great potential for future extended research. Many intriguing questions are suggested by any one of the frame-specific diagrams included in this paper, and they are raised without the benefit of other empirical data that could be brought together in a larger research project. The relations found here hint at several possible ways that they might "find life" in an actual setting. I am not claiming that beliefs are *determinates* of action, remember, but that their influence is great in the negotiation and definitions that pervade social interaction and direct its course.

Third and finally, the eliciting procedure and subsequent techniques for analysis seem very well suited for the development of more quantitative approaches to the study of this cultural phenomenon. I am not recommending that more mechanical techniques *replace* qualitative analysis as it is traditionally pursued, but that they can prove most useful in handling very complex or highly abstract inter-relations that more discursive methods are not equipped to deal with. Beyond this advantage, there seem very few other ways to do comparative analysis across as wide a range of cultural domains as is possible with a formal device of some kind.

SUMMARY OF FINDINGS

Using a substitution-frame technique for eliciting true-false judgements on propositions regarding crimes and criminality, we were able to discover several features of the belief system thus defined.

First, we were able to select those frames or dimensions of criminality most salient in discriminating types of crimes from one another. We found, for instance, that the class of "violent" crime was much easier for respondents to sort crimes with than those for which the victims were "old."

Taking the 50 most salient frames or categories, we were able to define how each was related to the other 49. Using a typology of set relations, we were able to describe the overall structure of those dimensions of criminality—which categories were subsets of others, which were in contrast to others, and how each would be placed on a graph representing these relations. Thus, each frame can be *defined* by its place in the total network of set relations.

Finally, the frame relations allowed us to compare the "routes" or "paths" of implication throughout the belief structure for several frames. In this way we were able to suggest the consequences that membership in a given category could have, through the inferences that are implied by the pattern of frame relationships.

In the way of a global description, what the analysis describes is a structure of implication for taking the types of *acts* people may engage in, and from those determining what *characteristics* may be ascribed to the person thus identified (e.g., if they committed a crime that required a weapon, then they are likely to commit other crimes as well).

Because of my insistence on the *social* nature of this belief system, and the fact that no respondent judged all of the possible statements, there arises the question of what status the belief system has as an object of research, and how it relates to the beliefs that a member of the culture may have, so let me clarify my understanding of what the belief system *is*.

First, the structure represented by Table 5 and subsequent graphs is an *abstraction* (or idealization)—it is implied by the pattern of respondents' judgements, not given directly from asking them. I see this as a virtue, as the more general the relation is, the less likely will a direct question about it elicit a meaningful response. On the other hand, abstracting relations in this way leaves open the possibility that respondents will explicitly deny an association thus derived. I do not believe that such a denial would invalidate the findings, but would rather give us an interesting paradox to consider. A similar paradox is reported by Shweder (1977), who asked respondents the likelihood of a person's being "tense" and "tolerant." One judge reported that, out of 10 people, 70 are tense and 75 are tolerant, but *then* reported that of those who were tense, only 10% (7) were also tolerant, a clear contradiciton (see Figure 16). Shweder takes this and other results to mean that people do not have a good ability to think "correlationally," but instead categorize by *resemblance* (a suggestion I will return to shortly). While I would not necessarily place the abstracted implications in a privileged position relative to explicit answers, there is little support for the converse. I would argue, too, that "real world" decision-making is probably influenced more by impressions formed by sums of specific elements than consciously-formed generalizations. In sum, the abstracted belief structure serves neither to predict an individual's responses nor to be confirmed by them, though we should be surprised to find gross discrepancies between the two.

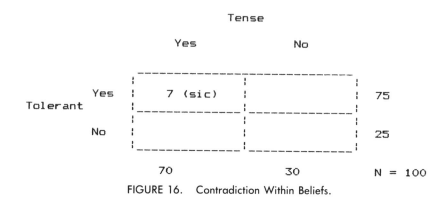

FIGURE 16.   Contradiction Within Beliefs.

The belief structure is an abstraction in another sense, and here I return to the analogy of a language's grammar, for individuals will *not* share the *same* knowledge of the social world, nor will any one of them have occasion to recall, in total, what he or she does know. Instead, specific paths of the system will be called up as they are judged relevant, and people will have differing interests in the system's parts. Society recognizes, as well, that some of its members will have greater knowledge or authority regarding specific aspects of the system, hence, experts are called in to establish some associations (e.g., how psychotics should be identified and treated). As with a grammar, there will be some who can declare the rules, some who won't know the rules, and some who want to change the rules, but this should not discourage our attempts to characterize the overall structure as best we can.

Another distinction between the belief system and a given individual's assertions lies in the remarks I gave in Section I concerning the belief system as a *medium* of social interaction; that it is specifically understood to comprise "what everyone knows;" that it is made up of "social facts" and known to be so. We need *not* assume that these beliefs are "internalized;" rather, the system is efficacious because people understand that it is *used* by others to make the various inferences and attributions. My understanding of beliefs is therefore close to Francesca Cancian's when, in her study of "norms," she assumed that "norms affect behavior by specifying what action will cause others to validate a particular identity.Therefore, beliefs that are perceived to be shared by a group will be related to action, while the *personal* beliefs of an individual may not be"

(1975: 135, emphasis added). A man who himself places no significance in one's wearing a beard may nevertheless elect to shave his off before going to a job interview, and this regard for social beliefs is probably just as strong as any that he accepts through "socialization." It is ironic that sociologists have spent the bulk of their time on those "personal" beliefs (e.g., religion, politics in our society) that have the least to do with social organization.

I must say, finally, that if the reader is left unconvinced by the arguments I have given regarding the status (or reality) of the abstracted belief system, there is nothing in the procedures I have described that forbids an examination of an individual's personal beliefs save time, money, and respondent fatigue. With sufficient resources, I would recommend letting the analysis distinguish (if it can) any sub-cultures represented by divergent beliefs. For example, I would be curious to know what might distinguish the structure for defendants (or convicts) from that of the officers of the court. Besides any difference in *content,* we might be able to differentiate them by whether the officers' system is more "distinctive," "rigid," or "coherent" than the criminals'. The comparative analysis could possibly reveal an "intermeshing" of the different belief systems— "equivalence structures," to use Anthony Wallace's (1969) phrase—so that each forms a part, like a puzzle piece, that forms a whole picture when brought together. But here again, I would be interested in belief systems as they are related to *actors* (or roles) rather than individuals.

In addition to these rather specific questions, there are, as well, a number of broader concerns that occurred to me upon seeing the results of this analysis.

First, one wonders whether the "bimodal" character of the belief structure (i.e., the two "streams") is specific to "criminality," or whether it is related to the perception of our judicial system as having a bimodal character of decision-making, i.e., a person's being guilty or not. If the belief system *does* reflect a major (perceived) characteristic of the domain it relates to, would we find the same bimodal structure in beliefs regarding admissions to college, hospitals, or promotions on the job? Would these belief systems split into typifications of who "gets in" and who does not, of who makes it and who does not? Would one or the other component be more finely differentiated? If such findings did arise, it would certainly be interesting to look for belief systems related to institutions that make "multiple choices." Perhaps the "coarse" structure of an institution reflects its charter in this way.

Another topic suggests itself when contemplating our belief system, and that is whether the implications it contains are followed only in the directions obtained in the data, or whether members will "incorrectly" make inferences in the wrong direction. The diagram in Figure 12 shows us that crimes attributable to mental illness are violent, but do people infer the converse—that someone who commits a violent crime is mentally ill, or that someone who is the "same as everyone else" would have only committed a crime that was "technically wrong?" Shweder's work has apparently convinced him that everyday inference does indeed make such "backward" inferences. He argues that "personality" attribution is fraught with this and other fallacies resulting in beliefs that "package" various attributes into superficially coherent wholes, and expectations that are rarely weakened by disconfirming evidence. If this characterization is accurate, our "belief structure" might be better shown as two separate "spheres" of unordered dimensions of criminality, such that any attribute locates the criminal or type of crime or motive in one or the other sphere.

I am curious, too, about how the beliefs depicted here relate to normative action. How does the "is" influence the "ought"? Does the fact that a person is convicted of a crime that "receives a severe penalty" have any bearing on whether he or she *will* receive a severe penalty? If so, how is that decision made? One can imagine a judge reasoning that, *because* this person committed a crime known to carry a severe penalty, he or she must be *really* deviant. Such circular reasoning would not be at all unusual, especially in those who deal with society's "deviants" (witch trials being a popular example).

David Sudnow's research (1965) suggests that public defenders will cooperate with prosecutors in finding a typification for a concrete case before them. If they succeed in finding such a typification, a routine plea-bargain can be struck—the alleged act becomes a "normal crime." The belief system here is closely related to this idea of typification, for although the court officers' own belief system would surely be "finer," the purposes it serves would be identical—to aid in the disposition of a case, to make, of a concrete case, a "typical" act. If we could describe the officers' beliefs in some detail would be better able to predict *when* a given defendant's case will be seen as normal or abnormal? I suspect so, but more important, such a study might yield finer distinctions than whether a crime is "normal" or not. Because the relevant official data are poor or non-existent, these typifications may be the most detailed information we can get that bears on this crucial aspect of the criminal justice system.

One can see from these suggestions alone that it would be possible to devote a lifetime to collecting and analyzing data of this sort, but to do so would defeat the purpose of the analysis. In concluding this chapter, then, I want to review *how* belief systems are related to social structure and social action.

It might be argued that, of all the sciences, sociology has been the most hampered by its desire to conform to a "scientific method," for its subject matter is the least amenable to the mechanistic image that such desires have fostered.

As I argued above, an approach that seeks to identify *action* as simple "behavior" does so in ignorance of the radical distinction between the two, a distinction high-lighted when we note that many different behavior displays (even *no* behavior) can accomplish the "same" act, and similarly, the "same" display can, at different times, be identified as different acts.

Once appreciating the distinction, we are left with the task of describing empirically what has been ignored, namely, *how* the social world is constituted. Using the analogy of the rules for a game or the grammar of a language, I argued that a culture provides its members with an implicit "scheme of interpretation" whereby members can ascribe actions to behavior through those interpretive rules, rules that link acts, actors, motives, and circumstances so as to give sufficient coherence to action that we may have expectations about one another's actions, or have interpretations handy should those expectations fail.

Thus, and this is my major point, the analysis and explanation of social action becomes of necessity a two-pronged approach: (1) an analysis of the a priori truths available to members as the scheme of interpretation—the belief system; and (2) an analysis of how that belief system is realized in any given setting—its instantiation.

The central concept of the "definition of the situation" therefore actually comprises these two aspects—the "necessary," or analytic truths shared by members of the culture, and the contingent facts having to do with their particular manifestations or specific interpretation. What is *contingent* for members can only be described or identified through use of what is *necessarily* true for them.

Let me illustrate my point here with the data at hand. We may speculate that, at one time or for a different sample, "homosexual acts" might have been placed in the category of "crimes attributable to mental illness." Our findings tell us that in the belief system, these crimes (mentally ill) are committed by people who "would commit other crimes as well" (see Figure 12). This presumed relationship could have something to do with the more specific belief (of some) that homosexuals are capable of child molestation. At any rate, beliefs regarding homosexuals (in our hypothetical case) would thus consist of the specific categorization of homosexual acts as crimes committed by the mentally ill, *and* the general (analytic?) belief that such people will commit other crimes as well. It is crucial to the understanding of how social belief systems work that the specific beliefs categorizing homosexual acts could be amended *without altering* the more fundamental structure that links mental illness with the commission of other crimes. To make the distinction between the belief system and its use even stronger, I may point out that the belief system itself may be appealed to for the purposes of reforming practices informed by it, as when, for example, homosexuals may collect data showing that they do not in fact commit "other crimes," and so should *not* be categorized with those *other* mentally ill people. Changing the beliefs about homosexuality, in other words, may be made possible by the strength of the beliefs underpinning our ideas about "criminality" on the whole. Progressive change may thus carry with it an "entrenchment" of less visible belief, beliefs that may legitimize the demand for change. The relevant belief system is therefore best described as being in a dynamic "tension" with the way it is used—its instantiation. A tension that contributes greatly to the phenomena of long-standing interest to sociology—domination, conflict, and social change.

There is little danger, then, that sociologists will restrict themselves to the exclusive study of belief systems, for those structures will tell us no more about who wins or loses than will the rules of a game. But in both cases, we cannot hope to understand what is happening without knowing them ourselves.

REFERENCES

Breiger, R.L., S. A. Boorman, and P. Arabie.
   1975   "An algorithm for clustering relational data with application to social network analysis and comparison with multidimensional scaling." Journal of Mathematical Psychology 12:328–383.
Cancian, Francesca
   1975   What Are Norms? New York: Cambridge University Press.
D'Andrade, Roy G.
   1976   "A propositional analysis of U.S. American beliefs about illness." In Keith Basso and Henry Selby (eds.), Meaning in Anthropology. Albuquerque, NM: University of New Mexico Press.
Kaufman, Felix
   1958   Methodology of the Social Sciences. New York: The Humanities Press.
Metzger, Duane, and G. E. Williams
   1963   "A formal ethnographic analysis of Tenejapa Ladino weddings." American Anthropologist 65:1076–1101.
   1966   "Procedures and results in the study of native catagories: Tzeltal firewood." American Anthropologist 68:389–407.
Saltz, Robert F.
   1981   "Finding Structure in Beliefs." Unpublished dissertation, University of Massachusetts.
Schweder, Richard A.
   1977   "Likeness and likelihood in everyday thought: Magical thinking in judgements about personality." Current Anthropology 18:637–658.

Stefflre, Volney, Peter Reich, and Marlys McClaren-Stefflre
    1971   "Some eliciting and computational procedures for descriptive semantics." In
            Paul Kay (ed.), Explorations in Mathematical Anthropology. Cambridge, MA:
            The MIT Press.
Sudnow, David
    1965   "Normal crimes: Sociological features of the penal code in a public defender
            office." Social Problems 12:255–276.

Three

Decision Making Under Threat of Disaster: An Experimental Simulation*

Robert K. Leik
Gregory A. Gifford
University of Minnesota

INTRODUCTION

This paper reports the results of a series of experiments conducted to test a Bayesian model of decision-making under threat of imminent disaster; specifically, under warning of an impending tornado. The experiments were conducted as part of a larger study of the dissemination of and response to warnings of natural hazards (see Leik et al., 1981, 1981).

The model derives from a tradition of rational individual decision-making (Von Neuman and Morgenstern, 1947, 1977; Luce and Raiffa, 1967; Bradley, 1976). In its "normative" or "prescriptive" form, a decision making model is a formal mathematical expression of the optimal decision strategy that can be used to make decisions. In the objective utility maximizing form, it assumes perfect objective knowledge of and control over (1) the likelihoods of events, (2) the available alternatives, and (3) the ability to generate a quantifiable order of preferences for the possible outcomes. Observed behavior generalized and abstracted into such a mathematical system comprises only a small portion of the decision-making literature. Findings from a variety of behavioral sciences indicate that, besides man's severe limitations as an information processor, other ubiq-

*This material is based upon research supported by the National Science Foundation under Grant No. PFR77-01452. Any opinions, findings, and conclusions and recommendations expressed in this paper are those of the authors and do not necessarily reflect the views of the National Science Foundation.

uitous influences militate against the use of an optimizing approach, even though it might often seem to be the ideal strategy for making decisions (Janis and Mann, 1977; Katona, 1953; Brim et al., 1962; Taylor, 1965; Etzioni, 1968; Miller and Starr, 1967; Vroom and Yetton, 1973; Simmons et al., 1973; Johnson, 1974; Steinbrunner, 1974).

Since people have only imperfect, perhaps unmeasureable, knowledge of and control over events and available actions, predicting individual decision-making behavior from the formal prescriptive model has had limited success. Questions typically asked in the literature are: (1) what strategies do provide an accurate descriptive model, and (2) to what extent are the definitions of events, alternatives, and outcomes affected by the different conditions under which decisions are made.

The first question has been addressed by attempts to delineate the various kinds of strategies used in decision-making. Given man's substantial limitations as an information processor, it has been found that, very often, the crudest, most ineffective strategies characterize the decision-making behavior of people who are facing major personal decisions. Whenever someone is looking only for an option which represents an improvement over the present situation, evaluation is usually confined to just two alternatives—a new course of action vs the present one. This "satisficing," rather than "optimizing," process is characterized by a series of sequential binary (i.e., two alternatives) choices (Janis and Mann, 1977). Each new possible course of action is considered against the current action for perceptible improvement.

A major part of an answer to the second question lies in a focus on the prescriptive model's assumption concerning the value people attach to the possible outcomes. Individuals are assumed to have a quantifiable set of preferences among the outcomes (P − C: which represents a subjective weighing of perceived possible payoffs against the possible costs for each action). If a given utility function does not represent some individuals' ordering of preferences, other outcomes of more importance to the individuals may be operating. Evidence exists from a variety of sources demonstrating the enormous influence of social institutions, habit, and tradition on decisions made by individuals. The influence of these psychological and sociological factors leads individuals to make decisions based on aspects of outcomes other than economic (Janis and Mann, 1977; Cook and Emerson, 1978). If an ordering of preferences based purely on economic utility is found to be incongruent with observed decision-making patterns, a shift in focus to social and/or more abstract values may provide a better description, which raises the question of the quantifiability of values.

We suggest that, rather than rejecting the assumption of a quantifiable order of preferences, we should undertake to construct value typologies. If we can express what values are important, it would not be necessary to abandon the expected utility model. The task of the researcher would become to list what outcomes are salient, and to control them either statistically or experimentally. That is, if we can hold constant what people know about the likelihoods of the appropriate events, and variably impose economic and non-economic values, expected utility theory could then be used to observe under what conditions non-economic values may subjectively outweigh economic values. The concept of outcomes, in expected utility theory, would then become broadened in scope beyond the classical economic sense, and the theory would gain generality.

Assuming a decision problem with two options then (A1 or A2—a binary decision), each option typically has two or more possible outcomes, based on the occurrence of certain events. For example, when an individual is confronted with a warning of an impending tornado, each has the option of ignoring the warning to continue routine behavior (A1), or responding with some form of protective action like seeking shelter (A2). If the storm misses (i.e., hypothesis H1 is true), the outcome for A1 would be the payoffs obtained from, for example, continued productivity (P1). If the decision was to take protective action (A2), the outcome would be the cost of wasting the time that could be spent with normal activities (C2). If the storm hits (i.e., hypothesis H2 is true), the outcomes for A1 would be in terms of costs—possible property damage, personal injury, or deaths (C1), whereas the outcomes for A2 would be the payoffs of savings in property, health, and/or life (P2). In this example, if the person knew the exact probability of the storm hitting (p(H2)), and could assign values (or utilities) to the costs and/or benefits associated with each outcome for each option, then a mathematically optimal decision could be reached by choosing that option with the highest expected utility.

The following equations represent how expected utilities are ideally established for each available option:

$$E(U/A1) = P1\ p(H1) - C1\ p(H2) \tag{1}$$

$$E(U/A2) = P2\ p(H2) - C2\ p(H1) \tag{2}$$

That is, there is an expected utility for each available action. The expected utility of continuing normal activity, $E(U/A1)$, is a comparison of the possible payoffs of A1 (P1), weighted by the probability that the storm will miss (P1 p(H1)), with the possible costs of A1 (C1), which are also weighted, but here, by the probability that the storm will hit (C1 p(H2)). If the probability that the storm will miss is very high (e.g., p(H1) = .99 and p(H2) = .01), the expected payoff for continuing normal activity would remain practically unaltered, whereas the expected cost would be almost nonexistent. Or, if the probabilities of the events were equal, whether the potential payoffs for continuing normal activity (P1) outweighed, in the person's mind, the potential costs (C1) would determine the expected utility of that action.

Similarly, the expected utility for the decision to take protective action, E(U/A2), is a function of how the possible payoffs of A2 (P2), weighted by the probability that the storm will hit (P2 p(H2)), compared to the possible costs of A2 (C2), weighted by the probability that the storm will miss (C2 p(H1)).

Most of the time, the objective probabilities of the rival hypotheses are unknown, and utilities are only qualitative feelings rather than exact known quantities. These perceptual imperfections have been accommodated in decision theory via the concept of "subjective expected utility" (Edwards, 1961). This concept reflects the idea that an accurate descriptive model of decision-making should focus on what is important to, and consciously or subjectively experienced by, the decision maker. If subjective estimates of the chances of the appropriate events are made and individuals have expressible orders of preferences among outcomes, then they can still have the feeling of rational decision-making by choosing the option with the maximum subjective expected utility.

Considerable research indicates that people tend to behave in terms of such a decision model for certain types of decisions but not for others. In fact, there are many decision strategies identified in the literature, with labels such as conjoint, disjoint, additive difference, lexicographic, additive, incrementalism, and elimination by aspects (Einhorn, 1970; Tversky, 1969, 1972; Miller and Starr, 1967). The list of strategies represents the search for accurate descriptive models, and is categorized by the conditions under which these less effective strategies emerge. For major or important decisions, as we indicated above, when there is an imminent deadline for an irrevocable decision, a "satisficing" strategy (Simon, 1976) frequently emerges where a large and often unmanageable domain of possible options becomes seen as a series of binary choices—at each point of which a "yes" or "no" is the response to a new suggestion or piece of information.

In a comprehensive psychological analysis of research on decision-making, Irving Janis and Leon Mann (1977) offer a "conflict-theory model" of "consequential" decision-making which could be characterized by a series of binary choices. Kunreuther et al. (1978), develop a similar model regarding whether people will purchase flood or earthquake insurance. Each major decision process begins with the generation of psychological stress from either the threat of negative outcomes or the threat of the frustration of valued objectives if stasis or no change in the current action is assumed. Once this kind of stress is present, Janis and Mann postulate the following process.

The first binary question is, "Are the risks serious if I don't change?" This substantive question poses empirical questions, the first of which is, what are the conditions affecting the individual's estimation of the seriousness of the outcomes if no change is made? There are two general factors: (1) variation in individual predisposition—some people may value a prestigeful position in a large corporation more than others; and (2) variation in external sources of information about potential losses from not changing. Perry et al. (1980), provide an elaboration of the psychological processes involved in perceiving personal risk. If the answer to the first question is "no," the present action will be continued—"unconflicted adherence"—and information processing is stopped. If the answer is "yes," a second question is raised concerning the seriousness of the risks if a change is made. That is, will changing result in the loss of valued goals? If the answer is "no," the first available alternative is adopted—"unconflicted change"—and there is no further consideration. If the answer is "yes," the search continues for a better alternative, and the third question is raised.

Since the individual is still open to new suggestions, the third question becomes: "Is it realistic to hope for a better solution?" The answer is again a product of individual predisposition and access to external information about other possible alternatives. At this point, the person has decided that (s)he may risk serious losses from continued stasis and from changing to the first available alternative. Now, if it seems that it is not realistic to hope for a better solution, the result is "defensive avoidance"— you just quit thinking about the problem. Thus, "no" answers to any of the questions, which are often considered in a matter of seconds, terminate the decision process prematurely, and result in less effective decision-making. If it seems realistic to search for a better alternative, the fourth and final question is asked leading to the most effective decision-making: "Is there sufficient time to search and deliberate?"

Conditioned again by variation in both predisposition (e.g., variation in cognitive abilities) and information about deadlines and time pressures, an affirmative answer to the fourth substantive question presumably leads to the most effective decision-making. If it appears as though there isn't sufficient time to continue the search, then panic or "hypervigilance" is the predicted result, although infrequently observed. If time, however, does seem to be available, "vigilance" in the appraisal and evaluation of information is predicted. The model, then, is useful in identifying points in the decision process at which binary choices are being made, with an emphasis on defining the conditions which militate against the most effective decision-making.

If we assume an uncertain deadline, then the empirical questions focus on the kinds of individual characteristics and information which lead to "vigilant" information processing. If we assume a decision problem with an imminent deadline for an irrevocable choice, the empirical questions focus on the kinds of individual characteristics and information which condition answers to question #3: whether it is realistic to continue to hope for better solutions than the one currently being considered. With time running out, it has become necessary to adopt one of the currently available options, rather than continue to search for other ones. Continued "vigilance" would be counter-productive. It has become necessary to make a decision on what is known now! The possibility that more useful information will be available should not be given subjective weight. You must change, or stay the same—now! The empirical problem area becomes: what contributes to continued unchange—"unconflicted adherence."

That is, if there is no time left for further consideration, and it is clear that the first available alternative does not risk serious losses, it is appropriate to adopt that first option. Under such circumstances, what contributes to not acting? One obvious influence is the estimation of the probability of the most serious outcomes ($p(H2)$). The history of one's experience with similar imminent choices, and their outcomes, will obviously affect the estimation of the probability of a hit by a tornado or hurricane, for example. In reinforcement schedule terms: for a given history of imminent decisions, as the proportion of that history resulting in "being hit" increases, the estimation of the probability of being hit in the future increases.

The other influence on waiting or not acting derives from both the kinds and amounts of information available from external sources. Just the quantity of information, "How frequently, in a given unit of time, is it available?" and the quality of the information, "Is it general (designed for a large audience), or is it specific and detailed?" will obviously influence the confidence and credibility attributed to the source. Given a history of similar imminent decisions, where the external information sources were consistently available as often as need be, and were as detailed as technically possible, any confidence in the usefulness of external sources would be higher than if the sources were consistently unavailable, inaccurate, and useless.

There remains one problem with maximizing subjective expected utility functions. Assuming that variation in outcome value is held constant, information which can be used to inform the subjective probability estimates is typically not available all at once, but rather becomes available only gradually, in successive bits and pieces. As new data are obtained, the subjective probabilities are changed, however inaccurately, and the implied decision changes as the utility function changes. Such a sequence of revisions of probabilities can be given optimal form based on probability theory, and can be related to a Bayesian process. The sequence is essentially:

Step 1   Establish decision criteria.
Step 2   Draw a new piece of information.
Step 3   Calculate a decision index based on all information thus far.
Step 4   If the index passes beyond decision boundaries, go to step 5. If not, go to step 2.
Step 5   Decide.

This routine, coupled with Bayes' Theorem, provides for gradual increase or decrease in confidence in a given hypothesis. That is, the subjective probability of that hypothesis will increase or decrease until an action can be chosen with reasonable assurance. Discussions of Bayes' Theorem can be found in Mosteller et al. (1961) or Bradley (1976). A short explanation follows.

If two events are independent, the probability of their joint occurrence is simply the product of their separate probabilities. If they are interdependent, however, then conditional probability statements are needed. Two versions of the same joint probability follow:

$$P(AB) = P(A/B)\ P(B) \qquad\qquad (3)$$
$$= P(B/A)\ P(A)$$

Suppose a disaster is imminent. There are two relevant hypotheses about the potential disaster—H1: There will be no disaster, and H2: There will be a disaster. There are two relevant actions associated with these hypotheses—A1: Continue normal activity, and—A2: Take protective action. Suppose that new information is continuously being received, one fact at a time. As each new datum is received, the probability that H1 or H2 is true can be reassessed in light of that new datum. Let $P(D/H1)$ be the probability that the new fact would be observed if H1 is true. Let $P(H1/D)$ be the probability that H1 is true given that new fact. Similar definitions can be used for $P(D/H2)$ and $P(H2/D)$. Using (3) above, we can write:

$$P(D,H1) = P(H1/D)\ P(D) = P(D/H1)\ P(H1) \qquad \text{and} \qquad (4)$$
$$P(D,H2) = P(H2/D)\ P(D) = P(D/H2)\ P(H2)$$

Leaving out the far left hand terms, we can express the above two lines as a ratio. The common P(D) factor will reduce to unity and can be omitted.

$$\frac{P(H1/D)}{P(H2/D)} = \frac{P(D/H1)}{P(D/H2)} \frac{P(H1)}{P(H2)} \tag{5}$$

The far right hand term in (5) is a ratio of the probabilities of the rival hypotheses: an odds ratio. Since it pertains to the hypotheses prior to receipt of a new datum, D, it is called a prior odds ratio. The other term on the right side is a ratio of the likelihood of observing D if H1 is true, to the likelihood of observing D if H2 is true. This is called a likelihood ratio. Finally, the left hand term is a ratio of the two hypothesis probabilities after observing D; hence, it is a posterior odds ratio. Letting $O(t)$ stand for the odds ratio at time t, $O(t+1)$ stand for the same odds ratio at time $t+1$, and $LR(t)$ stand for the likelihood ratio at time t, then equation 5 can be written as a time series which specifies optimal revision of the competing probabilities according to information in the data series, D.

$$O(t+1) = LR(t) O(t) \tag{6}$$

Equation 6 is a general version of Bayes' Theorem. Based on assumed payoffs and costs, it is possible to deduce what values of the posterior odds ratio constitute decisions points; that is, at what point the subjective expected utility of the chosen action will be positive. Also, if appropriate conditions obtain, there will be an area of indecision i.e., an area in which neither choice will be optimal. Rather than derive the equations for these decision points, it is preferable to note that there is one choice option not ordinarily considered: the decision to WAIT.

Assume that a decision to wait allows a nonzero chance to obtain more data which can inform the later decision to choose either course of action. By using a probability of obtaining a new fact prior to the (unknown) deadline for action, again a subjective probability, and a subjective estimate of how much difference that new datum might make in the current decision calculations, it is possible to derive a subjective expected utility for waiting. When compared with the existing subjective expected utilities for choosing either action at the present time, this new utility provides a basis for choosing whether to act now or to wait.

Let $E(U/A1)$ be the subjective expected utility of choosing decision 1 (no action) at time t. A similar definition holds for $E(U/A2)$. Also, let Dp represent the (discrete) change in the probability of H2 ("There will be a disaster") which a new datum will produce. Obviously, this change depends upon the probability of a new datum being obtained in time, designated R, and the diagnostic value of that datum. Given these terms, it is possible to show that the subjective expected utility of waiting exceeds E(U/A1) and E(U/A2), if:

$$Dp > \frac{(1\text{-}R)}{R} \frac{E(U/A2) - E(U/A1)}{P2 + C2} \tag{7}$$

when the current dominant choice is A2, taking protective action against the hazard. If an unknown series of future data inputs is considered, the new expression would be more complicated. The probability of waiting increases when other things remain equal, but the general character of the solution is not altered. For a more complete exposition of the "chronic imminence" formulation, see Leik and Kolman (1979). A brief proof of equation (7) appears in Appendix 1.

The terms contained in equation (7) involve R, the probability that new facts will be received prior to a deadline for action; E(U/A1 and E(U/A2), the subjective expected utilities associated with the action alternatives; and P2 and C2, payoff and cost associated with the dominant option (act) at time t. The left hand term is Dp, the rate that the subjective probability associated with the dominant hypothesis changes due to the new fact, D. This rate of change will depend upon the diagnostic value of the new datum. If a very informative message is expected, then Dp should be large and it would be rational to wait. If little new and/or useful information is expected, Dp will small in the future, and it would be rational to select the current dominant action. Thus, we can hypothesize that anything contributing to confidence in the usefulness and availability of future information (specifically, the amount and rate of information from a given source) will operate independently or additively to decrease the probability of protective action at any particular time in the decision process.

That is, as the rate of information flow from a source increases, confidence in the availability of more information from that source prior to deadline would increase. In addition, we would expect that, as the quantity of information from a source increases, confidence in the usefulness of information from that source would increase.

The amount of prior experience with similar imminent choices es expected to statistically interact with differences in the frequency and amounts of information encountered over that experience. Similarly, estimations of the probabilities of possible events are expected to interact with experiential histories. That is, the effects of quantity and quality of information, in terms of confidence in the source, accrue with experience. They cannot be expected to operate at first exposure.

The preceding discussion generates the following four hypotheses.

First, as indicated above, more complete and informative messages should generate confidence that more diagnostic information will still be available prior to deadline.

Proposition 1:

As the amount of information in a warning message increases, the probability of waiting for new information, rather than acting immediately, increases. Consequently, the probability of early protective action in response to a series of warnings decreases, as the amount of information in the warnings increases.

Intuitively, it may seem that faster message flow would produce faster action. In fact, just the reverse is predicted by equation (7). The right hand side contains the term (1-R)/R, which will be small if R is large. As the right hand side decreases, Dp will be more likely to exceed that expression; hence, waiting will be more rational. Consequently:

Proposition 2:

As the rate of information flow increases, the probability of waiting increases. Therefore, the probability of protective action decreases, as the rate at which warnings are issued increases.

The only remaining aspect of equation (7) which needs consideration is the initial value for E(U/A1) and E(U/A2). Since these are dependent only on payoff and cost considerations, along with initial subjective probabilities of the alternative hypotheses ("the storm will miss" vs. "the storm will hit"), and we are assuming fixed payoff and cost factors, there remains the question of initial values for subjective probabilities of the hypotheses. Obviously these will depend upon the experiences of the decision-maker. We have no basis for knowing those experiences. Empirical survey evidence from disaster research indicates that long term residents of an area (hence those with more experience with similar imminent choices) were less likely to respond to warnings with some form of protective action (Windham, Posey, Ross, and Spencer, 1977; Kendall and Clark, 1981). Consequently:

Proposition 3:

As the amount of prior experience of the decision maker with such decisions and information sources increases, the probability of protective action in response to a given warning will decrease.

In addition, we expect the sheer quantity of previous experience with similar imminent choices to interact with the proportion of the experiential history which resulted in the most serious outcomes (hereafter referred to as "proportion hit"). That is,

Proposition 4:
As the proportion hit (over prior experience) increases, the probability of protective action in response to a series of warnings will increase.

These propositions were tested experimentally in the research reported below.

METHOD

Method of Data Collection

Design.   The theoretical propositions were tested via an interactive computer-generated experimental simulation for the study of individual response to warnings of impending tornados. The nature of a simulation experiment is to study actual behaviors of subjects involved in simulated situations. This is in contrast to procedures which Cronkite (1980) has argued lack external validity. Her concern is with studies of how people think they or others would behave if they were in a hypothetical situation. Gifford (1982) discusses this distinction in greater detail. Evidence of external validity of experimental simulations comparable to those employed here can be found in Leik et al. (1982) and Ekker et al. (1982). The game required subjects to assume the role of management in a small manufacturing company, regulating the production in their plant. The management role was constructed to be extrinsically motivating. It provided continual problems to be solved, and the degree of success with which it was played determined the actual laboratory payment received. That is, the laboratory payment was determined exclusively by the final bank balance for the company achieved by the subjects.

While the subjects were engaged in management, three consecutive sequences of tornado warning messages appeared. Each sequence described the progression of a hypothetical tornado, from the point at which the first "official tornado warning" was issued, to the point where the tornado moved to its final disposition for the subject's company as either a hit or miss. After the issuance of each warning message, the subject was given the opportunity either to continue plant operation at the same rate of production, or take some form of protective action against the tornado (e.g., move stock from vulnerable areas, dismiss employees). The amount of descriptive information contained in the message (1), the rate at which the messages were issued (2), and the proportion of the subject's experimental history resulting in the most serious outcome (proportion hit) (3) comprise the independent variables experimentally manipulated. The variables were operationally defined as follows:

1. The amount of descriptive information contained in the messages assumed three values—high, medium, and low—which were defined as follows:

    3. The subjects in the high information group received in each message:

        (a) warnings which specified the location of the most recent sighting, by county and/or municipality in the Twin City seven county metropolitan area;

        (b) the approximate length of time it would take to reach Minneapolis, given its present course and speed (i.e., assuming subject's companies are located in downtown Minneapolis—this became an estimated time of arrival); and

        (c) a map outlining the seven county Twin City metropolitan area, showing the approximate location of the current plus any prior sightings of the tornado.

    2. The subjects in the medium information group received in each message:

        (a) warnings which specified the location of the tornado; and

        (b) the approximate time of arrival—but no map.

    1. The subjects in the low information group received in each message:

        (a) warnings which specified the location of the tornado only— no E.T.A. or map.

Message rate (2) and the proportion hit (3) were dichotomized, yielding a 2 × 2 factorial design for each of the three information groups.

2. The rate at which the warning messages were issued was defined as the frequency with which the messages were issued in a given unit of time. The two values were:

    a. fast = messages at four minute intervals, and

    b. slow = messages at eight minute intervals.

3. The proportion hit was defined as the proportion of the previous tornado warning sequences resulting in a hit on the manufacturing plant. The two values were:

a. (H)it/(M)iss/(H)it = where the first and third warning sequences were followed by a hit on the plant; and
b. (M)iss/(H)it/(M)iss = where only the second warning sequence was followed by a hit on the plant.

During the first sequence, of course, there was no prior history of being hit, so proportions for both groups were 0%. During the second sequence before the outcome for that sequence occurred, 100% of the experimental history for group (a) was a hit on the plant, whereas for group (b) it was still 0%. In the third sequence, however, the proportion for both groups became 5%. Consequently, when analyzing the affect of this variable, we will focus only on the decisions in the second sequence.

The amount of experience with the process of making similar decisions became a longitudinal variable, where subjects at the outset of the experiment had no previous experience with these decisions. By the third sequence, however, they had experience with two other similar decisions. By this time they had learned: what kinds of information to expect, how frequently it had been available, and how long it takes to effectively protect the company, along with many other things about managing their companies successfully.

The tornado sequences show reasonable real time approach of each storm. Actual timing of the messages shows minor random variation around the four or eight minute intervals, making the time between first warning and final outcome basically determinate, but unknown to the subjects. For each information level—high, medium, and low—the four treatments implied by the 2 x 2 design for message rate (2) and tornado history (3) were:

Treatment	Message Rate	Proportion Hit
1	fast	HMH
2	fast	MHM
3	slow	HMH
4	slow	MHM

For each message sequence, warnings occurred at the following approximate intervals:

Treatment	Sequence	Interval (in minutes)
1	1st	4 8 12 16 20 24 26.5 (Hit)
	2nd	4 8 10.6 (Miss)
	3rd	4 8 12 16 20 24 26.5 (Hit)
2	1st	4 8 12 16 20 24 26.5 (Miss)
	2nd	4 8 10.5 (Hit)
	3rd	4 8 12 16 20 24 26.5 (Miss)
3	1st	8 16 24 26.5 (Hit)
	2nd	8 10.5 (Miss)
	3rd	8 16 24 26.5 (Hit)
4	1st	8 16 24 26.5 (Miss)
	2nd	8 10.5 (Hit)
	3rd	8 16 24 26.5 (Miss)

The outcomes reported in parentheses at the end of each sequence occurred at the time immediately preceding it, such that there was a maximum of six warning messages sent.

After each message was issued, the subject was given the option of:

1. continuing full production, protecting nothing; or
2. Continuing production at ½ the rate at full production, while protecting saleable product; or
3. ceasing production completely, protecting supplies and product,
   and dismissing employees with pay.

If the tornado hit the plant, under option 1: all supplies and product, and
50% of the company's personnel were destroyed; under option 2: product
was protected (unless the tornado hit while products were being protected—a process which took about 30 seconds), but all supplies and 50% of
personnel were destroyed; and under option 3: supplies and product were
protected (unless the tornado hit during that process—which took about
1 minute), employees were dismissed, and there were no losses. These
options comprise the dependent variable—choice (Y). Payroll is regularly
assessed against the subject's bank balance, irrespective of whether the
plant is in production.

The demographic variables age, sex, marital status, and occupation
were recorded for each subject to statistically control in the analysis.

Subjects. One hundred ninety-eight adults were employed in the
experiments. Most were young (between the ages of 18 and 32) unmarried
students. Each was paid at least $5.00. An additional $1.00 was added to
their payment for every $5,000 they made for their company—to a max-
imum $10.00 payment.

Stimuli. A standardized verbal description of the operation of the manufacturing plant was given to each subject by the experimenter. The text for that description appears in Appendix 2. All subjects operated the same plant. That is, rates of production per employee, costs of supplies, and the price available in the market for the product were all the same for each treatment and information group. Assignment to information group was done sequentially, such that the high information group was filled first, the medium second, and the low third. Assignment to treatment was random until the number of cases in the cells became uneven, at which point cases were assigned to deficient cells.

Apparatus. Cathode ray tube computer terminals were used. Warning messages and company status were displayed on the screen of the terminal. Subjects operated their plants and responded to the tornado threats by interacting with the Fortran program constructed for these experiments through the terminals.

Procedure. When the subjects arrived at the lab, they were seated in a waiting room and asked to fill out the "Informed Consent" form, which also served as a record of their address, to which their lab payment was sent. During that time, the experimenter began the program. The date, time, information group to which the subject was assigned, case number, treatment, age, sex, marital status, and occupation were then selected and recorded for each case. After this information was entered, it disappeared at the top of the screen, and the subject was seated at the terminal. At this point, the subject was given the verbal instructions concerning his or her role in the experiment. Then, the program welcomed them to their new Minneapolis company, and gave them the opportunity to practice the operation of their plant for about 5 minutes. The practice was instituted to try to insure the subjects' success in the operation of their plant. If they were miserable failures at managing the plant, they might have been less likely to protect it from the threat of a tornado. Moreover, we wanted to insure that their "normal" activity represented the pursuit of valued goals, rather than struggling with a strange new experience. After the practice session, the tornado warning sequences were initiated.

Between warnings, and while their companies were in operation at some level of production, the subjects regulated production by buying supplies, hiring and firing personnel, and selling finished products. The program required only that they enter the quantities of supplies, product, and personnel they wanted. Accounting of the companies' costs and income was done and recorded automatically by the program. After each warning message, the three choices (Y) were given to the subjects.

TABLE 1. Modified Time-Series Design[a]

							Message Number								
Treatment	0	1	2	3	4	5	6	7	8	9	10	11	12	13	14
1	R	$X_{11}O_{11}$	$X_{12}O_{12}$	$X_{13}O_{13}$	$X_{14}O_{14}$	$X_{15}O_{15}$	$X_{16}O_{16}$	$X_{21}O_{21}$	$X_{22}O_{22}$	$X_{31}O_{31}$	$X_{32}O_{32}$	$X_{33}O_{33}$	$X_{34}O_{34}$	$X_{35}O_{35}$	$X_{36}O_{36}$
2	R	$X_{11}O_{11}$	$X_{12}O_{12}$	$X_{13}O_{13}$	$X_{14}O_{14}$	$X_{15}O_{15}$	$X_{16}O_{16}$	$X_{21}O_{21}$	$X_{22}O_{22}$	$X_{31}O_{31}$	$X_{32}O_{32}$	$X_{33}O_{33}$	$X_{34}O_{34}$	$X_{35}O_{35}$	$X_{36}O_{36}$
3	R		$X_{12}O_{12}$		$X_{14}O_{14}$		$X_{16}O_{16}$		$X_{22}O_{22}$		$X_{32}O_{32}$		$X_{34}O_{34}$		$X_{36}O_{36}$
4	R		$X_{12}O_{12}$		$X_{14}O_{14}$		$X_{16}O_{16}$		$X_{22}O_{22}$		$X_{32}O_{32}$		$X_{34}O_{34}$		$X_{36}O_{36}$

[a] The design is not a pure time-series design, since there are not parallel observations across all treatments.
X_{ij}: represents subjects' exposure to tornado warning message for the ith sequence and the jth message.
O_{ij}: represents the observation of the subjects' choice after the tornado message for the ith sequence and the jth message.

Since the first sequence of warning messages consumed around 26½ minutes, the second about 10½, and the third about 26½ once the practice session was ended, the time required to go through the three warning sequences was about 63 minutes. After each of the three sequences, the outcome of the tornado for their plant was reported to the subjects by the program. When the tornado missed their plant, that fact was reported to them, and they were permitted to continue plant operation. When the tornado hit their plant, the computer reported "D-i-s-a-s-t-e-r . . . the tornado has struck your plant," after which a breakdown of its losses was reported to them and recorded according to the schedule described above.

Subjects were permitted to make two business decisions before the status of their plant was reported to them. That is, after two decisions, the company's bank balance, available supplies, product, and personnel were reported to the subjects. This constituted one business cycle. The above information on the status of the company was automatically recorded after each cycle. The mean number of cycles completed was 31 for all treatments. Any losses incurred to the company from the tornado were also automatically recorded. Of the 198 subjects who were paid, 197 yielded data where at least 7 cycles were completed. One subject never completed any cycles, strongly indicating that (s)he never attributed much value to the plant or the experiments.

At the end of the third tornado warning sequence, the program informed the subjects of their lab payment and thanked them. At this point, each subject was debriefed. That is, they were quizzed as to whether they discerned the purpose of the experiment, and then they were informed in as much detail as they desired.

Table 1 is a time series design diagram showing the sequencing of exposure to the warning messages (X_{ij}: where i = the treatment and j = the message number) and the recording of the subject's choice (Y) (O_{ij}).

Measurement of Response Rate

The choices available to the subjects after each warning comprised the dependent variable: response to warning. The level of measurement of the response variable was inherently ordinal. Interval level scores for options 1 and 3 can be arbitrarily set without introducing problematic measurement error. Let these options have scores of 0 and 1 respectively. To score option 2 as .5, midway between 1 and 3, would probably somewhat underrepresent the actual degree of response. Selecting that option, which protects finished products, is likely to indicate a greater psychological change than changing between the two levels of protective action. Although selecting option 3 also protects supplies and personnel, from a purely economic viewpoint these are easily replaced. The products, however, symbolize the tangible fruits of their efforts and their sole incentive. The net result of equal interval scoring of choice Y should be to render statistical tests of significance for tests about mean level of response slightly conservative, making it more difficult to reject the null hypotheses. The equal interval scores of 0, .5, and 1 were therefore adopted. Although not technically a probability, the mean response score can be interpreted as a probability of protective action.

RESULTS

The propositions specified that experience (a longitudinal variable), rapid message flow, more complete message content, and a low proportion hit all induce subjects to delay defensive action. We must remember that the same variables were expected to contribute to a reduction in the probability of protective action when the deadline is uncertain, as well as when a deadline is imminent for an irrevocable choice. When the deadline is uncertain (i.e., time seems to be left to gather more information), waiting for more information is appropriate.

However, when a deadline is imminent for an irrevocable choice, waiting reflects inappropriate decision making. If an alternative is available that will eliminate the risk of serious losses, it is not wise to continue to search for better ones. If these factors were operating independently, they would suggest the following data comparisons:

1. For each level of experience, rate of message flow, and proportion hit, response curves for subjects exposed to the more complete messages should be lower than response curves for those exposed to the less complete messages (See Figure 1).
2. For each level of experience, amount of information, and proportion hit, response curves for subjects receiving messages at the fast rate should be lower than response curves for subjects receiving messages at the slow rate (See Figure 2).
3. For each level of amount of information, rate of message flow, and proportion hit, response curves for experienced subjects (i.e., curves for the third sequence) should be lower than response curves for inexperienced subjects (i.e., curves for the first sequence) (See Figure 3).
4. For each level of amount of information, rate of message flow, and experience, response curves for subjects exposed to the lowest proportion hit should be lower than response curves for those exposed to the highest proportion.

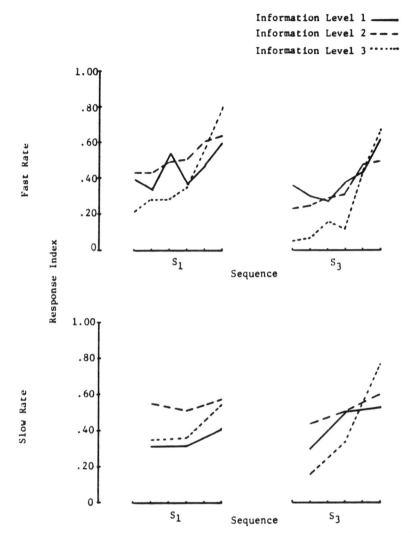

FIGURE 1. Response Rate by Information Level, Controlling Experience and Rate of Flow of Information.

Response curves are presented first according to the preceeding suggested comparisons. Note that the same curves are reused in Figures 1–3 so as to facilitate different comparisons.

A variety of formal conclusions can be reached from Figures 1–3, which contain the response curves, and Tables 2–7, which summarize the results of two different types of analysis of variance. For certain comparisons, ordinary analysis of variance will be appropriate. However, when

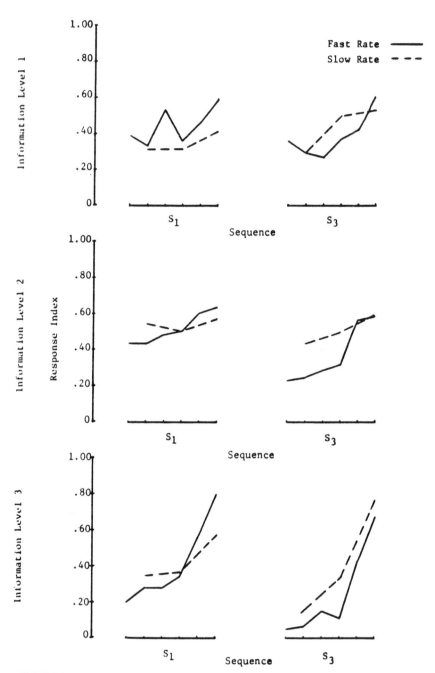

FIGURE 2.   Response Rate by Rate of Flow of Information, Controlling Information
Level and Experience.

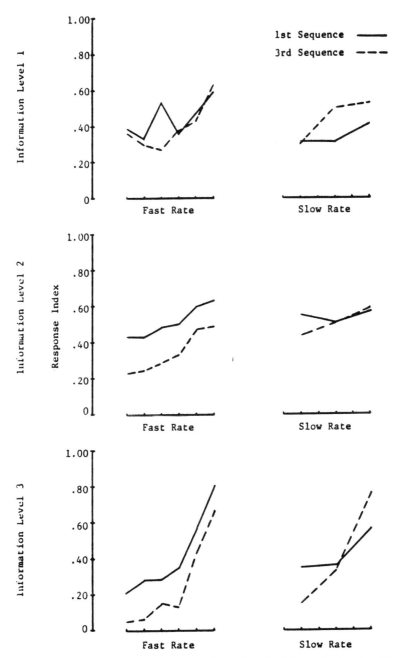

FIGURE 3.   Response Rate by Experience, Controlling for Information Level and Rate
of Flow of Information.

all data points for a given tornado sequence are analyzed, or when trends or averages are compared across sequences, it is necessary to remember that each subject contributed to each successive measurement. Consequently, the over time data are of the form of a repeated measurement experiment.

The MANOVA program of SPSS allows transformations of such repeated measurements into a polynomial function over time. The coefficients of each polynomial term are then used in place of the original data, for subsequent analysis. For a six warning sequence, then, the procedure provides, for each subject, a mean response over time, a coefficient for a linear time trend, a coefficient for a quadratic time trend, and so forth through a fifth power term in the polynomial. Each of these coefficients constitutes a single dependent variable for that subject, eliminating the over time interdependence of the original data. It then becomes possible to analyze these independent components within the analysis of variance design of the experiment to determine whether manipulated variables affected the time trends of the subjects' responses to warnings. This procedure will be referred to as a repeated measures analysis of variance.

TABLE 2.   Effects of Experience, Information Level, and Rate on Response Curves Over Time

Sequence 1

			Information Level		
			Low	Medium	High
Rate	Slow	Mean	.34 *	.53 *	.42 *
		b(LIN)	.07 n.s.[a]	.00 n.s.	.15 *
		b(QUAD)	.04 n.s.	.05 n.s.	.08 n.s.
	Fast	Mean	.42 *	.52 *	.47 *
		b(LIN)	.18 *	.13 *	.36 *
		b(QUAD)	.08 n.s.	.00 n.s.	.16 *

Sequence 3

			Information Level		
			Low	Medium	High
Rate	Slow	Mean	.44 *	.51 *	.42 *
		b(LIN)	.17 *	.12 *	.43 *
		b(QUAD)	− .07 n.s.	.01 n.s.	.11 *
	Fast	Mean	.43 *	.38 *	.28 *
		b(LIN)	.23 *	.28 *	.43 *
		b(QUAD)	.07 n.s.	.08 *	.21 *

TABLE 2. (continued)

Source		df	Analysis of Variance Hyp. S Sq	Error S Sq	Hyp. Mn Sq	Error Mn Sq	F	P
			Sequence 1[b]					
	Mean	1/186	.08	16.92	.08	.09	.84	.360
Rate	b(LIN)	1/186	1.09	15.40	1.09	.08	13.22	.000
	b(QUAD)	1/186	.03	9.89	.03	.05	.49	.483
	Mean	2/186	.61	16.92	.31	.09	3.36	.037
I.L.	b(LIN)	2/186	1.27	15.40	.63	.08	7.67	.001
	b(QUAD)	2/186	.28	9.89	.14	.05	2.66	.073
Rate	Mean	2/186	.07	16.92	.03	.09	.36	.695
by	b(LIN)	2/186	.09	15.40	.04	.08	.53	.591
I.L.	b(QUAD)	2/186	.15	9.89	.07	.05	1.40	.249
			Sequence 3[b]					
	Mean	1/186	.39	12.98	.39	.07	5.61	.019
Rate	b(LIN)	1/186	.26	17.60	.26	.09	2.75	.098
	b(QUAD)	1/186	.54	11.84	.54	.06	8.53	.004
	Mean	2/186	.36	12.98	.18	.07	2.55	.081
I.L.	b(LIN)	2/186	2.30	17.60	1.15	.09	12.14	.000
	b(QUAD)	2/186	.87	11.84	.43	.06	6.81	.001
Rate	Mean	2/186	.15	12.98	.08	.07	1.10	.334
by	b(LIN)	2/186	.19	17.60	.10	.09	1.02	.363
I.L.	b(QUAD)	2/186	.03	11.84	.02	.06	.26	.772

* $p \leq .05$

[a] No significance.

[b] Experience is represented by Sequence 1 vs. Sequence 3. Comparable time points for fast and slow message rates were transformed into a polynomial function of time (mean, linear, and quadratic components) and analyzed by a multivariate analysis of variance (SPSS MANOVA). F tests pertain to whether the specified effect has influenced the mean response, linear and quadratic slope over the curve of response to warnings. Six cases were randomly deleted from treatments to equalize cell frequencies for this and all subsequent analyses.

We will summarize the results of the repeated measures ananlysis of variance first. Because the different rate groups had unequal numbers of observations per given sequence, the effect of rate could not be analyzed if all observations were included. Therefore, we included only the three observations in the analysis which were taken at the same times until deadline (i.e., 012, 014, 016 for the first sequence, and 032, 034, 036 for the third sequence). The results of this analysis appear in Table 2.

Next we will shift the focus from the probability of protective action to the mean waiting time until the first protective action. Using mean waiting time provides us with the opportunity to summarize general changes in response time across the comparable tornado warning sequences (i.e., 1st and 3rd). Because all data were recorded in the computer by lapsed time from the start of each tornado sequence, a mean waiting time for each sequence was easily calculated. These data appear in Table 3.

Finally, we will focus again on the probability of protective action, but at specific points in each sequence. Tables 4–7 summarize the results of the simple analysis of variance where the change in the probability of either early or late protective action across successive sequences was the dependent variable.

Table 2 presents evidence on Propositions 1 and 2. If information level was operating additively, the curves would be parallel, with the highest information level group exhibiting the lowest curve and mean throughout each sequence and for each rate. Similarly, if rate was operating additively, the curves for each rate would be uniformly different, with the fast rate exhibiting the lowest curve and mean throughout each sequence and for each information level.

Figures 1 and 2 provide a breakdown of response curves by information level and rate. Even a very cursory review of those figures suggest that these variables produce different trends, although it is unclear whether they produce different means. Looking at Table 2, it is clear that information level and rate do not interact on any components in the polynomial for either sequence.

In the first sequence, the means do not appear to systematically vary with rate. Although information level produces significantly different means in the first sequence ($F = 3.36$, $p = .037$), they do not systematically decline with increases in information level. Both variables produce significantly different linear coefficients, with the highest information level and the fast rate producing the largest coefficient ($b = .36$). Rate does not affect the quadratic coefficients significantly, as all but one do not significantly differ from zero. Information level comes close to generating different quadratic coefficients, producing a significant slope for the fast rate group exposed to the highest amount of information ($b = .16$).

In the third sequence, the means for the fast rate are significantly lower over all than for the slow rate ($F = 5.61$, $p = .019$). Increasing information level, when combined with the fast rate, also produces systematically decreasing means (.43, .38, .28), although it is uncertain whether the differences are significant when both rates are included in the test ($F = 2.55$, $p = .081$). Increasing rate produces increasing linear trends, with the exception of the high information level group, which is probably part of the reason that it is uncertain whether the test of rate on thelinear coefficients is significant ($F = 2.75$, $p = .098$). Increasing information level almost uniformly produces increasing linear coefficients ($F = 12.14$, $p = .000$). Information level and rate both significantly affect the quadratic coefficients ($F = 6.81$, $p = .001$; and $F = 8.53$, $p = .004$), such that the largest quadratic coefficient is evident for the highest information level and the fast rate (.21), the combination of treatments which produced the most accelerated pattern of protective action.

In sum, only in the third sequence were the expectations of the first and second propositions supported. They called for an additive relationship between message rate and quality, with respect to their affect on the probability of protective action. A given sequence of disaster warning messages, varying systematically by availability (frequency) and quality (detail) was predicted to produce concommitant variation in the probability of protective action. As the message sequences became more frequent and detailed, the likelihood of protective action as a response to any given message was expected to decline. Only in the third message sequence were there systematic and additive affects of increasing frequency and detail over the entire response curve, a finding which suggests that variation in message availability and quality have independent affects on the probability of protective action, but only after previous exposure to making similar decisions and using information sources of similar availability and quality.

If the probability of protective action decreases uniformly by increasing information quality and availability, the overall time waited until the first protective action should also increase over time (i.e., across the warning sequences). That is, there is one waiting time for sequence 1, and one for sequence 3, for each subject. These two times produce a mean for the two sequences, and an estimated linear trend. With only two observations, no higher order terms can be estimated.

When these two observations are analyzed as a polynomial, the linear coefficient is proportional to the difference between waiting times across the first and third sequences. An analysis of the mean waiting time across the sequences would not test whether the changes in the waiting times from the first to the third sequences were significantly different from treatment to treatment. Only by estimating a linear coefficient for each subject, and using that as a dependent variable, can we test whether the treatments produce different changes. Table 3 summarizes the results of this analysis.

Clearly, the group exposed to the most informative messages at the fast rate produced the largest linear increase in waiting time ($b = 4.42$) from the first to the third sequences. Conversely, those exposed to the least informative messages at the slow rate actually exhibited a decrease in waiting time ($b = -1.32$). The summary table indicates that information level and rate affect independently the mean waiting time, such that those exposed to the most detailed and available information sources exhibit the greatest increase in waiting time until first protective action ($F = 5.99$, $p = .003$; $F = 7.70$, $p = .006$, respectively).

TABLE 3.   Effects of Experience, Information Level, and Rate on Waiting Time Until First Protective Action

			Information Level					
			Low		Medium		High	
Rate	Slow	X(1)[a]	16.13		9.94		16.05	
		X(3)[a]	14.25		12.38		18.31	
		b(LIN)	− 1.32	n.s.	1.72	*	1.59	n.s.
	Fast	X(1)	8.75		8.57		12.63	
		X(3)	10.19		13.06		18.88	
		b(LIN)	1.01	n.s.	3.12	*	4.42	*

Analysis of Variance

Source of variation	Sum of squares	df	Mean squares	F	P
Within cells	5661.63	186	30.44		
Info Level (IL)	364.56	2	182.28	5.99	.003
Rate	234.38	1	234.38	7.70	.006
IL By Rate	15.44	2	7.72	.25	.776
Total	6276.01	191			

* $p < .05$.
[a] Experience is represented by Sequence 1 [X(1)] vs. Sequence 3 [X(3)]. Repeated measures Analysis of Variance (SPSS MANOVA) was used to transform S1 and S3 waiting times in minutes into a polynomial function of time (mean and linear components only). F tests pertain to whether a specified source of variation has influenced the linear slope b(LIN) between S1 and S3.

Finally, we can test Propositions 3 and 4. If the amount of prior experience a decision maker has with similar decisions and information sources operates independent of variation in the quality and availability of those sources, all second sequence curves would be lower than all first sequence curves; and all third sequence curves would be lower than all first and second sequence curves. If prior experience was operating as stated above, all changes in the probability of either early or late protective action would have negative values (e.g., 021 − 011 < 0 for the fast rate, and 022 − 012 < 0 for the slow), and no experimental variables would differentially affect those values. (Obviously, for those exposed to the slow rate, there was only one opportunity to respond in the second sequence. That response was used for both early and late time analyses.)

If proportion hit interacts with experience, those hit in the first sequence should exhibit no change if not an increase, and those missed in the first sequence should show the largest decline. Table 4 summarizes

TABLE 4. Change in Early Response Across Sequences (2 to 1) — by Rate, Information Level (IL), and Disaster History (DH).

Source of Variation	Sum of Squares	df	Mean Square	F	Significance of F
Main Effects	2.586	4	.646	3.332	.012
Rate	.949	1	.949	4.893	.028
Information Level	1.531	2	.766	3.946	.021
Disaster History	.105	1	.105	.544	.462
Two Way Interactions	1.345	5	.269	1.387	.231
Rate IL	.406	2	.203	1.047	.353
Rate DH	.814	1	.814	4.195	.042
IL DH	.125	2	.062	.322	.725
Three Way Interactions					
Rate IL DH	.510	2	.255	1.315	.271
	.510	2	.255	1.315	.271
Explained	4.441	11	.404	2.081	.024
Residual	34.922	180	.194		
Total	39.363	191	.206		

N = 192

the three-way analysis of variance, where the changes in the probability of early protective action from the first to the second sequence comprised the dependent variable.

This analysis indicates that both information level and rate significantly affect the change in the probability of early protective action, but the influence of rate is a byproduct of its interaction with disaster history. That is, only among those exposed to the slow rate is there an increase in the probability of early protective action (+ .29) from being hit in the first sequence. Moreover, being missed by the first tornado does not significantly reduce the probability of early protection. It must be remembered that early action in the second sequence is not precisely comparable to early action in the first, since the first messages issued in the second sequence indicate a much more imminent tornado. This accounts for the overall positive change (.13).

Information level, however, significantly affects the changes in early response from the first to the second sequence (F = 3.946, p = .021). Those exposed to the lowest information level show almost no change (.02), whereas for those in the medium group, there is a substantial increase in early protection, but those exposed to the highest amount of information exhibited the largest increase. Obviously, with respect to changes from the first to the second sequence, Proposition 3 is not confirmed. Prior experience with similar decisions and information sources does not operate independent of the quality and availability of the sources.

With respect to Proposition 4, proportion hit ("Disaster History") also does not operate quite as expected. Although it does not have a main effect (F = .544, p = .462), it does interact with rate (F = 4.195, p = .042). The effect is such that, if the rate is fast, proportion hit has virtually no effect. When the rate is slow, however, although both "Disaster History" groups exhibit increases in early protection, the experience of being hit by the first tornado does signficantly augment that increase.

When we look at the change in the probability of late protective action from the first to the second sequence, disaster history and rate again produce a significant interaction effect (F = 3.324, p = .070). This change overall is .04. The effect is almost indistinguishable from that which occurred on changes in early action, such that only among those exposed to the slow rate did the experience of being hit by the first tornado significantly increase the probability of late protective action from the first to the second sequence (.21). Being missed by the first tornado did not affect this change (− .01), nor did being hit or missed affect this change, among those exposed to the fast rate (0.0 and − .02 respectively). Information level does not significantly affect this change.

Table 6 summarizes the analysis on the change in early protective action from the first to the third sequence. Information level (F = 3.555, p = .031) and "Disaster History" (F = 3.555, p = .061), both significantly affect this change. Message rate did not affect this change. Overall, the probability of early protective action decreases from the first to the third sequence (− .12). Information levels medium and high both produced an identical augmentation of this reduction (− .17). The experience of being missed by the first tornado also further reduced early protection in the third sequence (− .17), even though they were hit by the second one, whereas being hit by the first one produced an almost negligible change (− .07).

Table 7 summarizes the analysis of the change in late protective action from the first to the third sequence. Here message rate produces the only significant effect. The fast rate of message flow significantly reduces the probability of protective action at the last possible opportunity from the first to the third sequence (F = 6.236, p = .013).

Summarizing Tables 4–7, we must remember that the second sequence was only 10.5 minutes long, that those in the slow rate group experienced only one warning message, and that that occurred when the tornado was only 2 minutes away from the plant. Since the choices for this group at this time became the observations for both early and late time analyses, it is not surprising that the interaction evidenced between

TABLE 5.   Analysis of variance: Change in Final Response Across Sequences (2 to 1) — by Rate, Information Level (IL), and Disaster History (DH).

Source of Variation	Sum of Squares	df	Mean Square	F	Significance of F
Main Effects	1.531	4	.383	2.707	.032
Rate	.574	1	.574	4.061	.045
Information Level	.268	2	.134	.948	.389
Disaster History	.689	1	.689	4.871	.029
2-Way Interactions	1.324	5	.265	1.873	.101
Rate IL	.289	2	.145	1.022	.362
Rate DH	.470	1	.470	3.324	.070
IL DH	.565	2	.283	1.998	.139
3-Way Interactions					
Rate IL DH	.065	2	.033	.230	.795
	.065	2	.033	.230	.795
Explained	2.921	11	.266	1.878	.045
Residual	25.453	180	.141		
Total	28.374	191	.149		

N = 192

TABLE 6.   Analysis of variance: Change in Early Response Across Sequences (3 to 1) — by Rate, Information Level (IL), and Disaster History (DH).

Source of Variation	Sum of Squares	df	Mean Square	F	Significance of F
Main Effects	1.443	4	.361	2.728	.031
Rate	.033	1	.033	.246	.620
IL	.940	2	.470	3.555	.031
DH	.470	1	.470	3.555	.061
2-Way interactions	.486	5	.097	.735	.598
Rate IL	.128	2	.064	.483	.618
Rate DH	.293	1	.293	2.216	.138
IL DH	.065	2	.033	.246	.782
3-Way interactions	.148	2	.074	.561	.571
Rate IL DH	.148	2	.074	.561	.571
Explained	2.077	11	.189	1.428	.164
Residual	23.797	180	.132		
Total	25.874	191	.135		

TABLE 7.   Analysis of variance: Change in Final Response Across Sequences (3 to 1) — by
Rate, Information Level (IL), and Disaster History (DH).

Source of Variation	Sum of Squares	df	Mean Square	F	Significance of F
Main Effects	1.607	4	.402	2.287	.062
Rate	1.095	1	1.095	6.236	.013
IL	.135	2	.068	.386	.681
DH	.376	1	.376	2.143	.145
2-Way interactions	1.345	5	.269	1.532	.182
Rate IL	.760	2	.380	2.165	.118
Rate DH	.293	1	.293	1.668	.198
IL DH	.292	2	.146	.830	.438
3-Way interactions	.219	2	.109	.623	.538
Rate IL DH	.219	2	.109	.623	.538
Explained	3.171	11	.288	1.641	.091
Residual	31.609	180	.176		
Total	34.780	191	.182		

rate and "Disaster History" (Tables 4 and 5) are almost indistinguishable. Given this fact, Table 5 should be given the most weight, since either response in sequence 2 is most parallel to a final response. That is, aligning an early response in sequence 2 with an early response in sequence 1 would be erroneous given the greatly unequal distances away from plant indicated in the early messages in sequence 1, and the early ones in sequence 2.

Information level, then, interacts with experience to produce a significant reduction in early protective action (See Table 6), whereas it does not affect changes in final protective action. The rate at which messages are issued, however, interacts with experience to produce a significant reduction in protective action at the last possible opportunity (See Tables 5 and 7). "Disaster History" (proportion hit) interacts with experience and message rate such that, among those exposed to the slow rate, the experience of being hit by the first tornado slightly increases final protective action from the first to the second sequence, whereas being missed does not affect this change. With respect to changes in early protection from the first to the third sequence, however, "Disaster History" interacts with experience alone such that, although the change overall was a reduction in protective action, being missed by the first tornado further reduced early protection. Those hit by the first tornado also showed a reduction in early protection from first to third sequences, but it was not significantly above the mean reduction.

DISCUSSION

When subjects are inexperienced, fast message rate produces a greater likelihood of protection prior to deadline (i.e., see Figure 2). If that finding were to hold across increased experience, then the Bayesian analysis would be refuted and the implication for warning policy would be to issue warnings at frequent intervals. Assuming that responses to actual warnings are similar in form to those generated in our experiments, it would be reasonable to recommend that new residents in an area subject to a particular hazard, if they have no prior experience with that hazard, might best be given frequent warnings.

The balance of the data, however, provides a quite different picture. With respect to the influence of the variables information level and rate, we find that increasing rate produces uniform decreases in the (mean) curves of protective action only in the third sequence. Moreover, we also find that information level is the variable most closely associated with the degree to which those curves increase and accelerate with the passage of time (See Table 2). The results in Table 3 indicate that these variables operate additively on the waiting time until first protective action, effectively simulating the intuitively reasonable process of learning to postpone unnecessary defensive action, when good quality information sources are available and there is plenty of time left to gather information for a later decision.

To interpret the influence of these variables more discretely, we need to separate changes in protection over time, at early points in a given sequence, from late points. In our experiments, decreases in protective action at early points reflect an appropriate response. As subjects gain experience in these simulations, it becomes clear that closing the plant in response to the first message is unnecessary. The entire process of protection takes a maximum of one minute, and a subject in any treatment group can be confident that at least one more opportunity to decide will be available before the tornado passes, at least for the first and third sequences. Reductions in protective action at late point in sequences 1 and 3 represent a willingness to sacrifice the community welfare for the profit that may be gained in the interim before the passage of the tornado.

Therefore, although all experimental variables were included in analyses summarized in Tables 4–7, interpreting the influences of information level and rate on changes in early and late protective action can only be done using the results of the analyses reported in Tables 6 and 7, which compare sequences of comparable length. Tables 4 and 5 should be used to discuss proportion hit ("Disaster History") only.

Tables 6 and 7 indicate that information level, not rate, reduces early protection, whereas only rate reduces late protection. One possible interpretation for this result could be that each tornado warning message sequence is considered anew, each to be evaluated on its own with respect to quality and availability. If so, the quality of a source can be ascertained from the first message. If it contains very detailed information, and at least one or two more messages can be expected in time, it becomes less necessary to take action immediately. Conversely, if that first message contains only a verbal description of the tornado sighting at some remote, frequently unknown municipality, it may seem less certain that a high quality piece of information will be available in the future.

The availability of a source of information, however, cannot be obtained from the first message. Particularly if that message does not contain any indication of a time until deadline, and/or if the present message sequence has been preceded by others of much shorter duration, the first message provides no basis for assessing the probability that new data will be available prior to deadline. If each sequence is evaluated independently as to availability, any confidence in the availability of sources producing messages frequently could be generated only after exposure to a regularized succession of messages (i.e., toward the end of our experimental sequences).

One possible means of experimentally researching this question would be to vary the quality and availability of the information source across warning message sequences. The control group would then be exposed to message sequences of constant quality and availability. If the control group exhibited greater reductions across sequences with increasing quality and availability, we would conclude that, with respect to the present experiments, each messge sequence is not evaluated independently, and the interpretation would become more complex.

This interpretation is not inconsistent with the finding that experience with making similar imminent decisions, using information sources of similar quality and availability, reduces the likelihood of protective action. It only suggests that the similarity of one source used in one decision to another source used in another decision, with respect to quality and availability, is a question the decision maker must resolve anew with each new decision sequence. The quality of a source is immediately obtained from the first message; the availability is not. Once those characteristics are established for a given source, previous experience with sources of similar characteristics can be used to determine their future usefulness.

If the trend evident in these data were to continue with longer histories of exposure to warnings, it is likely that good–quality, rapid warnings would lull more people into so reducing their response that they would delay beyond deadline. To clarify this point, refer back to Figure 2.

Whereas the curves of response for the upper portion of the figure tend to be flat and somewhat chaotic, those for information level 3, especially the fast flow curve for sequence 1 and both curves for sequence 3, are steep and regular. The one dip in the fast flow curve for sequence 3 corresponds to an apparent drifting off course of the storm shown in that sequence. These curves, then, show clear non-linear shift from an early indifference to the warnings to an almost last minute acceleration of the likelihood of taking action.

Taking these findings back to the subjective expected utility formulation for waiting, equation (7), the predictions made by the propositions are generally confirmed. The finding that waiting for more information was induced primarily among the experienced subjects who were provided with the most complete (i.e., highest) information levels and available (i.e., rapid) warning messages indicates that the variables (1) amount of information, (2) message rate, (3) experience, and (4) the proportion of one's history most serious, rather than operating independently (i.e., linearly, and additively), are operating interactively. That is, confidence in the future utility of high quality available information sources can only be gained from a history of exposure to and use of those sources in making similar decisions.

Looking at equation (7), a partial explanation for the findings can be obtained.

$$Dp > \frac{(1\text{-}R)}{R} \frac{E(U/A2) \; - \; E(U/A1)}{P2 \; + \; C2} \tag{7}$$

Those experienced in the processing of tornado warning sequences, when provided with the most complete and available pre-disaster information, are probably in the best position to use whatever diagnostic information becomes available. Conceivably, others, who have no experiential basis from which to evaluate tornado warning information, do not know what to expect from it, and find it difficult to use. Their confidence in the usefulness of future information is diminished. The experienced, however, provided reasonably detailed prognostic warning information at relatively frequent intervals, come to believe that the probability of useful warning information being available in subsequent messages (Dp) is large. The term Dp was defined as the rate that the subjective probability associated with the dominant hypothesis is perceived to change with the addition of the new fact, D. When very informative messages are expected, Dp was predicted to be large. We found that future messages were expected to be informative among those with enough experience in using similar information. They apparently weighed heavily the belief that upcoming messages would arrive soon enough and be sufficiently complete to allow them to react in time. It seems as if this belief outweighed (1) the belief that a useful message would not arrive in time, $(1 - R)/R$, and (2) the expected utilities associated with either of the other two options (i.e., to not change or to protect), the far right term in the equation.

Experience can be interpreted as having the effect of increasing the cognitive resources the individual brings to the warning information. As individuals gain experience in evaluating the hazard information to decide on when protective actions are appropriate, they become more rational in their response to each piece of information, and less likely to show immediate response to the first indications of the presence of a possible threat. The implication of this is that the most experienced residents in a community subject to a given threat would be most resistant to official recommendations and more autonomous in their decisions.

Similarly, the proportion of one's history resulting in the most serious outcomes must condition the way the amount of prior experience operates on the decision process. When the decision is imminent, and when it is less certain that future messages will be available, if the first experience with a tornado was a hit, there is a substantial increase in the likelihood of protective action. A plausible interpretation may be that, assuming unavailability of future information, when "all" past histories resulted in the most serious outcomes, the subjective probability of a hit for the next scenario is higher than if all past histories did not result in a hit.

When the first scenario resulted in a miss, however, there was virtually no change in the likelihood of protection from the first to the second sequence. If the outcomes of the experimental scenarios were the only factors influencing subjects' estimated probabilities of a hit on the plant (i.e., $p(H2)$), that subjective probability would be 0.0, and we would expect a large decrease in final protective action from the first to the second sequence.

We suggest that, without an indication to the subjects that the probability of a plant being hit by a tornado in the simulations is the same as the probability of an actual tornado hitting a real location, the experience of being missed in the first scenario does not produce a subjective $p(H2)$ = 0.0. It is likely, instead, that when they were missed the first time, knowing that these scenarios were set up for experimental reasons, they expected some kind of worst case scenario to occur sooner or later.

One possible way to explore this possibility would be to provide subjects, at the outset of the experiments, with the explanation that the behavior of the simulated tornados was designed to parallel, as closely as possible, that of actual tornados; and that some geographical areas are more subject to the threat of tornados than others. With this information in mind, they would then use outcomes of all prior experimental scenarios to estimate the likelihood that their area is subject to the threats.

Finally, if pre-experiment experience with actual tornado warnings was being transferred to the simulation setting, the confidence attached to the simulated warnings (intentionally worded as if they were issued by the National Weather Service) could be affected by non-experimental experience. If this were the case, we would need case histories on the number of tornado warnings actually experienced, and the number for which a tornado appeared in the predicted area. A ratio of the latter over the former, even subjective estimates, would provide a measure of the perceived likelihood that a warning indicates the eventual occurence of a tornado in the area. Statistically controlling these "perceived accuracy" measures would allow us to test whether they are affecting the confidence in the simulated warnings. Both of these possible added controls in our experimental procedure have been introduced in subsequent work.

Our final very important issue should be mentioned concerning the external validity of the findings. It is obvious that magnitudes of the costs and payoffs imposed by the experiment are not parallel to those that exist under the conditions that the experiment attempted to simulate. When the experimental focus is on outcomes such as personal injury and possible death, it would be impossible, not to mention unethical, to impose the actual magnitude of those outcomes. To the extent that this lack of extreme outcomes in the laboratory creates large subjective discrepancies between real and simulated tornados, the utility of waiting for information would be much less in the real as opposed to the simulated experience.

APPENDIX 1

Proof of Equation 7

1. Assume that taking protective action is the dominant choice at time t. That will be true if $E(U/A2,t) > E(U/A1,t)$, where t indicates time. Let the expected utility of A2 at time $t+1$ be designated $E(U/A2, t+1)$. For convenience, let p stand for $p(H2)$, the dominant probability. If p changes to $p + Dp$ from time t to time $t+1$, but costs and payoffs are fixed, then:

$$E(U/A2,t+1) = P2\ (p + DP) - C2\ (1 - p - Dp) \qquad (1)$$
$$= E(U/A2,t) + Dp\ (P2 + C2)$$

To calculate the expected utility of waiting at time t, note that "successful" waiting means that new information has been obtained, which has altered p to $p + Dp$. The probability of new information on which a decision can be made occurring prior to the deadline is R. If no new information is obtained in time, waiting will have produced inaction, by default, and have the same outcomes as choice A1. The probability of this occurring is $1 - R$. Therefore,

$$E(U/WAIT,t) = R\ (E(U/A2,t+1) + (1 - R)\ E(U/A1,t) \qquad (2)$$

Substituting (1) into (2), and omitting t, since all terms will now pertain to the same time, gives:

$$E(U/WAIT) = R\ [E(U/A2) + Dp\ (P2 + C2)] \qquad (3)$$
$$- (1\text{-}R)\ E(U/A1)$$

By hypothesis, $E(U/A2) > E(U/A1)$. If $E(U/WAIT) > E(U/A2)$, it will also exceed $E(U/A1)$. This will occur if $E(U/WAIT) - E(U/A2) > 0$.

$$E(U/WAIT) - E(U/A2) = R\ Dp\ (P2 + C2)$$
$$- (1 - R)\ [E(U/A2) - E(U/A1)] \qquad (4)$$

Consequently, $E(U/WAIT) > E(U/A2)$ if:

$$Dp > \frac{(1\text{-}R)}{R} \frac{E(U/A2) - E(U/A1)}{P2 + C2} \qquad (5)$$

Q.E.D

Note that either a sufficiently large positive change in Dp or a large enough negative change to make E(U/A1) > E(U/A2) can satisfy equation seven. The former implies waiting so as to be more confident in the final choice; the latter implies waiting in the event that new data might argue against the current predilection to take protective action.

2. The solution is simpler if inaction (A1) is the current dominant choice. In that case, not getting new information prior to deadline also results in inaction (although deciding not to take protective action, hence closing the decision making process, is quite different from waiting and continuing to monitor data in the hope of a safer future decision). For this case, it can be shown that waiting is always optimal if p is expected to decrease (favor inaction even more), or if p may increase a sufficient amount to make protective action the dominant choice. Remembering that p refers to p(H2), the methods used in section 1 of this appendix will produce:

$$E(U/WAIT) - E(U/A1) = -R \, Dp \, (P1 + C1) \qquad (5)$$

Therefore, E(U/WAIT) > E(U/A1) if Dp is negative (i.e., more in favor of deciding not to take protective action), since R and the P and C terms are all assumed to be positive. If Dp is positive and large enough, taking protective action is again implied, and the utility of waiting question returns to the first part of this appendix.

Equation (7) in this paper and the proof above are different from Leik and Kolman (1979) in one minor respect. In their presentation, option A2 was inaction, whereas A1 was an active option, which changes certain terms in the equation, but not the basic solution. It should be recognized that many binary choices have two "action" options, which would require that the derivation of Equation (7) incorporate a different assumption about the consequences of waiting too long (beyond deadline) before choosing a course of action.

APPENDIX 2

Experimenter Instructions to Subjects

E. AFTER ENTERING SUBJECT INFORMATION, SEAT THEM AND THEN HAVE THEM WAIT FOR VERBAL IN-

STRUCTIONS. THE FOLLOWING SHOULD BE *DIRECTED TO ALL SUBJECTS EXCEPT WHERE NOTED.*

1. Your task will be to manage a computer-simulated small business. As in any real business, your goal should be to try to maximize the profit of your company as much as possible.

   E.   Have subjects enter a ''1'' now.

2. You start out with $1674 (simulated dollars), and lab payment corresponds to the amount in the bank at the end of the session such that, for approximately every $20,000 in the bank, an additional $1.00 is added to the minimum $5.00 lab payment that we guarantee you for your participation.

   Assume that you can spend more money than you have. The bank will loan it to you at a certain interest rate, but feel free to do so if you wish.

3. Assume that the companies and all divisions are located in downtown Minneapolis. They are composed of three departments—A, B, and C. Department A is responsible for the initial assembly of part of the product, producing what the computer calls Department A's ''units on hand.'' Those units are then transferred to Department B, which then combines them with their supplies, producing Department B's ''units on hand.'' Those are then transferred to Department C, which performs the final inspection of the product, making it available for sale.

4. While you are regulating your company, you will receive messages that suggest that hypothetical tornadoes may threaten your company. You will be given options after each message concerning whether you would like to take any protective action against the threats.

   E.   Instruction #5 is only for those in the *high information condition,* i.e., if Information Level = 1.

5. After each tornado message and before your choices appear, a map of the seven county Twin City metropolitian area will appear. Assume that the company and all divisions are located where the ''X'' appears. The numbers that appear on those maps indicate where the tornado was last sighted—the larger the number, the more recent the sighting.

6. Assume that, for the purposes of this simulation, tornados can hit downtown areas—there is no such thing as an urban heat island, and that they can more in any direction.

---

*E: Denotes instructions to experimenter.

REFERENCES

Bradley, J.V.
 1976 Probability; Decision; Statistics. Englewood Cliffs, NJ: Prentice-Hall.
Brim, O.G., D. C. Glass, D. E. Lavin and N. Goodman.
 1962 Personality and Decision Processes. Palo Alto, CA: Stanford University Press.
Campbell, D.T., and J. C. Stanley
 1963 Experimental and Quasi-Experimental Designs for Research. Chicago, IL:Rand McNally.
Cook, Karen S. and Richard M. Emerson
 1978 "Power, equity, and commitment in exchange networks." American Sociological Review 43 (October): 721–739.
Cronkite, R.
 1980 "Social psychological simulations: An alternative to experiments?" Social Psychological Quarterly 43:199–216.
Edwards, Allen L.
 1967 Statistical Methods. 2nd Edition. New York: Holt, Rinehart, and Winston, Inc.
Ekker, K., S.A. Leik, R.K. Leik, and G. A. Gifford.
 1982 "Computerized Experiments in Family Decision Making: The Mt. St. Helens Study." Paper presented at the 10th World Congress of Sociology, Mexico City, Mexico.
Einhorn, H.J.
 1970 "The use of nonlinear, noncompensatory models in decision making." Psychological Bulletin 73:221–230.
Etzioni, A.
 1968 The Active Society. New York: The Free Press.
Gifford, G.A.
 1982 "Role Differentiation, Role Conflict, and Decision Making Under Stress: Experimental Simulations of Official Warning Decisions and Implications for Medical Diagnosis." Unpublished PhD dissertation, Minneapolis, MN: University of Minnesota.
Janis, Irving L., and Leon Mann
 1977 Decision Making—A Psychological Analysis of Conflict, Choice, and Commitment. New York: The Free Press.
Johnson, R.J.
 1974 "Conflict avoidance through acceptable decisions." Human Relations 27:71–82.
Katona, G.
 1953 "Rational behavior and economic behavior. Psychological Review 60:307–318.
Kendall, S.D., and J.P. Clark
 1981 "Household studies." Part 3 in R.K. Leik, T.M. Carter, J.P. Clark, S.D. Kendall, G.A. Gifford, W. Bielefeld, and K. Ekker (eds.), Community Response to Natural Hazard Warnings, Final Report. Minneapolis, MN: University of Minnesota.
Kunreuther, H., R. Ginsberg, L. Miller, P. Sagi, P. Stovic, B. Borkan, and N. Katz.
 1978 Disaster Insurance Protection. New York: Wiley.
Leik, R.K., and A.S. Kolman
 1979 "Models of the decision to conserve." Pp. 65–91 in M. Lewis (ed.), Research in Social Problems and Public Policy, Vol. 1. Greenwich, CT: JAI Press.
Leik, R.K., T.M.Carter, J.P. Clark, S.D. Kendall, G.A. Gifford, and K. Ekker
 1981 Community Response to Natural Hazard Warnings, Summary Final Report. Minneapolis, MN: University of Minnesota, and National Technical Information Service PB82-11187.

Leik, R.K., T.M. Carter, J.P. Clark, S. D. Kendall, G.A. Gifford, W. Bielefeld, and K. Ekker
    1981   Community Response to Natural Hazard Warnings, Final Report. Minneapolis, MN: University of Minnesota.

Leik, R.K., S.A. Leik, K. Ekker, and G.A. Gifford
    1982   Under the Threat of Mt. St. Helens: A Study of Chronic Family Stress. Minneapolis, MN: University of Minnesota.

Luce, R.D., and H. Raiffa
    1967   Games and Decisions. New York: John Wiley and Sons, Inc.

Miller, D.W., and M.K. Starr
    1967   The Structure of Human Decisios. Englewood Cliffs, NJ: Prentice-Hall.

Mosteller, F., R. Rourke, and G. Thomas, Jr.
    1961   Probability with Statistical Applications. Reading, MA: Addison-Wesley.

Perry, R.W., M.K. Lindell, and M.R. Greene
    1980   Evacuation Decision-making and Emergency Planning. Seattle, WA: Battelle Human Affairs Research Centers.

Simmons, R.G., S.D. Klein, and K. Thornton
    1973   "The family member's decision to be a kidney transplant donor." Journal of Comparative Family Studies 4:88–115.

Steinbrunner, J.D.
    1974   The Cybernetic Theory of Decision. Princeton, NJ: Princeton University Press.

Taylor, D.W.
    1965   Decision Making and Problem Solving. In J. March (ed.), Handbook of Organizations. Chicago, IL: Rand McNally.

Tversky, A.
    1969   "Intransitivity of preferences." Psychological Review 76:31–48.

Von Neuman, J., and O. Morgenstern
    1977   Theory of Games and Economic Behavior. Princeton, NJ: Princeton University Press. (1st Edition, 1944)

Vroom, V.H., and P.W. Yetton
    1973   Leadership and Decision Making. Pittsburgh, PA: University of Pittsburgh Press.

Winer, B.J.
    1962   Statistical Principles in Experimental Design. New York: McGraw-Hill Book.

Windham, G.O., P.J. Possey, and B.G. Spencer
    1977   Reactions to Storm Threat During Hurricane Eloise. Report #51 from the Social Science Research Center, Mississippi State University.

Four

A Two-Process Theory of Social Behavior

Richard Ofshe
Kenneth Christman
University of California, Berkeley

INTRODUCTION[1]

Choice and Stimulus-response Theories

The question of how individuals construct their social behavior is a core problem for social psychology and a major problem in the social sciences. Presently, the social sciences provide, as solutions, two different models of the organization of behavior, separate in their approach, equal in their aspirations. One model treats individual behavior as the result of choice between alternative courses of action based on a self-conscious evaluation of probable consequences. The other model treats behavior as a response to coincident stimuli unmediated by choice or evaluation (Harré and Secord, 1972:89).

There is no anomaly in the existence of two contradictory models, since controversy is as characteristic of scientific disciplines as mortality is of scientific theories. The anomaly lies in the failure of these two models to compete, and of either to show signs of an impending demise. Despite their contradictory claims, there has been no major and continuing confrontation between these two models of man.

---

[1]Limitations on the research to be discussed: This paper is designed to introduce a theoretical approach to a certain problem in social psychology. Rather than attempt to report how much of the literature we think we can already subsume, we will restrict ourselves to certain classic experiments and, even then, often to starting points in research traditions. In many cases, we could considerably extend the discussion; however, the present analysis is, we hope, sufficient to make our point.

The mutual inattention of "choice" and "S-R" theories can be explained by reference to the history of the two models.

The History of the Rational Model of Man

The belief that behavior is the result of choice has a far longer history than we need reconstruct. By the 18th century, the choice model had been harnessed to the system of philosophical argumentation through which it entered the social sciences; indeed, it established the social sciences as more than a branch of ethical philosophy. This system, which we will call "natural law" philosophy, had four typical characteristics:

1. The necessity of the existence of some phenomena, usually social, was demonstrated as a deduction from a set of axioms.
2. The axioms were assertions about individual psychology.
3. Prominent among these axioms would be the propositions that individuals were:
   (a) "Rational," i.e., chose behavior on the basis of an evaluation of probable consequences.
   (b) "Hedonistic," i.e., evaluated alternatives in terms of their implications for the individual's pleasure or pain.
4. An underlying harmony in the affairs of men is assumed. Thus, that which must be, i.e., is a "natural law," must be good (Taylor, 1960, ch. 1; Schumpeter, 1954, ch. 2).

As this method of argumentation was assumed to provide a "rational" method by which ethical issues could be settled, it was frequently employed to advocate particular governmental policies. In practice it was used largely to explain characteristics of major political and economic institutions (MacPherson, 1962; Schumpeter, 1954; Blaug, 1968; Taylor, 1960).

This system of theorization led directly to the development of modern economics (Blaug, 1968, ch. 16; cf. also, Schumpeter, 1954:133–134). Although the assumption that individual behavior is the result of choice is ubiquitous in the social sciences, this assumption is made most self-consciously in modern economics.[2]

---

[2]Modern economists have attempted to replace assumptions of individual choice with the use of indifference curves. However, the method of indifference has been used only to produce propositions that could be deduced from traditional rationalist assumptions. Therefore, as Routh points out (1977:243–246), the method of indifference has not so much replaced as restated the traditional choice assumptions of economics.

From economics, rigorous attention to the implications of choice models has made a moderately successful invation of the other social sciences in the last twenty years. The collective result of this invasion is known as "exchange theory" (Heath, 1976:2–4). This invasion resulted both from economists' attempts to explain phenomena characteristically assigned to other disciplines (Downs, 1957; Olson, 1965) and from social psychologists' and sociologists' (Thibaut and Kelly, 1959; Siegel and Foraker, 1960; Siegel and Foraker, 1960; Blau, 1965; Homans, 1961; Ofshe and Ofshe, 1970) becoming interested in the possibilities of explaining social behavior by using choice models.

Exchange theory and economic theory have maintained the penchant of natural-law philosophy for examining behavior in institutional contexts. Economists are concerned with behavior in the firm and in the marketplace. Exchange theorists have examined such issues as partisan politics in representative governments (Downs), the formation of organized interest groups (Olson), and the conditions under which bureaucrats will subvert institutional rules to aid each other (Blau). Thus, choice theorists have concentrated on life situations in which tangible and important rewards and punishments are clearly dependent on the individual's behavior.

The History of the "S-R" Model of Man

The S-R model of man has a considerably shorter history than the choice model. It originates with behaviorism, which, in turn, is closely tied to the development of American psychology in the late 19th century. American psychology inherited its emphasis on experimental methodology from contemporary German psychology; however, German psychology was "structuralist," that is, psychology was assumed to be the study of the contents of consciousness. American psychology was strongly influenced by Darwinism and the Darwinian treatment of the organism as an entity adapting to its environment. Accordingly, American psychology became largely "functionalist." It defined itself as the study of how organisms emit behavior in an environment (Boring, 1950:505–508; cf. also Woodworth and Sheehan, 1964, ch. 2). Since Darwinism posited the identity of the evolutionary process undergone by all organisms, a concomitant of American psychology's functionalism was an interest in animal behavior. Animal behavior was assumed to be fundamentally similar to human behavior, but possibly simpler and more easily analyzed (Kantor, 1969:359–360; Chaplin and Krawiec, 1974:236–238; Boring, 1950:622–624). "Morgan's Canon" was an early result of the new animal psychology. Morgan argued that, for reasons of parsimony, psychologists should not attempt to explain animal behavior as the result of higher mental processes if they could be explained as the result of less complicated processes (Chaplin and Krawiec, 1974:327). John B. Watson, another animal psychologist, extended Morgan's appeal to parsimony by arguing that psychologists should dispense with all concepts referring to unobservable mental processes, and concentrate on studying the more reliable data gained by observing behavior and its relationship to its environment (Boring, 1959:641–642). This was the origin of the psychological school known as behaviorism.

Behaviorism was closely linked to Darwinism. Darwinism, in turn, implies that behavior is adaptive; that is, behavior is regulated by its future consequences. Therefore, Watson from the beginning was concerned to demonstrate that behavior could be shown to be adaptive even if assumed to be under stimulus control and unmediated by unobservable mental processes such as evaluation of future consequences (Hernnstein, 1973:102–104). Although Watson's attempt to develop an S-R theory of adaptive learning was quickly superseded (Woodworth and Sheehan, 1964:125–126; Chaplin and Krawiec, 1974:238–239), it did establish learning as the central problem in behaviorism. Tolman's purposive behaviorism, Hull's mathematical theories of intervening variables, and Skinner's theories of operant conditioning, the three major schools of S-R theorists that developed after Watson, all treat learning of new and adaptive responses as their central concern (Hernnstein, 1973:98–99).

We need not speculate on why learning by (usually) infrahuman subjects has remained the central concern of S-R theorists. The fact is, it has. For methodological reasons, behaviorists have preferred the study of easily defined and measured, relatively molecular behavior in laboratory conditions in which discrete, simple characteristics of the stimulus field can be manipulated. Such issues as the integration of simple into more complex behavior, the functioning of the organism in non-laboratory situations, and, in particular, the behavior of humans in non-laboratory situations in which the distribution of major rewards and sanctions is determined, have not played a prominent role in their research. Thus, although S-R theories have claimed the ability to explain all aspects of human behavior (Homans, 1961; Emerson, 1972; Staats, 1975; Burgess and Bushell, 1969; Skinner, 1953, 1974), they are seldom involved in analyzing those aspects of human behavior which have normally concerned choice theorists.

The Two-Process Approach in Cognitive Psychology

The very different interests of "choice" and "S-R" theorists in the social sciences is the basis of their mutual inattention. In practice, the proponents of the two different models seldom attempt to invade each other's bailiwicks. Choice theorists do not attempt to study the acquisition of relatively simple behavior by human or infra-human subjects. S-R theorists seldom attempt to explain the functioning of the marketplace. In practice then, these two models have divided human behavior into two categories, although their proponents certainly do not advocate such a bifurcation.

It appears this bifurcation has occurred for purely historical reasons. Nevertheless, the recent development of the two-process approach in cognitive psychology suggests that human behavior is actually the result of two very different types of constructive processes, and that these constructive processes correspond to the processes of social behavior construction hypothesized by "choice" and "S-R" theorists. The basic assumptions of the two process approach in cognitive psychology are that: (a) the operations of mind are operations that involve the processing of information; (b) the processing of information can be divided into two systems:

(1) a system of relatively simply connatural or overlearned "preattentive" processes that convert the raw material of sensory information into responses or more sophisticated representations that are available to higher thought processes; (2) these "higher thought processes" themselves. These thought processes are typically considered equivalent to what is experienced phenomenologically as consciousness. They are assumed to allow the evaluation and purposeful manipulation of information and behavior.

A history of the two process approach in cognitive psychology provides an overview of the development of the field itself. In fact, the foundation for the two-process approach is present in a seminal work in cognitive psychology, *Plans and the Structure of Behavior* (Miller, Galanter, and Pribram, 1960), and subsequent work has developed ideas first presented there.

Cognitive psychology is the area of psychology concerned with explaining the faculties of mind (e.g., perception, memory, speech). It is of fairly recent origin, having only developed late in the 1950s, when it became apparent that the newly developed electronic computer engaged in processes that were analagous to those that must occur in the human mind. Both the mind and the computer seemed in some sense to manipulate "symbols" that were representations of the external environment. Both seemed to operate as systems in that their operations were those of mutually dependent components. The existence of the computer, whose separate operations were designed and so well understood, gave hope that operations of mind could be modeled using computer simulations to test their sufficiency.

Crucial in securing the acceptance of the mind-computer analogy in the late 1950s was Miller, Galanter, and Pribram's *Plans and the Structure of Behavior* (1960). The basic contention of the book was that human behavior could not be conceptualized adequately in terms of stimulus-response chains as attempted by Behaviorists. Rather, it argued that the "fundamental building block of the nervous system is the feedback loop" (Miller, Galanter, and Pribram, 1960:26–27). Such a loop consists both of operating and test mechanisms that establish, respectively, the operations to occur and the circumstances under which they will occur. Such loops, in turn, may be imbedded within larger loops. A system of such TOTEs, so-called (for Test-Operate-Test-Exit), is called a "plan." Miller, Galanter, and Pribram argue that human behavior consists of the activation of such plans, and that thought is largely directed to their construction.

For our purposes, the crucial part this argument is the implicit distinction that is drawn between types of plans. Some plans, it was argued, are accompanied by a continual evaluation of their likely consequences (Miller et al., 4960:62–63). Furthermore, such plans are relatively flexible and are continually being modified in response to changing conditions (pp. 77–79). Other plans, what we might normally call "skills and habits," are so well learned that they are automatically activated under appropriate circumstances. Such plans do not seem to require, and indeed may be resistant to, conscious monitoring (pp. 89–90).

This distinction, between plans that are flexible, conscious, and evaluated with respect to their likely consequences, and heavily over-learned and inflexible plans, is the core distinction of any two process approach. It was, however, a relatively minor issue for Miller, Galanter, and Pribram, and little noticed by their readers. It had considerable subsequent impact, but not, surprisingly, on the study of behavior. Cognitive psychologists have been more interested in explaining mental faculties such as perception than in explaining the link between these faculties and behavior. Consequently, this distinction was transformed into a distinction between types of perceptual processes by Neisser (1966).

It was Broadbent (1958) who established that the amount of information that the individual can consciously attend to is far less than the amount various sensory receptors are capable of relaying. He argued that the bottleneck caused by the narrowing of channel capacity between sense organs and consciousness is controlled by a "filter" that permits only a relatively small proportion of sensory information to enter consciousness. This filter operates by discriminating between incoming signals on the basis of gross sensory characteristics (e.g., the sensory channels in which they occur). Manipulation of the information contained in the sensory stimuli to produce representations of the external environment was presumed to occur only after the stimuli have passed the filter and entered focal attention. This idea, that attention is in some sense "selective," can be traced back to Wundt (1907). Broadbent made the problem of selective attention a central concern of cognitive psychology. However, his theory was quickly outmoded as evidence accumulated indicating that filtering frequently involved the semantic content of sensory information. For instance, subjects proved capable of recognizing and attending to their own name when it was presented to them in one sensory receptor while they were occupied in monitoring the inputs from another receptor (Moray, 1959; cf. also Triesman, 1960).

Results like these led to Neisser's creation of what was formally referred to as a "two-process" theory of perception. Neisser relied upon several assumptions also used by Miller, Galanter, and Pribram:

1. mentation is an active or constructive process;
2. familiar operations of mind require relatively little processing capacity, and can occur without the intervention of consciousness;
3. what is experienced phenomenologically as consciousness is a particular operation of mind that allows great flexibility and creativity by employing considerable information processing capacity to accomplish certain mental tasks.

Neisser differed from Broadbent in assuming that complex information processing occurs prior to the intrusion of sensory inputs into consciousness. These pre-attentive processes "form segregated objects and help to direct further processing" (Miller et al., 1960:94). Thus, sensory information is presumed to be translated into representations long before entering consciousness. Focal attention or consciousness "then makes more sophisticated analyses of the chosen object" (p. 94).

Thus, in this view, the distinction between "pre-attentive processes" and "focal attention" becomes one between two ways in which information is processed. Interestingly, Neisser argued this distinction can be applied to "higher mental processes" as well. In thought, a "primary process," analogous to the pre-attentive mechanisms of perception, makes an array of crudely defined "objects" or "ideas" that tend to follow the lines of information in memory. In alert and wakeful individuals, "secondary processes of directed thought," rather like focal attention, select among these crude ideas and develop them (Miller et al., 1960:302). Their development is serial, and is carried on by an executive system analyogous to the executive routine of a computer program.

This two-process approach of Neisser's distinguished between (a) complex processes that precede consciousness but are themselves heavily overlearned or connatural and not responsive to conscious intent, and (b) a level of processing that is flexible, rational, and directly responsive to what one might call the "will." It therefore recapitulated Miller, Galanter, and Pribram's distinction between consciously conceived flexible plans and heavily overlearned "skills." Indeed, it even treated perception in the same way as Miller, Galanter, and Pribram treated behavior—as primarily a constructive process in which percepts are the result not only of sensory information but also of pre-existing methods of categorizing, schematizing, and structuring information. Nevertheless, Neisser's theory was an account of mental faculties, not of behavior, although he did suggest at one point that it might be applicable to behavior as well. (Miller et al., 1960:286)

Current theorizing about memory and attention draws heavily on Nesser's two-process model (Lachman, Lachman, and Butterfield, 1979:199–200) (e.g., Schneider and Shiffrin, 1977; Shiffrin and Schneider, 1977; Posner and Snyder, 1974). It is typically argued that well learned tasks require little attention (Underwood, 1974; Ostry, Moray, and Marks, 1976) and that consciousness constitutes a kind of bottleneck in information processing that is normally bypassed (Posner and Snyder, 1974). Because cognitive psychologists are relatively uninterested in behavior, the two-process model has been largely restricted to explaining characteristics of these faculties (cf., however, Anderson, 1975:163–173, who argues this model can be extended to the explanation of behavior).

The Two-Process Approach and Research on Social Perception

Since Miller, Galanter, and Pribram, the two-process characterization of human functioning as the result of both relatively complex but inflexible pre-attentive mechanisms and flexible conscious processes has had relatively little influence on the psychologist's view of behavior. It has nevertheless had some impact on social psychologists' study of the perceptions that accompany social behavior.

The study of social perception—one's attribution to and evaluation of both oneself and others—has been the social psychological growth industry of the 1970s. Given how active cognitive psychology has been in the study of perception, it is not surprising that the 1970s saw the development of a self-consciously "cognitive" social psychology (Carrol and Payne, 1975) devoted to transferring principles and methods developed in cognitive psychology to social psychology.

Much of the work done on social perception makes fairly explicit use of ideas developed in or related to the two-process approach in cognitive psychology. This work can be divided into three groups:

1. The two-process approach was first applied to perception to explain certain of the operations of selective attention (Neisser, 1966). The concept of selective attention has recently been used in research on individual self-evaluation. In its original formulation, the theory of "objective self-awareness" postulated that any stimuli reminding the individual of his own status as an object of perception (e.g., a mirror image of the

individual, a tape recording of his voice, knowledge that he is being watched) will tend to attract attention to self. All other types of stimuli will tend to focus attention elsewhere. (Duvall and Wicklund, 1972). In this formulation, a person attending to self is typically assumed to find shortcomings in self that lead either to avoidance of self-focusing stimuli or discrepancy reduction through attempts to make one's traits compatible with one's aspirations. In a later work, Wicklund (1975) argues that states of objective self-awareness are occasionally desirable. This occurs whenever a person has recently experienced an obvious success of some type. Carver (1979) further revises this theory of self-awareness by arguing that: (a) self-evaluation and discovery that one's attributes fail to meet some behavioral standard leads to negative affect only when the person perceives that he or she can alter his or her present characteristics so that they meet the standards; (b) one need postulate no "drive" constructs, since one need only assume a cybernetic "matching-to-standard" process which leads subjects engaged in self-evaluation to modify their characteristics to accord with behavioral standards.

2. The two-process approach to perception treats perception as a constructive process using not only sensory information but also well learned or connatural methods of categorizing, schematizing, or structuring information. It has been suggested that such "schemata" are crucial in structuring attributions and evaluations of self and the social environment.

Abelson (1976) suggests that the concept of "script" can be applied to the individual's understanding of his social environment. A script is a system of propositions describing the course of events likely to be encountered in certain types of situations (Schank and Abelson, 1977). They facilitate understanding by allowing inferences to be drawn about relationships between events, even though the relationship, or the events, themselves may not be observed and not communicated by others.

A number of other social psychologists use similar assumptions about the nature of "episodic memory" to explain specific research findings.

Cantor and Mischel (1977) propose that individuals characterize themselves and others using not logically bounded categories but a system of propositions about what the typical member of a class should be like. Such a system of propositions describes a prototypical class member. A person who is very much like the prototype on a number of dimensions is considered to belong to the relevant category. This determination does not require consideration of all potentially relevant dimensions nor a consideration of the category's boundaries.

Markus (1977) argues that individuals typically possess internally coherent systems of propositions or beliefs about some but not all of their own characteristics. These "self-schemata" are used to facilitate judgements and decisions about the self. They provide easily retrieved behavioral evidence consistent with relevant self-judgements, produce confident predictions about one's own behavior and traits, and decrease the likelihood that particular information contradicting a schemata will be viewed as symptomatic.

Tesser (1978) argues that similar schemata potentially exist for any relevant social domain—concerning either self or other. He argues that thinking about any doman increases the likelihood that beliefs about that domain will develop schemata-like properties (i.e., will develop into a set of mutually relevant and consistent propositions describing some domain). Consequently, thinking about a domain tends to increase consistency between beliefs, including evaluative beliefs about the domain. In consequence, thinking about a domain tends to lead to a polarization of attitudes towards that domain.

3. The two-process approach to perception assumes that focal attention is reserved for aspects of the environment that are important. Taylor and Fiske (1978) borrow this assumption in order to explain why subjects in many attribution experiments impute causal significance to those elements of the experimental situation that are more salient (this position is partially retreated from in Taylor, Crocker, Fiske, Springer, and Winkler, 1979).

They argue that aspects of experimental situations are frequently mundane and uninteresting. In consequence, they are unlikely to engage the subject's attention. In research on causal attribution, this results in no attributions being constructed during the course of the experiment. Such attributions are constructed only later, when the experimenter asks that they be provided. Not surprisingly, due to a lack of attention, much of what occurred during the experiment is not readily remembered. Therefore, subjects attribute causal significance to those events they are most likely to remember—events that are novel or made perceptually prominent.

In all three groups, the two-process approach has been applied to perception, not to behavior. Although not incompatible with Miller, Galanter, and Pribram's treatment of behavior as either intelligent and flexible or heavily overlearned, this work is also compatible with a model in which behavior is always the result of conscious choice and evaluation, although, due to capacity limitations, such choice may be based on very incomplete knowledge.

The Two-Process Approach and Research on Social Behavior

A model of behavior similar to Miller, Galanter, and Pribram's two-process approach is clearly present only when social psychologists argue that certain social situations are so well learned that they can be responded to with little need for thought. Labels proposed for such situations and/or their associated responses include "frames" (Goffman, 1974), "episodes" (Harre' and Secord, 1972), "caricature" (Thorngate, 1976), and "habituation" (Berger and Luckmann, 1966). However, the social psychologists just mentioned, with the exception of Thorngate, are relatively less interested in social behavior as it becomes less thoughtful. Therefore, they cannot really be considered to be interested in importing the two-process approach to behavior into social psychology.

Langer and her colleagues may be considered to have first brought the major elements of the two-process approach to behavior into social psychology. Langer's debt to Miller, Galanter, and Pribram, or to the research on social perception cited above, is unclear. Langer has clearly been influenced by research on scripts in speculating that behavior, like ways of processing sensory information, might be well learned and require little or no thought (Langer, Blank, and Chanowitz, 1978; Langer, 1979b).

Essentially, Langer argues that social behavior can be either "minded" or "mindless." Minded behavior is precisely that, behavior which is the result of conscious choice. "Mindless" behavior is merely an unfolding of previously acquired behavioral scripts, given appropriate situational cues, and does not engage consciousness. Langer argues that much of social behavior, although ostensibly thoughtul, is actually mindless. She uses this assumption to generate research on: attributions, responsiveness to requests, availability of "mindless" behavior to introspection, and illusions of incompetence.

Attributions. Langer (1979b) argues that the scope of attribution theory may be severely limited by the fact that people frequently fail to pay attention to social situations and, therefore, frequently fail to make attributions during social interaction. This speculation results in the research reported in Langer and Newman (1979).

In Langer and Newman (1979), as in Taylor and Fiske (1978), attributions are viewed as post-hoc reconstructions. As in the latter article, it is argued that attributions are "minded" reconstructions of what occurred when the subject was paying little attention to relevant experimental manipulations (i.e., when the subject was "mindless"). It is argued that this approach can be used to explain the classic Asch (1946) and Kelley (1950) finding that subject's evaluation of another was heavily influenced by information provided them about the other's supposed "warmth" or "coldness" of personality.

Langer and Newman argue that subjects typically fail to attend closely to the characteristics of the other when required by the experimenter to evaluate the other after the experiment ends. Therefore, they will be dependent on the summary evaluations of "warmth" or coldness" provided by the experimenter when required to evaluate the other. Consequently, Langer and Newman correctly predict that subjects who retain little information about the other's behavior when the other was present will be the subjects who are influenced by information about the other's warmth or coldness.

Langer and Imber (1979) extend these ideas by arguing that people, made mindful of characteristics they normally pay little attention to, will interpret these characteristics as atypical. To test this prediction, subjects are allowed to view a videotape of a confederate after being informed that the confederate was either normal or statistically deviant (i.e., a homosexual, a millionaire, divorced, a cancer patient, or an ex-mental patient). In addition, half of the subjects informed that the confederate was normal were warned before viewing the video-tape that they would be asked to evaluate the confederate, and were asked to pay close attention to his behavior. After viewing the videotape, subjects were asked to evaluate the confederate's general characteristics and the extent to which his demeanor was typical. It was hypothesized that subjects asked to pay close attention to the confederate's demeanor, or merely believing the confederate was unusual, would pay close attention to the confederate's behavior and, consequently, evaluate his behavior as atypical. This prediction proved correct.

Responsiveness to Request. Langer, Blank, and Chanowitz (1978) provide the initial attempt to test the idea that certain social behavior is "mindless." It is argued that people may respond only to the syntactical "appropriateness" and not the semantic content of a request, if the request requires little effort to comply with. This hypothesis is assessed in three separate field experiments.

In an initial experiment, level of effort required to comply with the request and the syntactic and semantic structure of the request are varied. The request may be: (a) short, (b) syntactically longer but without increased semantic content, (c) syntactically longer and with increased semantic content. It is predicted that merely increasing syntactic length will increase compliance for a request that is easily fulfilled, to the same extent as will increased length and semantic content. However, for a more demanding request, increased length without increased semantic content will not increase compliance, although increased semantic content will increase compliance. These predictions prove correct.

Availability of "Mindless' Behavior to Introspection. Langer and Weinman (1979) investigate the availability of "mindless" behavior to introspection. In a series of three experiments, it is demonstrated that: subjects confronted with a familiar sentence with a mistake in it (e.g., Mary

had aa little lamb) are typically unaware of the error, yet believe they
have read the sentence accurately; subjects reading a familiar rather than
an unfamiliar poem of similar meter and length rate themselves as more
confident of understanding the poem, but did worse on objective measures
of comprehension of the poem; subjects, on discussing a familiar as opposed to a novel issue, show less articulate speech if asked to think about
the issue before speaking. This suggests, as discussed below, that it is
difficult to bring well-learned behavior under conscious control. If subjects
were aware of this difficulty, we would presume they would resist any
attempt to make them think about the well-learned topic. It is suggested
that the apparent willingness to think about the topic indicates a failure
to discover the debilitating effects of overlearning through introspection.
These three experiments all suggest that subjects respond to familiar stimuli
in unthinking ways, yet are unaware of the extent to which the reaction
to these stimuli is "mindless."

Illusion of Incompetence.   Langer and Weinman (1979) suggest that
attempts to gain conscious control over well-learned, mindless behavior
will result in performance decrements. Langer and Imber (1979) support
the same conclusion. In this experiment, subjects of varying familiarity
with a task are given labels that suggest the subject has been subordinated
to another subject. It is assumed this labeling will lead to doubt about
competence at the task. They will therefore attempt to bring their behavior
under conscious control. It is suggested this will lead to performance decrements if the task behavior is well learned, but not otherwise. It is also
suggested these decrements will be alleviated for subjects provided with
a written list of the components of the tasks, so that the task may be more
easily consciously controlled. These predictions prove correct.

    In a somewhat similar experiment, Chanowitz and Langer (1980)
demonstrate that, when subjects are told about certain types of (non-existent) perceptual deficits, but led to believe the deficit will not be relevant
to them, a later discovery that they have the deficit leads to performance
decrements. No such decrements occur if the subject is asked to either
think about the perceptual deficit or is led to believe he might have it.
The implication is that subjects accept information about the deficit mindlessly and, thus, uncritically, if simply told about it. A more critical evaluation of the deficit and its implication occurs if it seemed personally
relevant, or if the subject is simply asked to think about the deficit. If
information about the deficit is critically evaluated, subjects discover ways
to avoid it and do not suffer performance decrements. If uncritically accepted, the information does create such a decrement.

    The results reported by Langer and Imber support Langer's con-
tention that subjects, led to question their competence on well learned

tasks, or forced to bring performance of such tasks under self-conscious control, experience severe performance decrements that may lead to negative self-evaluations. Chanowitz and Langer demonstrate that potentially self-deprecatory information may also be accepted uncritically in heavily overlearned environments. Langer (1979a) argues that such negative self-evaluations may be typically aroused in individuals placed in socially impoverished environments that quickly become all too familiar to them, such as nursing homes.

Shortcoming of Langer's Approach.   Although all of these experiments are undoubtedly of interest, all suffer from the same flaw. Simply put, Langer fails to provide us with an explicit theory of "minded" and "mindless" behavior. The research is an attempt to test predictions derived from assumptions that are never made explicit, although they seem, to the extent they can be reconstructed, fairly plausible given the success of the two-process approach in cognitive psychology. Since the theory providing Langer's predictions is unknown, the predictions themselves are necessarily ad hoc.

Ad hocness is a problem for two reasons. First, choosing between alternative explanations involves consideration of the scope, specificity, and empirical adequacy of the theories providing them (Lakatos, 1970). In the absence of explicit theories, there is simply no basis on which to choose between competing plausible explanations of a phenomena. This is perhaps particularly troublesome in social psychology, which is beset with a plethora of plausible although ad hoc explanations for any conceivable finding (Freese and Rokeach, 1979).

In addition, in the absence of an explicit theory, the formal logical structure of an explanation is difficult or impossible to trace. Internally inconsistent assumptions, non-sequitors, and circular arguments are difficult or impossible to detect under these circumstances.

It is not difficult to find examples of both kinds of problems in Langer's work. For example, in the second and third experiment reported in Langer, Blank, and Chanowitz (1978) (cf. above), subjects are shown to be more likely to acquiesce to requests that can be shown to be structurally similar to those with which subjects are familiar. Langer et al. argue that subjects are mindlessly acquiescing to requests that are syntactically familiar, precisely because of this familiarity. One can just as easily explain these findings by assuming that subjects are self-consciously using structural consistency with past communications to estimate the legitimacy of the request. In the absence of an explicit theory of known scope, parsimony, etc., providing one or both of these rival explanations, there is no basis on which to choose between these equally plausible alternatives.

In Chanowitz and Langer (1980), subjects are assumed to mindlessly and uncritically accept information proffered them about perceptual deficits. However, Langer (1979b) and Langer and Newman (1979) both argue that subjects frequently fail to retain information when behavior is mindless. One must wonder if this is not an internal contradiction in Langer's concept of mindlessness. In the absence of an explicit theory, it is impossible to say.

Self-Perception Theory

Self-perception theory does not explicitly draw on the work of cognitive psychologists, or cognitive social psychologists. However, implicit within self-perception theory is a model of human functioning that resembles the model of man explicitly employed in the two process approach.

Self-perception theory originated as an explicitly "Skinnerian" psychological theory. Bem (1972) argued that a theory that viewed both the individual's behavior, and his verbalizations about his own internal states, as under the control of the external situation, was capable of providing a far more parsimonious explanation of the results in a variety of attitude change experiments than the explanation provided by cognitive dissonance theorists.

The attitude change experiments of most concern to both Bem and cognitive dissonance theorists were "forced-compliance" experiments (Bem, 1972:17–22). In these experiments, subjects were asked to rate themselves on some attitude, were then induced to engage in some behavior that contradicted their professed attitude, and then were asked to again rate themselves on the attitude. These experiments revealed the famous "reverse-incentive" effect. Subjects given greater inducement to engage in a counter-attitudinal behavior showed comparatively little change in attitude during the experiment. Subjects given less inducement to engage in the same behavior revealed considerably more attitude change.

Cognitive dissonance theory (Festinger, 1957) presumes there is an inherent tendency for individuals to maintain congruence between their various attitudes and actual behaviors. It explains the tendency of subjects given low inducements for compliance in a forced compliance experiment to change their attitudes towards conformity with their "counter-attitudinal" behavior as a result of this tendency to maintain congruence. Subjects given greater inducement do not exhibit such marked attitude change, because their behavior "follows from" the large compensations they were given.

Bem objected to this cognitive dissonance explanation for two reasons: it is not clear why, in the cognitive dissonance formulation, a counter-attitudinal behavior could "follow from" a large inducement, and why this should reduce dissonance; also, concepts such as "consonance," "dissonance," and "dissonance reduction" presume complex (though largely undefined) unobservable mental processes. However, an explanation of the results in these experiments, far more parsimonious in terms of the mental processes it hypothesizes, can be provided using a more "Skinnerian" approach.

Self-perception theory denies that these attitude change experiments manipulate internal states called "attitudes" which are available to introspection. Instead, it treats the subjects' post-experimental report of their own attitudes as a self-attribution subjects provide using: (a) knowledge of their own previous behavior, particularly in the experiment itself, and of the conditions under which the behavior occurred; (b) previously socialized interpretations of the relationship between internal states, environmental contingencies, and behavior.

Self-perception theory assumes that subjects are referring to their behavior during the experiment to determine what their attitudes must actually be. Subjects given a large reward to engage in some behavior assume their performance reflects this reward, and not an attitude towards the behavior. Subjects given a small reward to engage in the behavior will assume their performance reflects their attitudes rather than the reward. Consequently, subjects in a forced-compliance experiment are more likely to report attitudes congruent with their supposedly "counter-attitudinal" behavior if given only a low inducement. These subjects will then appear to have experienced attitude change.

Self-perception theory denies individuals the ability to discover by introspection at least some attitudes the individual believes are available to introspection. It views self-reports about such attitudes as primarily under the control of external stimuli. Yet, in spite of its professed Skinnerian heritage, self-perception theory also presumes individuals are using their memory of previous behavior and the circumstances under which it occurred to "infer" what their own attitudes must be. By positing such an inferential process, self-perception theory presumes the individual capable of self-directed and intelligent problem-solving activity, but it is not explicitly discussed. Bem has also been reticent about the following issues: (1) whether all or only some individual behavior and verbalization may be treated as under the control of external cues; (2) whether the propositions of self-perception theory may be extended to behaviors other than self-attribution. Consequently, it is difficult to infer from self-perception theory to an explicit model of behavior production. Nevertheless, the theory's ability to posit both intellectual inference processes and the control of behavior by situational factors, rather than by internal states available to introspection, does suggest individual action to be a combination of intelligence and non-aware responsiveness to external cues. Such a model of behavior is strikingly similar to the two-process model of Miller, Galanter, and Pribram (1960).

Overview

The purpose of this chapter is to present an explicit, albeit simple, model of social behavior production consistent with Bem's self-perception theory and the two process approach in Miller, Galanter, and Pribram. This theory is designed to solve the problem of ad hoc explanation that results from Langer's failure to develop an explicit model of behavior production. We shall call this theory "Two-Process Theory."

Two-process theory borrows freely from work done by other social psychologists. It differs in that it is an attempt to state propositions that, up to now, have been presented only in a rudimentary or implicit form, it treats variation in conscious self-conscious self-control over behavior as a variation in the loci of regulation of behavior, and it emphasizes the role of time in the explanation of social behavior. The last point is particularly important. We shall suggest that explanations using two-process models lend themselves to, and indeed require, that the temporal aspects of social interaction be emphasized.

Due to the paucity of research in the interplay of habit and thought in social behavior, two-process theory is minimally specified. The concept and crucial mechanisms are outlined. The theory has been elaborated sufficiently to account for the research findings discussed here.

Plan of the Chapter

Two-process theory is presented in the next section. The remainder of the chapter is devoted to a discussion of empirical work to which it seems applicable.

Certain experiments or series of experiments are a continuing source of fascination for the social psychologist. We treat four such programs of research: the Festinger-Carlsmith experiment (1959), Berger et al.'s (1977) work on status characteristics and influence in small groups, Latane and Darley's bystander-intervention experiments (1970), and Milgram's obedience-to-authority experiments (1974). We shall argue that the results in these experiments can be explained using two-process theory.

The strategy we employ is simple. Our minimally specified theory is used to generate "analytic models" of these experiments; that is, the basic theory is applied and additional assumptions consistent with the basic theory and the present state of social psychological knowledge are introduced to provide an explanation of the results in the experiment. In each case, a two-process-based analysis is developed. The evaluation of the theory rests on how well the model organizes findings from already completed research.

The order in which these four areas of social psychological research are discussed is not arbitrary. Rather, certain of the ideas developed in each section are re-encountered in subsequent sections. The Festinger-Carlsmith experiment is discussed first. We, as Bem (1972), will see the so-called reverse-incentive effect as actually a phenomenon of post hoc attribution. The phenomena of post hoc attribution will play some role in our discussion of the next three areas. We next discuss the development and maintenance of dominance orders in small groups. We propose that dominance orders are adequately explained as the filling of a set of roles that define a group structure. The concept of group structure also figures in our interpretation of certain prominent bystander-intervention experiments. We also see these experiments as manipulating the difficulty of arriving at a problem solution in a time-dependent situation. We view Milgram's work on obedience to authority as fundamentally similar to these bystander-intervention experiments.

TWO-PROCESS THEORY

Preliminary Assumptions—Behavior and Situation.

Behavior will be treated as composed of discrete identifiable units which we shall label "bits." More molar behavior shall be thought of as the display of a series of bits. We shall label such a series of bits a "string."

Situations in which behavior occurs will be treated as having distinctive components, for which different strings are produced. We will consider those components of a situation towards which a particular string is oriented to comprise a distinct "facet" of the situation. A situation may have more than one facet, and a person may produce more than one string simultaneously. For example, consider a person talking to some second person on the phone while in the presence of a third party. The person may employ a tone and verbal content appropriate to indicating obsequious agreement to the second person. Simultaneously, the person may employ a facial expression to communicate (to the third person) a rather lower opinion of the demands of the second.

Strategic and Reactive Behavior.

Two-process theory, like choice and S-R theories, is a theory that explains why one string, rather than any other, is produced by some individual in a particular situation.

Choice theorists assume that bits are organized into strings by the actor's construction (choice) of one string from a number of possible alternative strings on the basis of an evaluation of their future consequences.

S-R theorists assume that bits organized into strings are readily available to the actor due to prior learning. Strings are initiated when the actor receives appropriate inputs and without conscious intervention.

In mixed models, strings can be considered the result of either type of process. That is, behavior and situation may be mediated by conscious, complex information-processing strategies oriented to achieving some goal. Behavior may also be well-learned behavior mediated only by relatively simple non-conscious processes. In social psychology, Langer and her colleagues have tended to label these two types of behavior "minded" and "mindless," respectively.

The terms minded and mindless tend to focus attention on the different qualities of the mental processes assumed to produce these two categories of behavior. Unfortunately, differences in the mental processes used in organizing behavior are inherently difficult to detect. Therefore, we suggest it is more profitable to think of behavior as differing in its locus of regulation. "Minded" behavior is more appropriately seen as goal-oriented; hence controlled by (perceived) future consequences.[3] "Mindless" behavior is more appropriately seen as responsive to cues in the environment; hence as under the control of contemporaneous stimuli.[4] To emphasize this crucial difference in external versus internal control and future versus present orientation, we shall employ the terms "strategic" and "reactive" to identify the two types of behavior.

Since strategic behavior is presumed to be the result of self-conscious decision-making, we will assume that individuals can discover both the internal and external events that control strategic behavior by introspection. In contrast, it appears that the external events that control reactive behavior or any internal events that might precede the behavior are not available to introspection (Langer and Weinmann, 1979).

Situational Factors and the Organization of Behavior

Identifying two types of behavior raises the issue of when either can be expected to occur.

Most social psychologists who have employed a mixed model have assumed that reactive behavior occurs in situations that are sufficiently familiar for responses to them to be well learned (Taylor and Fiske, 1978:280; Berger and Luckmann, 1966:50–56; Langer, 1979b). We will therefore assume that for the competent adult (i.e., an individual who has

---

[3]Perception of future consequences is, of course, no more easily directly measured than any other mental event. However, we can use actual environmental contingencies to provide a measure of perceived contingencies.

[4]The assumption that reactive behavior is under stimulus control need not suggest that reactive behavior is inflexible or only relatively simple. Research on the social behavior of animals (cf. Etkin, 1964; Thorpe, 1966; Schein, 1975; Wilson, 1975) suggests that such behavior is complex, flexible, and highly adaptive. No one, however, has suggested that such behavior is conscious or intelligent.

TABLE 1.   Characteristics of Facet and Behavior Produced For It.

Situation Problematic	Situation Novel	
	yes	no
yes	strategic	strategic
no	strategic	reactive

the ability to produce the behavior typically used in his culture), reactive behavior is produced for facets of a situation that are not novel. We will consider a facet of a situation not novel when its occurrence is typical for the culture in question (and therefore likely to be familiar to the individual) or there is evidence that the individual has encountered the facet before.

In addition, we speculate that even well-learned behavior can be brought under conscious self-control (albeit with difficulty; cf. Langer and Imber, 1979) when it is relevant to some goal. Therefore, we will assume that behavior will be reactive only if it is not relevant to achieving some valued resource or avoiding some sanction.

It seems unlikely, however, that much thought will be required if such goals are easily obtained (cf. Langer, 1979b). Therefore, we will assume that behavior is strategic when it is produced for a "problematic" facet of the situation. We define a facet as problematic if it is relevant to a goal-achieving which requires some effort, or if the achievement of that goal would be judged doubtful by an observer.

In short, we argue that a facet's being neither novel nor problematic is the necessary and sufficient condition for behavior produced for it to be reactive. We argue that a facet's being either novel or problematic is a sufficient condition for the behavior produced for it to be strategic (cf. Table 1).[5]

Time and Two-Process Theory.

The adoption of the mixed model of man has major consequences for how one goes about explaining individual social behavior. Time, in particular, comes to play a central role in any explanation.

The reason why this is the case can be well illustrated by reference

---

[5]Obviously, one of the key assumptions made in this argument is that the discrimination of a facet into the novel or purposive categories does not require consciousness. Part of socialization, we suggest, is learning to make this type of discrimination and activate consciousness when the situation warrants.

to some work done by Spence and his students, and later by Ross (Ross, 1971; Kimble, 1971). Although this research was originally conceived in S-R terms, it eventually became a classic example of the use of the mixed model of man.

Spence was originally concerned with the extinction of an eyeblink response (CR) conditioned to a tone (the CS) through its pairing with a puff of air to the eye (the UCS). Spence predicted that extinction of the CR would proceed at a rather slower rate if the UCS were presented with some delay after the CS during extinction than if it were omitted altogether. An experiment conducted with human subjects in which the CR was developed through an 80% partial reinforcement schedule confirmed these prediction. A subsequent experiment in which the CR was developed through a 100% reinforcement schedule found no difference between omitted- and delayed-USC extinction procedures (Ross, 1971:166). This greater resistance to extinction on a delayed-UCS extinction schedule following partial reinforcement was labeled the Partial Reinforcement Effect (PRE) (Ross, 1971:171–172). A subsequent study also revealed a precipitous performance drop for subjects on the CR within one or two trials if they were shifted from a continuous to partial reinforcement schedule (Ross, 1971:167).

Spence and his students adopted a mixed model to explain these results. They hypothesized that subjects became aware of the CR and its relation to environmental contingencies when the switch from continuous to partial reinforcement, or delayed-UCS extinction schedule, occurred. They argued that this had not occurred in the original experiment when a switch from partial reinforcement to delayed-UCS extinction was made, since this change in environmental contingencies was far less dramatic. Once subjects became aware of the CR, it was voluntarily inhibited.

This interpretation was supported by a variety of experiments which revealed that infra-human subjects (e.g., rabbits, pigeons, fish) and human retardate subjects failed to demonstrate the PRE (Ross, 1971:172).

In order to test this hypothesis further, the original experiments were repeated with a "masking task" designed to distract the subject's attention. Subjects were instructed that the experiment was concerned with the effects of distraction upon performance in a problem-solving situation. They were given the task of predicting, upon the lighting of a centrally located signal lamp, which of two small lamps would light next. They were told that distraction was to be provided by a tone and an air puff directed to the eye. Actually, the tone and airpuff were the CS and UCS, respectively, and these experiments repeated the earlier experiments' sequence of reinforcement and extinction (Ross, 1971:168–169). It was predicted that if subjects were becoming aware of the CR due to the sudden shift from a continuous reinforcement to a partial reinforcement or delayed-UCS extinction schedule, the masking task should distract their attention and prevent this awareness. Subjects would then fail to inhibit the CR cognitively, and the PRE should not be observed. This prediction was borne out.

Spence et al.'s work is interesting because a close examination reveals what a crucial role time plays in their theorization. According to Spence and Ross, conditioning in the original experiment (without masking task) proceeded uneventfully until there was a dramatic shift in environmental contingencies that shifted subject attention to their emission of the CR. The CR was then consciously inhibited. In other words, the CR had been reactively produced. At that point in *time* in which environmental contingencies shifted, subjects became aware of the CR and inhibited it. The CR (or its lack) had become strategic. Furthermore, if a masking task was being performed *simultaneously,* such a shift in the locus of regulation of the CR did not occur.

These experiments are important because they reveal the importance of considering the temporal coincidence of events (behavioral and otherwise) if they are to be explained successfully using a mixed model. Furthermore, they provide an example of a phenomenon, "process change," that will play a central role in our interpretation of all the research discussed in the next four sections. Process change is a shift in the locus of regulation of the behavior, oriented to a particular facet of the situation. Process change may involve either a shift from strategic to reactive or reactive to strategic behavior.

We assume that the locus of regulation of behavior is sensitive to the current novelty and problematicity of the relevant facet. If a facet that supports strategic behavior is altered sufficiently to support reactive behavior, we would expect behavior to shift from strategic to reactive. The opposite change in situation would produce a change in behavior from reactive to strategic. This implies that attention can be quickly shifted away from non-purposive, non-novel facets of the situation, and that discriminations of alterations in the situation that are sufficient to attract consciousness do not require consciousness.

Two-process theory suggests that process change must be a ubiquitous part of social life. For instance, if one spends sufficient time in a novel situation, it becomes increasingly familiar and behavior in it increasingly likely to be reactive.[6] Similarly, a person's learning that a facet

---

[6]This point is of particular interest to social psychologists, since it significantly increases the scope of the inferences that may be drawn from experimental social psychological research. For typical subjects, an experiment is a novel situation. Initially, behavior in it is likely to be strategic. However, if facets of the experimental situation (e.g., requests from others, task assignments) take an ordinary, even mundane, form, behavior is likely to shift from strategic to reactive within a short period of time. This allows inference to be made to non-experimental situations which, presumably, are even more routine and so likely to engender reactive social behavior.

he or she believed relevant to some goal is, in fact, not, would change the facet from problematic to non-problematic and behavior in relation to it from strategic to reactive.

The eyeblink experiment also provides an example of a "masking task." We presume that, if attention is focused on one aspect of a situation, it is less likely to be shifted to another facet of the situation that would, in the masking task's absence, support strategic behavior.

The implication of having concepts such as process change or masking task is to enhance further the centrality of time. Both concepts prevent our ruling out the possibility that seemingly similar behavior at different points in time are the result of entirely different processes, and must be explained using entirely different principles. Whether a behavior can be treated as strategic or reactive depends on the duration of the behavior and the coincidence of other events over time.

Spence's experiments are of interest not only because of light they shed on process change. Kimble, in interpreting these results, argues that they suggest what we might call the principle of the "conditional autonomy" of reactive behavior. Kimble points out that, while humans are able to inhibit reactive behavior, such behavior typically proceeds without conscious intervention (Kimble, 1971:85). In other words, reactive behavior continues as long as the appropriate elicitors exist in the environment, or until the individual chooses to stop it. For instance, the CR developed and proceeded uneventfully in the eyeblink conditioning experiments (above) until the subject chose to suppress it, or the eliciting conditions were withdrawn and it extinguished. This suggests a principle of inertia: in explaining reactive behavior, we need not refer to self-conscious processes to explain why they continue. This principle itself reintroduces the concept of time. We assume that reactive behavior continues until a decision to suppress it is made or the situation alters. Given process change, such a choice is frequently easily made, and there is little time-lag between the situation altering sufficiently to produce strategic behavior and the choice of the new behavior actually occurring. We might expect greater time-lag if the situation is complex or ambiguous and therefore confusing. Furthermore, Langer and Imber (1979) suggest that heavily over-learned behavior may be relatively more difficult to bring under conscious control. The time required to replace or suppress such behavior should be correspondingly increased.

We will find that the concept of "process change" and consequently the consideration of time will be central in our interpretation of all the research to be discussed below. This is appropriate. Reactive behavior can be explained by some variety of S-R model. Strategic behavior can be explained using some type of choice model. Process change, however, can be treated only by some variety of mixed model such as two-process theory.

THE FESTINGER-CARLSMITH EXPERIMENT

The Experiment

The Festinger-Carlsmith experiment (1959) is famous for revealing the "reverse-incentive" effect. Festinger and Carlsmith interpreted this effect as a cognitive dissonance phenomena. Bem (1972) later demonstrated that the effect could just as easily be explained using self-perception theory. We will find that Bem's account bears some resemblance to Spence and Ross's account of the PRE. We, therefore, suggest that the reverse incentive effect, like the PRE, can be interpreted using two-process theory. Indeed, we will find most of the two-process theory interpretation already present in Bem's self-perception account. Finally, we will suggest that the Festinger-Carlsmith experiment provides an example of a type of misattribution effect that frequently characterizes the work not only of "lay" but also professional social psychologists.

The major manipulation in the Festinger-Carlsmith experiment involved the experimenter's inducing subjects to act as his confederates by telling another subject (actually a confederate) that a series of tasks were interesting although the subject had just completed them and knew they were quite boring. The subject was offered either a large or small monetary reward for his "assistance." After making his speech, the subject was interviewed to determine his attitude toward the dull tasks he had had to perform. The experiment revealed the "reverse incentive" effect; low-compensation subjects expressed significantly more favorable attitudes towards these tasks than had high-compensation subjects.

The Self-Perception Explanation of the Experiment

Bem's explanation of the reverse-incentive effect is derived from the basic tenet of self-perception theory: "Individuals come to 'know' their own attitudes, emotions, and other internal states partially by inferring them from observation of their own overt behavior and/or the circumstances in which this behavior occurs. Thus, to the extent internal cues are weak, ambiguous or uninterpretable, the individual is functionally in the same position as an outside observer, an observer who must necessarily rely upon those same external cues to infer the individual's internal states" (Bem, 1972:2).

Time plays a crucial role in Bem's explanation. He implicitly distinguishes four major events occurring over four successive periods in the course of the Festinger-Carlsmith experiments:

(T1)   subjects, under experimenter's direction, perform a series of boring tasks;

(T2)   subjects are offered either small or large monetary reward to tell the confederate the experimental tasks are interesting;

(T3)   subjects tell the confederate the tasks are interesting;

(T4)   subjects declare their attitudes toward tasks during interviews.

Bem argues that, when subjects at T4 were asked what their attitudes were towards the tasks performed during T1, they either lacked, or, at least, could not discover by introspection, such attitudes. They comply with the interviewer's request by attempting to discover their attitudes in the same way that an outside observer would. They review their behavior and other "external cues" relevant to these tasks. There are two obvious external cues: the favorable speech the subject made to the confederate, and the amount of monetary compensation received for the speech. Bem explains the reverse-incentive effect as the result of subjects who had been promised large rewards being likely to conclude that their endorsement of the tasks was motivated by the monetary reward, and not by a favorable attitude towards the tasks. In contrast, subjects promised a small reward will be less likely to reason that their endorsement was motivated by a monetary reward, and more likely to conclude their endorsement represented a "real" favorable attitude towards the task. Thus, subjects promised less to give a favorable speech will be likely to report more favorable attitudes towards the task.

The Two-Process Theory Interpretation of the Experiment

Bem's self-perception interpretation of the Festinger-Carlsmith experiment makes two important implicit assumptions. First, Bem's explanation assumes that subjects incorrectly identify the situational factors controlling their behavior. Second, Bem's explanation assumes that subjects at T4 are using an apparently complex cognitive faculty in order to solve a problem.

The reason why we argue that Bem makes these assumptions may not be readily apparent. Let us, therefore, review parts of his argument.

Bem's argument assumes that subjects use the magnitude of the monetary incentive to determine if it was this incentive or an actual attitude that motivated them to agree to act as the experimenter's confederate. This implies that subjects felt that the experimenter's request was not a sufficient condition to induce them to act as a confederate, and that either a monetary incentive or their own positive attitude was necessary to insure their compliance.

However, Bem's explanation also assumes that such an attitude towards the task was either weak or altogether lacking. Therefore, attitude seems unlikely to have influenced subject compliance.

Similarly, monetary reward does not seem to have motivated subject compliance. Subjects invariably acceded to the experimenter's request no matter what magnitude of monetary reward they were offered.

Therefore, it does not seem that either attitude or monetary incentive induced subjects to act as a confederate. It appears that, contrary to the subject's own opinion, the experimenter's request, per se, was sufficient to produce subject compliance.

Thus, subjects, in assuming that either the monetary incentive or their own attitude produced their compliance, incorrectly identify the factors controlling their own behavior.[7]

Bem's argument also assumes that subjects at T4 impose a post hoc explanation on their acquiescence to the experimenter's request in order to reconstruct their attitudes. Since subjects produce this explanation only by employing some hypotheses about the factors controlling their behavior at T2 (as just discussed), it appears that subjects reconstruct their attitudes through the use of rather sophisticated cognitive faculties at T4.

There are certain obvious parallels between these assumptions and Spence and Ross's explanation of the PRE. Just as Bem assumes his subjects are unaware of the factors controlling their acquiescence to the experimenter's request, Spence and Ross assume that subjects are unaware of the relationship between the factors controlling their behavior (tone (CS), puff of air (USC)) and their response (the eyeblink responses (CR)). Bem assumes that cognitive faculties come into use in response to a direct question about a (nonexistent) attitude. Spence and Ross assume that subjects become aware of, and consciously inhibit, the eyeblink response in response to a dramatic shift in environmental contingencies. In both cases, consciousness is assumed to intrude only when the situation becomes "problematic" (a term we use here only in a loose sense). These similarities suggest that the Festinger-Carlsmith experiment, like the Spence-Ross experiments, can be understood using two-process theory and, in particular, the concept of process change. In fact, the Festinger-Carlsmith experiments do seem to fulfill the necessary and sufficient conditions for process change to occur, and the reverse-incentive effect can easily be explained using the concept of process change.

During T1 in the Festinger-Carlsmith experiment, the subject performs a series of dull, repetitive, and simple tasks. The subject's only social behavior is acquiescence to the experimenter's continuing requests

---

[7]Bem is aware that the self-perception theory implies the individual's pervasive unawareness of the factors controlling his own behavior. To the question, "Why do people have such an illusion of freedom?" he provides the not unilluminating answer, "Why not?" (Bem, 1972:37). We add to Bem's response, "Because." (Cf., above and below.)

that he perform one more in a series of tasks. Since this behavior is continually repeated, the subject's interaction with the experimenter soon lacks novelty. The subject performs adequately throughout the interaction with the experimenter simply by acquiescing to the experimenter's request. Whatever rewards (or sanctions) are available in the situation, they are available to the subject without great effort. Thus, the social situation cannot be considered problematic. The social situation fulfills the necessary and sufficient conditions for behavior oriented to it to be reactive.

The social aspects of the situation at T2 simply repeat the salient characteristics of interaction during T1. The subject is requested to perform a new task—act as the experimenter's confederate—but this is simply the latest in a series of requests. The social situation is not novel.[8]

Subjects are told that a large or small monetary reward is contingent on their performing the new task. However, the request was so organized that subjects were aware, prior to hearing of the monetary incentive, that the new task was not very effortful. It involved only a few minutes spent in the company of, and a short speech made to, another subject (cf., Festinger and Carlsmith, 1959:205). Thus, the social situation cannot be considered problematic at T2. Social interaction with the experimenter remains reactive.

At T4, the subject is given the task of communicating the attitudes formed at T1. Bem argues such attitudes were not formed. Therefore, such attitudes simply cannot be produced by the subject. However, there is considerable evidence that subjects are motivated to comply with experimenter demands (Rosenthal, 1976). Thus, at T4, the social facet of the situation can be considered problematic, and subject's social behavior should be strategic (i.e., there is some reward contingent on the outcome of the situation, *and* it cannot be effortlessly attained).

In summary, social behavior at T1 and T2 is reactive. Social behavior at T4 is strategic. Process change occurs.

Bem's assumption, that attitude towards the experimental task performed at T1 is lacking, is consistent with the contention that social behavior at T1 was reactive. One would expect individuals to form attitudes only towards phenomena that they evaluate. If subjects' agreements to perform the experimental tasks are reactive, there is no reason for subjects to evaluate these tasks. Therefore, there is no reason for subjects at T1 to form attitudes towards the tasks.

The assumption that subjects are unaware of the factors controlling

---

[8]Note that the social situation is not novel at T2, because of what happened during T1. If subjects were requested to act as confederates when first entering the experiment, they would respond strategically.

their social behavior at T2 is also consistent with the assumption that such behavior is reactive. Two-process theory predicts that the factors controlling reactive social behavior cannot be discovered by introspection.

Finally, we may note that Bem's account assumes the subject's use of certain cognitive faculties at T4. This is what we would expect, given that subject's social behavior at T4 is strategic.

The two-process theory interpretation of the reverse-incentive effect is fundamentally similar to Bem's self-perception interpretation. It simply supplements the self-perception interpretation by explaining several points that the self-perception interpretation only assumes—why subjects don't form attitudes towards the experimental tasks at T1; why subjects misidentify the factors controlling their behavior at T2; why subjects so blithely unaware of their own prior motivations and attitudes are so capable of complex problem-solving behavior at T4. The concept of process change is central in this account.

Implication of the Two-Process Theory Analysis of the Festinger-Carlsmith Experiment

The two-process interpretation of the reverse-incentive effect sees it as the result of subjects acting strategically to (mis-) interpret prior reactive behavior. A similar explanation could be applied to any of the experiments mentioned by Bem (1972) as exhibiting self-perception effects, if two requirements are met: (a) the subject is assumed to incorrectly identify the phenomena controlling their behavior; (b) the behavior in question and the motivation for it could be discovered by the subject. Zimbardo et al. (1969), for example, meets these requirements. Valins (1966), in which subjects' inability to discover their symptoms of physiological arousal result from the inadequacy of human interoceptors, does not.

There is evidence to suggest that this kind of post hoc misattribution phenomena is ubiquitous in social psychological experimentation.

Taylor and Fiske (1978) review a considerable body of evidence that suggests that individuals impute causal control over their own and other's behavior to environmental events that are more "salient" in the situation. They suggest this is the result of subjects paying little attention to the experimental situation and, therefore, remembering only salient events when later asked to name the factors that influenced their own or other's behavior. Obviously, Taylor and Fiske's argument is not far removed from our interpretation of the Festinger-Carlsmith experiment.

Langer and Newman (1979) interpret the classic Asch (1946) and Kelley (1950) experiments in very similar terms. In these experiments, individuals were shown to be heavily influenced in their evaluation of some other person by the information that the other was considered to have either a "warm" or "cold" personality. Langer and Newman argue that this influence is due to subjects paying little attention to the behavior of the other. Then, when the subject is later asked to evaluate the other, the only information available to the subject is his or her information about the supposed "warmth" or "coldness" of the personality.

Langer and Newman replicate these warm/cold studies using a design in which subjects are given information about the other's warmth/coldness, listen to the other give a speech, and then evaluate the subject's personality. As predicted, subjects who could successfully answer questions about the evaluatee's speech (i.e., those who paid attention to the speech) were not influenced by the warm/cold manipulation.[9]

The ubiquity of post hoc misattribution in experimental research suggests that it is a process of considerable interest.

Fiske and Taylor suggest it is of interest precisely because the relatively unengaging laboratory situations created by social psychologists are mirrored in many equally routine situations encountered by individuals in the real world (1978:278–279). Thus, post hoc misattribution may be a very common part of social life.[10]

While we agree with Fiske and Taylor's argument, we believe that the actual mechanisms of the post hoc attributions made by subjects in the Festinger-Carlsmith experiment may be of peculiar interest because of what it tells us about the thought processes of social psychologists.

In Festinger-Carlsmith, subjects reconstruct their attitudes by speculating about the factors controlling their behavior. Thus, they operate, in fact, as "lay" social psychologists (Heider, 1958). What is interesting about their reconstruction is that it assumes their behavior is a result either of the incentives in the situation (i.e., monetary rewards) or their own desires (i.e., attitudes towards the experimental task). They do not analyze their behavior as a response to social cues, although evidence suggests this would have been appropriate. In other words, the subjects analyzed reactive behavior as though it were strategic.

It seems reasonable (and the Festinger-Carlsmith experiment certainly suggests) that much of the lay social psychologist's implicit theo-

---

[9]There are also superficial similarities between the position taken by Nisbett and Wilson (1977) and that espoused here. However, Nisbett and Wilson believe that all subject's accounts of their motivation, thought processes, etc. are post hoc reconstructions, and that all operations underlying cognitive processes are unavailable to introspection. We, in contrast, argue that, while operations may not be available, conscious calculation certainly is available to introspection but frequently does not accompany social behavior.

[10]Ineed, one suspects that Schacter's (1965) account of emotion, and the restatement thereof by Hochschild (1979), treats emotions as post hoc labels of a few relatively undifferentiated physiological arousal states. The labels are accompanied by attributions of causal significance and knowledge of appropriate responses.

rization would be based on introspection. We suspect (based partly on our own introspection!) that professional social psychologists also make considerable use of introspection. Introspection is far too convenient a tool not to employ.

Yet reliance on introspection poses a very clear hazard. As only strategic behavior is available to introspection, our experience of our own strategic behavior provides the only model of behavior that we can discover through introspection. Therefore, introspection leads one to treat individuals as more cognitively active than they are.

This argument suggests that, as a general principle, social psychological theories based only on introspection cannot be considered adequately supported. All theoretical schools that rely heavily or almost exclusively on introspection (e.g., "verstehen" sociologies, symbolic interactionism, phenomenology) are suspect. Although introspection undoubtedly will continue to be used by social psychologists, there is a need for the critical evaluation of even the most intuitively "obvious" of social psychological propositions using publicly available evidence.

THE GENESIS AND MAINTENANCE OF DOMINANCE ORDERS IN SMALL GROUPS

In the early 1950s, Bales and his colleagues revealed that small group interaction was characterized by the development of stable dominance orders (Bales et al., 1951; Heinecke and Bales, 1953; Bales and Slater, 1955; Slater, 1955). That is to say, they found that certain members of a discussion group in an experimental setting will participate more, be more influential, and be more highly evaluated by other members of the group. Strodtbeck, James, and Hawkins (1957) reveal that position in the dominance order is positively related to social status.

These findings have been replicated in numerous other experiments (Borgatta and Stimson, 1963; Norfleet, 1948; Hurwitz, Zander, and Hymovitch, 1960; Katz and Benjamin, 1960; Zander and Cohen, 1955; Torrance, 1954; Katz, Goldston, and Benjamin, 1958; Ziller and Exline, 1958; Strodtbeck and Mann, 1956; Croog, 1956). Indeed, the discovery that there are stable group structures can be considered a classic finding in social psychology.

Expectation States Theory and Dominance Orders

Berger, Fisek, Norman, and Zelditch (1977) represent the most sophisticated attempt to date to explain why dominance orders occur. They argue that individuals possess a variety of "status" characteristics. A "status" characteristic is an individual characteristic that others will use to develop expectations about the individual's performance on a task. "Specific" status characteristics influence other's expectations about performance on a specific task. "Diffuse" status characteristics influence other's expectations for a variety of tasks. Those status characteristics that Berger et al. identify as "diffuse" tend to be characteristics usually identified as contributing to an individual's social status (e.g., race, education).

Berger et al. argue that a person's possession of status characteristics leads others to impute to the person greater competence. A person who is perceived as more competent will tend to be more positively evaluated, more influential, and be allowed to participate more in a group (i.e., he will be dominant in the group). This "expectation states" theory explains the development of dominance orders in small groups and the relationship of dominance to social status by, in effect, arguing that perceived competence produces dominance and that individuals of higher social status are likely to be perceived as more competent.

An impressive body of evidence supports expectation states theory. The evidence can be divided into six categories:

1. There is research that indicates that group participant's influence and participation rate and others' evaluation of his or her performance are associated in small groups whose members are relatively homogeneous in social status (Borgatta and Stimson, 1963; Bales et al., 1951; Hienecke and Bales, 1953; Bales and Slater, 1955; Slater, 1955; Norfleet, 1948).
2. There is evidence that these three measures of dominance are highly associated with participant's social status, both in experimental groups whose members are relatively heterogeneous (Strodtbeck, James, and Hawkins, 1957; Hurwitz, Zander, and Hymovitch, 1960; Katz and Benjamin, 1960; Zander and Cohen, 1955; Torrance, 1954; Katz, Goldston, and Benjamin, 1958; Ziller and Exline, 1958; Strodtbeck and Mann, 1956), and in naturally occurring groups (Croog, 1956).
3. Berger et al. (1977) (and the conceptually similar Tuddenham, MacBride, and Zahn, 1951) show that one can increase or decrease the influence of another (fictitious) individual on the subject by manipulating either the subject's expectations about the other's competence or the subject's information about the other's social status.
4. There is evidence that expectations develop around prominent social characteristics and roles (Gold, 1952; Hatton, 1967; Katz, Epps, and Axelson, 1964; Preston and Bayton, 1941; Dion, Berscheid, and Walster, 1972).

5. There is evidence that expectations about performance are associated with dominance in groups that have existed for some time (Whyte, 1943:14–25; Harvey, 1953; Sherif, White, and Harvey, 1955; Gold, 1958; Lippit and Gold, 1959).

6. There is some evidence that higher status members of naturally occurring groups that have existed for extended periods of time have greater influence (i.e., husbands in families and boyfriends in dating couples are more influential than wife or girlfriend (Strodtbeck, 1951; Heiss, 1962; March, 1953).

Shortcomings of the Evidence Supporting Expectation States Theory

Although the quantity of evidence supporting expectation states theory is impressive, there are considerable limitations on the quality of the support offered.

The evidence that the three measures of dominance are associated with each other and social status is limited precisely because it shows only association. Although there does seem to be a persistent relationship between these variables, the evidence does not bear on their temporal relationship. This evidence is not relevant to expectation states theory's contention that differential attribution precedes differential influence and participation, and that influence or participation could be manipulated by manipulating attributions.

Berger et al. (1977) present research that addresses the issue of temporal ordering. Subjects in most experiments were asked to determine whether there is more black or white in a series of complex black-and-white patterns (the two were present in equal proportion). They are made aware of the competence on this task or the social status of another subject and of this subject's answer. They are given an opportunity to revise their answer to accord with the second subject's. Proportion of subjects' answers revised is a measure of the second subject's social influence. The second subject's social influence is found to be related to subjects' beliefs about his or her competence or social status. However, the extent to which one is entitled to infer from this experiment to group interaction is limited by the fact that face-to-face interaction never occurs. Indeed, the second subject may not even exist, and his or her supposed "answers" were communicated indirectly. The Berger et al. experiments then necessarily control away a variable other research suggests is crucial—assertiveness.

The evidence that expectations develop around prominent social roles only demonstrates that such expectations exist; it doesn't demonstrate that they are typically activated in small group interaction. Although Berger et al. do demonstrate such expectations being activated, this demonstration occurs, as just noted, only when interaction is limited to an exchange of very specific information. Evidence that individuals with higher social status are more influential, or that dominant individuals are more highly evaluated in groups that have interacted over long periods of time, is balanced by data not consistent with expectation states theory. Such effects become weaker as groups grow older and individuals interacting over long periods of time apparently develop special areas of competence (Leik, 1963; Heiss, 1962; March 1953; cf. Berger et al., 1977:18, for a review of this evidence). This suggests that the dominance-relevant processes operating in long-established groups may be very different from those operating in the short-term discussion groups that social psychologists study in experimental settings. Therefore, we will assume that the account of group dominance-order formation and persistence offered here is limited in scope to group interaction of relatively short duration.

Behavioral Style as an Alternative Explanation of the Acquisition of Dominance

An alternative explanation of the development of dominance orders in small groups has been developing in social psychology. This we might call the "behavioral-style" theory. This theory views an individual's position in a dominance order as a result of the individual's assertive behavior.

The behavioral-style theory is based on evidence that a subject's self-assertion can influence all three measures of dominance:

1. Attributions: Lucas and Jaffee (1969), Jaffee and Lucas (1969), Reilly and Jaffee (1970), Regula and Julian (1973), Bavelas, Hastoff, Gross, and Kite (1965), Gitter, Black, and Fishman (1975), Leik (1965), Fisek and Ofshe (1970), and Lee and Ofshe (1981).
2. Influence: Moscovici, Lage, and Noffrechoux (1969), Moscovici and Lage, 1976), Nemeth, Swendlund, and Kanki (1974), Nemeth and Wachtler (1974), Richardson, Dugan, Gray, and Mayhew (1973), and Lee and Ofshe (1981).
3. Participation: Rosa and Mazur (1979), Willard and Strodtbeck (1972), Koomen and Sagel (1977), Nemeth, Endicott, and Wachtler (1976).[11]

---

[11]The experiment by Nemeth, Endicott, and Wachtler is interpreted as providing evidence that assertiveness leads to participation, because males are shown to participate more in the jury discussion only if they chose the head seat at the jury table significantly more often than expected by chance.

A number of these experiments yield results that directly contradict expectation-states theory. Several show not only that behavioral style influences dominance, but also that it is more effective than variation in the two causal variables treated as crucial by expectation-states theory: social status (Gitter et al., 1975; Nemeth, Endicott, and Wachtler, 1976; Leik, 1965; Lee and Ofshe, 1981) and competence (Lucas and Jaffee, 1969; Jaffee and Lucas, 1969; Regula and Julian, 1973; Richardson et al., 1973). Several experiments also suggest that attributions (Fisek and Ofshe, 1970; Jaffee and Lucas, 1969; Lucas, 1969; Reilly and Jaffee, 1970; Regula and Julian, 1973) and influence (Richardson et al., 1973[12]) are the result of differential participation rather than vice versa.

Of all these experiments, the most interesting are Lee and Ofshe (1981) and Richardson et al. (1973).

Lee and Ofshe conduct an experiment specifically designed to evaluate the effects of social status and assertiveness on influence and attributions. Subjects were shown a videotape of other supposed subjects (actually confederates) engaged in a mock jury deliberation on the size of settlement in the case. One, the "target," argued for a very low compensation in the case. The text of the verbal argument was standardized for all three confederates. The target's behavioral style in the presentation of his argument (e.g., tone of voice, volume, rate of speech, posture, gestures, etc.) was varied. Subjects were also given differing information about the discussants' occupational statuses. Subjects were asked to choose again the level of compensation to be awarded in the case. Subjects were also asked to rate the target on various evaluative dimensions. Influence was measured as the monetary difference in the size of subject's initial and final awards. After influence was measured, attributions of competence and judgements of quality of argument were obtained. Only behavioral style influenced attributions of competence or judgements of quality of argument. Only behavioral style had an effect on interpersonal influence. Both behavioral style and status influenced attributions of confidence and assertiveness and perceived influence. Thus, behavioral style seems to have been far more important than status in influencing either attributions or interpersonal influence.

Interestingly, although social status does not effect actual influence, subjects subsequently asked to rate influence assume that discussants of higher social status are more influential. This suggests that, as noted earlier, expectations do develop around prominent social roles. These expectations are not activated during the subject's listening to the simulated jury dis-

---

[12]Jaffee, et al. (1970) suggest that this occurred even though subjects could keep track of the success rate in this experiment. Internal evidence also suggests subjects could keep track of the success rate in Richardson et al. (1973).

cussion. However, when asked about influence later, subjects do provide the culturally appropriate stereotype.

In Richardson et al. (1973), competence was shown to strongly effect influence when participation was not allowed to vary. When, however, individuals could gain increased participation through self-assertion, the effect of competence on influence is swamped by the effects of differential participation.

Since Berger et al. (1977) demonstrate that manipulation of beliefs about competence and social status effect influence when behavioral self-assertion is precluded, these findings suggest that the results of Berger et al. cannot be used to infer to situations in which self-assertion is possible (i.e., small group interaction).

Shortcomings of the Behavioral Style Explanation

A number of the experiments supporting the behavioral style explanation place a great many artificial constraints on the interaction allowed to occur (Regula and Julian, 1973; Moscovici and Lage, 1976; Moscovici, Lage, and Noffrechoux, 1969; Nemeth, Swendlund, and Kanki, 1974; Gitter et al., 1975). Although a similar criticism has been made of Berger et al. (1977) and the support it provides expectation states theory, this criticism is not as serious in this case. The findings in all these experiments have been replicated in less restrictive experimental designs.

A more serious shortcoming of the behavioral style theory is theoretical. The behavioral style theory, as stated so far, is unable to explain a number of findings that expectation states theory can explain quite simply:

1. the association of position in a dominance order and social status;
2. why less dominant individuals acquiesce to the creation of dominance orders;
3. why dominance orders tend to be stable over time.

In addition, the behavioral style theory, unlike expectation states theory, fails to predict the order in which influence, attribution, and participation become differentially distributed.

Two-Process Theory and the Development of Dominance Orders in Small Groups

The limitations of the behavioral style approach can be surmounted. It is possible to suggest an account of the genesis and maintenance of dominance orders that is consistent with currently available evidence and that can explain the phenomena listed above. To do so requires use of available evidence on the development of dominance orders over time and two-process theory.

The Development of Dominance Orders Over Time

The evidence pertaining to the development of dominance orders over time can be summarized in six propositions:

1. Dominance orders in newly formed groups are extremely unstable but develop in the direction of stability;
2. Acquisition of a dominant position in a group is frequently due to acts of self-assertion at the very beginning of group interaction;
3. Self-assertion at the beginning of interaction is a consciously chosen strategy;
4. Greater self-assertion is a result of greater motivation;
5. High-status individuals are more likely to assert themselves early in interaction;
6. Differential attributions associated with dominance follow, rather than precede, the development of a stable dominance order.

We will discuss this evidence in the same order as the propositions are listed above.

1. Only two experiments provide information on the development of dominance orders over time: Fisek and Ofshe (1970) and David (1972).

In Fisek and Ofshe, three male undergraduates formed problem-solving groups. Subjects were all male freshman at Stanford and had not met previously; thus, there seems no reason to expect great variation in social status or perceived competence. Participation rate was monitored for the entire 40-minute session, which was treated as consisting of 1 one-minute and 13 three-minute segments.

Fisek and Ofshe report that by the final segment all groups had developed marked participation-rank orders (i.e., there was considerable interpersonal variation in participate rates, and participation rank had been stable for at least several segments. Furthermore, participation rank in the last segment was associated with rank for the entire experiment).

Some groups displayed significant difference in participation rates quite early. In these groups, participation rank in the first seven minutes was highly associated with rank in the final segment. In other groups, the variation in initial participation rates is much less. In these groups, initial participation rank is much less closely associated with final participation rank. Fisek and Ofshe label the first type of group "initially differentiated" and the second "initially undifferentiated." In both types of groups, a period of considerable stability in participation rank eventually develops.

David (1972) reports an attempt to replicate certain results reported in Bavelas et al. (1965). Bavelas et al. attempted to increase the participation rate of low-participation subjects in a homogenous discussion group by reinforcing them for speaking. They found this manipulation extremely effective in increasing target subject's participation rates. The comparable subjects in control groups displayed considerable stability in participation rates, and were less highly evaluated.

David extended this experiment by adding a second discussion group for target subjects and their controls.

David placed female undergraduate subjects in three-person discussion groups that met three times. The subjects who participated least in the first discussion session were designated "target subjects." One-half of the target subjects had their participation reinforced during the second and third discussion session. The other one-half acted as controls and were not reinforced. The reinforced target subjects, like their counterparts in Bavelas et al., showed a considerable increase in participation rate. Their control's participation was stable.

After these three discussion periods, target subjects (experimental and control) were placed in new three-person discussion groups with new subjects who had not previously participated in the experiment. During this fourth discussion period, control and experimental target subjects did not differ markedly in participation rate. Controls accounted for a mean of 36% of verbal output, while the experimental target subjects accounted for 29%. Neither group of subjects showed participation rates greatly different from the 33% we would expect if participation were randomly distributed between targets and other participants in the new group. Obviously, this implies that participation rate in the first group had no influence on participation in the second.

In Fisek and Ofshe, participation rate may be seen as a measure of dominance. Fisek and Ofshe's results show that stable dominance order follows some period (of varying duration) of instability.

A similar interpretation may be made of David. In David, once participation rates were established in the first session, they were stable unless the experimenter intervened. However, upon the formation of the second group, the dominance order had to be formed anew.

2. The construction of a group dominance order appears to be tied to particular acts of self-assertion at the very beginning of group interaction.

In Rosa and Mazur (1979), a "glance-hierarchy" established in the first seconds of mutual contact was found to predict participation rank in three-person discussion groups. The subject who first averted his eyes from the other during mutual dyadic contact prior to the discussion tended to be lower in participation. If subjects could not see each other, then the subject who spoke first tended to participate most in the group.

In a simulated jury study, Strodtbeck et al. (1957) reveal that one-third of all jury foremen were those who managed to speak first when the discussion began. Nemeth and Wachtler (1974) show that the actual act of choosing the head seat at the time when a simulated jury first sits down at the jury table leads to an increase in subsequent influence. Nemeth, Endicott, and Wachtler (1976) show that male subjects have more influence in simulated mixed gender juries in those particular juries in which they are more likely than females to select the head seat at the beginning of discussion. In Fiske and Ofshe (1970), for initially differentiated groups, participation rate differences can be traced to the initial minute of inter-action.

3. Koomen and Sagel (1977) suggest that acts of self-assertion to gain dominance are strategically organized.

Koomen and Sagel extend an earlier study by Willard and Strodtbeck (1972). Willard and Strodtbeck hypothesized that subjects' ability to re-spond quickly in interaction would increase their participation rates in discussion groups by allowing them to quickly "get the floor" during gaps in conversation, and by convincing others they were self-confident. Sub-ject's ability to get the floor was measured by Latency of Verbal Response (LVR). LVR was measured by elapsed time between last word of a sen-tence stub and subject's first word in completing the stub for a series of stubs administered prior to the experiment. Willard and Strodtbeck found that, as predicted, low LVR was associated with high participation rates in four-person discussion groups.

Willard and Strodtbeck conceive of LVR as a relatively stable char-acteristic of the individual's behavioral repertoire. Koomen and Sagel show otherwise. They measure LVR prior to discussion, in a manner similar to Willard and Strodtbeck. They then put subjects into two-person dis-cussion groups in which participation rate was measured, and LVR was measured again. Two conditions—a competitive and cooperative condi-tion—were created by telling subjects either to look for more and better arguments and attempt to persuade the other, or to be particularly ac-cessible to each other's viewpoint and attempt to solve differences of opinion.

Both conditions essentially replicate Willard and Strodtbeck's find-ings; LVR (premeasured) is again highly associated with participation rates. Furthermore, in the competitive condition, LVR (in discussion) is highly correlated with participation rate and LVR (premeasured). How-ever, in the cooperative condition, LVR (in discussion) is not significantly associated either with participation rate or LVR (premeasured). In other words, in both conditions, LVR (premeasured) is closely connected to high participation, but only in the competitive condition does high participation appear to result from very rapid response time (LVR) during actual interaction.

Low LVR is likely to be an effective technique in competitive groups. However, it would be somewhat "off-putting" in cooperative groups. Since the use of LVR varies with changes in subject's instructions (i.e., their cognitions), not with the actual setting of the discussion, and, furthermore, since its use varies with the subject's goals, it appears that low LVR is a consciously chosen strategy. Low LVR is, of course, an assertive behavior.

4. If the use of self-assertive techniques is a consciously chosen strategy to gain dominance, we must ask why certain individuals choose to employ such strategies when others do not. Differential motivation appears to be the answer.

In David (1972), participation rank in one discussion group did not predict participation rate in the next. This suggests differential dominance need not reflect great differences in competence or skills, but rather differences in some relatively evanescent characteristic.

Nemeth et al. (1976) found that females were as likely to participate as males in discussions, only if they had to commit themselves to a long review of evidence before joining the discussion. They, therefore, suggest that differential motivation, a suitably evanescent phenomena, causes differential participation (p. 303) (cf., also Rosa and Mazur, 1979:35).

Willard and Strodtbeck's findings can be easily explained if we assume that differential motivation leads to increased participation. LVR (premeasured) can be seen as a measure of motivation; subjects who are more highly motivated complete the prediscussion sentence stubs used to measure LVR with suitable alacrity. They also attempt to achieve dominance in both competitive and cooperative conditions, but use low LVR only in the former condition (in which it will be effective). This is why LVR (pre-discussion) is *always* associated with participation, but LVR (in discussion) is associated with participation *only* in the competitive condition.

5. Higher status individuals appear more likely to assert themselves early in group interaction.

Strodtbeck et al. (1957) report that: (1) jury foremen are more likely to come from high-status backgrounds, and (2) one-third of all foremen were the first in their group to speak. Unfortunately, Strodtbeck et al. do not provide any measures of the association of social status and being the first in a group to speak.

Nemeth, Endicott, and Wachtler report that, in a large proportion of their simulated juries, males were considerably more likely than females to choose the head seat at the jury table. In these groups, and these groups only, males participated more than females.[13]

6. Fisek and Ofshe (1970) found that more positive attributions were associated with greater participation only in initially differentiated groups. There was no such association of attribution and participation in initially undifferentiated groups. Both types of groups eventually develop stable participation rank orders, but the initially differentiated groups do so earlier. Fisek and Ofshe conclude on the basis of this evidence that differential attributions become associated with dominance only after a stable dominance order has existed for some time.

Two-Process Theory in the Explanation of the Development and Persistence of Dominance Orders

Two-process theory suggests an account of the development and persistence of dominance orders that is consistent with the available evidence.

The evidence cited above tells us four things about the structure of group interaction when a group first forms. At the very beginning of group interaction, there is not a stable intercorrelated rank-ordering of participation, attribution, and influence. In other words, a dominance order is not immediately available. However, a stable dominance order will eventually arise, and often does so fairly quickly. Dominant position in this dominance order is based on acts of self-assertion that occur at the very beginning of group interaction. Such acts of self-assertion seem to be consciously chosen.

These facts can be accommodated if we realize that, when a group first forms, although all individuals have the ability to occupy a dominant role, it is not clear who will actually occupy this role. Development of a group interaction structure comprises a facet of the situation that is then necessarily "novel;" there are no cues immediately available to group members to tell them how to apportion roles in the group. Individual be-

---

[13]There are a number of plausible and not mutually exclusive explanations of why higher social status would cause self-assertion at the beginning of group interaction:

1. Higher status individuals may have a self-image (of being more intelligent, forceful, etc.) that leads them to believe it appropriate for them to speak forcefully during a discussion.
2. They may place a higher value on occupying a dominant position in a group discussion.
3. They may be more motivated to "do well' in experimental situations.
4. They may have acquired greater skill in self-assertion and organizing group interaction without violating politeness rules; possibly through work (if managerial) or education (if college-level).

havior oriented to this facet will be strategic. Some individuals will consciously choose to assert a claim to a dominant role in the situation by simply engaging in behavior that demands deference from other group members.

In other words, the situation at the beginning of group interaction provides all group members with a problem to solve. An individual who asserts himself is, in effect, offering a problem solution.[14]

It is not surprising, given this view of claiming a dominant position as a strategic process, that more motivated individuals will make these claims. Presumably, one has to wish to occupy a dominant role in order to go to the trouble to claim one. Nor does it seem surprising that higher status individuals are more likely to view themselves as persons who can more *appropriately* make such a claim.

This view also explains why initial acts of self-assertion are so important in claiming a dominant role. Once an individual claims a dominant role, another's claiming the same role will provoke conflict. If the person in the dominant position has not violated politeness rules, it may be fairly costly to challenge his position, since such a challenge will conflict with the group's discussing the task at hand and appear rude or pushy.

By this view, the formation of a dominance order in a group is a kind of competition between individuals who claim dominant roles. Why, we might ask, does the competition eventually end and the dominance order eventually stablilize?

An obvious explanation could be borrowed from expectation-states theory: once a dominance order is established, differential expectations develop around it (Whyte, 1943:14–25; Harvey, 1953; Sherif et al., 1955; Slater, 1955; Gold, 1958; Lippit and Gold, 1958). The expectation that a person will be more or less competent sustains the person's position in the dominance order. As Fisek and Ofshe demonstrate, a stable system of differential attributions becomes associated with participation only after a stable dominance order has existed for some time; this explanation does not seem tenable.

If we assume that the maintenance of a dominance order is reactive, we can explain both their stability over time, and Fisek and Ofshe's finding that differential attributions become associated with participation, only if the dominance order has been stabilized for some period of time.

Evaluation of other's performance are collected only after group in-

---

[14]We do not wish to imply that individuals see the problem encountered as one of forming a dominance order. This is a term appropriate to the perspective of the scientific observer. To the participant, the problem is more likely seen as, "May I speak now?" or "May I interrupt now?" Acts of self-assertion really represent the individual's answer to these questions—both for themselves and others.

teraction has concluded in small group research. If the maintenance of the group structure is reactive, it is unlikely that the group structure, per se, leads subjects to develop evaluations of other's performance. Such evaluations are post hoc, occurring only when the experimenter asks the subject to provide attributions. Thus, the situation is the same as analyzed in the previous section's discussion of the Festinger-Carlsmith experiment. Subjects must use "external cues" to reconstruct nonexistent attitudes. A dominance order, if stable over a sufficient period of time, gives subjects a relatively obvious "external cue" which they can use to produce post hoc evaluations of other's performance. High-participation subjects are assumed to have positive qualities. Low-participation subjects are assumed to have more negative qualities. Thus, attribution will be closely associated with participation, which, in turn, is associated with dominance. If a stable dominance order does not develop, or exists only for a short time, differential participation will be less obvious and unlikely to guide evaluations of other's performances. Attributions will then be unrelated to dominance.

Increased participation, per se, probably also leads directly to increased influence. After all, we should expect that hearing an opinion expressed more frequently would increase the likelihood of its being adopted. As noted earlier, there is also considerable evidence that the very acts of self-assertion that accompany dominance increase influence.

This explanation of the development of an attribution order implies that process change follows the establishment of a dominance order. A dominance order is developed strategically and maintained reactively. To understand why this would be the case requires some discussion of what dominance orders are and why they exist. This discussion will also allow us to understand why we earlier used the term "role" to refer to positions in the dominance order, and why a dominance order that is reactively maintained should tend to be stable.

Jaffe notes that a significant characteristic of man as a social being is his inability to effectively speak and listen simultaneously (1978:55–56). Orderly interaction requires that some process exist by which individuals can be prevented from speaking simultaneously, and "control of the floor" can be exchanged. Recent research has revealed the existence of a complex system of cues employing tone, gesture, direction of gaze, facial expression, and particular speech sequences that govern turn-taking in dyadic interaction (Duncan and Fiske, 1978, ch. 11; Rosenthal, 1976). The results reported in Rosa and Mazur (1979) suggest such cues are also present in larger groups where, if anything, they would be more needed.

The allocation of turns does not seem to be equal to all group members. This can be explained in part by the need for some individual to act as a "moderator" or adjudicator in assigning speaking turns. This function is probably fulfilled by the individual labeled the "group leader" in the literature. We need not assume that the moderator explicitly assigns turns, or that allowing interaction to be orderly is the only goal the moderator pursues in the situation. We do argue that the patterns of behavior that act as cues to organize orderly group interaction are well learned by competent adults, since they are a typical part of interaction. The moderator's position in the group can be described as a "role". By the term "role," we refer to a pattern of behavior that competent adults in a culture learn to emit under certain appropriate conditions.

The person engaged in the moderator's role may be primarily concerned with trying to influence others, providing himself or herself with a favorable self-image through increased participation or some other form of self-aggrandizement. All this is possible if one occupies the role of moderator, since its occupant acquires considerable control over the floor. However, one cannot continue to occupy this role without challenge if one seems impolite. One would seem impolite if one did not give others a chance to speak or garner others' opinion. In other words, one can participate more in a group only if one acts partly to actually allow an orderly flow of interaction—as the "moderator."

A dominant or "moderator" role is immediately available in group interaction. It is available because all group members have already learned how to act as moderators and how to defer to some other individual acting as moderator. The beginning of group interaction is novel because it is not clear who will acquire this role. However, once the role is acquired through self-assertion, the organization of group interaction (not necessarily its content) can proceed reactively. Since it appears that claiming a dominant role is a strategic process, the very fact that the situation now allows the organization of interaction to be reactive is a sufficient condition for roles not to be exchanged. In other words, the dominance order will be stable.

This account assumes that there are no major rewards dependent on dominance. This is typically the case in small group research. If there were rewards, we might expect rival claims to the dominant position to be pressed for some time and the stability of the dominance order to be much delayed or eliminated.

Given this interpretation, Berger et al.'s (1977) experiments that manipulate one subject's perception of another's social status, so manipulating social influence, are shown to be irrelevant to the development and maintenance of dominance orders. As suggested earlier, they are irrelevant because they eliminate all interpersonal interaction. What they do is provide subjects with a problem to solve (the black-white pattern discrimination) which is novel and, in fact, insoluble. The only seemingly relevant information available to subjects is the opinion of the (supposed) other subject and information relevant to determining the competence of this other. Two-process theory suggests that subjects will operate strategically and (as observed) employ this information. This does not mean such information will be employed when group interaction actually occurs.

BYSTANDER INTERVENTION

A wide variety of experiments on "bystander intervention" have been performed in the last fifteen years. This section is not devoted to explaining the results of all these experiments. Indeed, we suspect such experiments actually manipulate a wide variety of conditions and require a wide variety of explanations.

Three of the most prominent of these experiments, the "lady-in-distress" experiment, the "epileptic-seizure" experiment, and the "smoke-filled-room" experiment, however, are very similar. These three experiments are probably responsible for providing the issue of bystander intervention with much of its present prominence. They are reported in Latané and Darley (1970) and are the most dramatic of the early experiments on bystander intervention.

We will suggest that these experiments can easily be analyzed by using the concepts of two-process theory and by further developing the concept of group structure suggested in the previous section.

Design of the Experiment

The design of these three experiments is basically similar. One or more individuals are placed in a situation in which a somewhat ambiguous event, conceivably an "emergency," occurs. Latané and Darley are interested in the proportion of subjects who respond to the crisis. In all experiments, a relatively limited amount of time, two to six minutes, is available before the experiment is concluded. Latané and Darley manipulate the number of individuals present to confront the crisis. In addition, a subject may by placed with "passive" confederates who do not respond to the crisis or to the subject's attempts to initiate interaction. Latané and Darley find that, in general, the presence of more subjects leads to a lower response rate. The presence of passive confederates also depresses responding.

Latané and Darley argue that intervention is depressed by the presence of the bystanders because this leads to a "diffusion of responsibility." There is evidence internal to these experiments that contradicts this interpretation.

The Concept of "Group Structure" and the Explanation of Bystander-intervention Effects

In the last section, we suggested that turn-taking in group interaction is governed in part by a system of interpersonal cues, and that such cues are typical of group interaction. Individuals, therefore, are not typically aware of producing or responding to these cues.

These cues allow control of the floor to be exchanged with little conflict. In other words, they allow a "group structure" to form. By this term "group structure," we mean only an orderly pattern of group interaction.

In all three experiments to be discussed, subjects will find themselves in physical spaces with distinct boundaries, and in the presence (auditory and, in two of three cases, visual) of no more than six other persons. Certain internal evidence suggests that when an emergency occurs, subjects react as if they are in more than a mere aggregation of individuals. Subjects act as if they are in an incipient group.

Latané and Darley observe that, once one subject in the situation responds, others feel no need to respond (1970:48). In addition, in the "lady-in-distress" experiment, in comparing the reaction of bystanders who are strangers with those who are friends, Latané and Darley note behavior that suggests subjects are attempting to cue each other in such a way as to form a group structure. "[Strangers] . . . often glanced furtively at one another, [each] apparently eager to discover the other's reaction, yet unwilling to meet eyes. . . . Friends, on the other hand, seemed better able to convey their concern nonverbally and often discussed the incident and arrived at a mutual plan of action" (Latané and Darley, 1970:64).

The assumption that the subjects make some attempt to transform those present into a group which would respond to the seeming emergency allows an explanation of the findings in these three experiments. The findings include several that contradict the "diffusion-of-responsibility" explanation.

From the point of view of two-process theory, these experiments produce situations in which an anomalous event suddenly occurs and produces strategic behavior. The subject is confronted with the problem of responding to this event in two basically different situations. The subject may be alone, or he may be in the presence of others. In the first case, the subject need respond expeditiously only to the seeming emergency. In the second, the subject is given the additional problem of finding the socially correct way of responding to an anomalous event when others are present. Here, we are not interested in response rate in the first condition: we will take it as a given. We are interested in explaining why the presence of others could lower the response rate.

Ability to respond in the bystander-intervention experiments is largely time dependent. Subjects must make some response in a limited amount of time (two to six minutes in the experiments discussed here) or be considered nonresponding. Any condition that makes deciding on an appropriate response take longer will, therefore, produce a lower response rate. The additional problem of determining the appropriate way of responding in the presence of others will, therefore, decrease response rate.

The extent to which the presence of others will decrease responding, however, is highly variable. Because of the identity of the other(s) present, the subject may find himself confronted with two entirely different problems.

If one or more individuals present obviously possess particular competence to deal with the situation, the socially appropriate behavior for all others present is also obvious. They will provide whatever assistance is requested. Such a situation is encountered in one variation of the "lady-in-distress" experiment: in this case, presence of others would have little effect on response rate, because one person would obviously be "in charge."

In most variations of the bystander-intervention experiments, however, bystanders are a rather homogeneous group. Subjects are faced with the problem of activating the polite sequence of events that allow decisions to be arrived at in a group with no formal leadership. An initial, probably reactive (as it is heavily overlearned [Langer and Imber, 1979]) exchange of nonverbal cues allows those present to engage each other in an exchange of information directed to arriving at a consensus on the appropriate response. We need not require this exchange of information to be a fairly obvious verbal one. In certain circumstances, such nonverbal acts as a glance and a lifted eyebrow may be sufficiently eloquent.

The difficulty of initiating polite information exchange varies with the characteristics of those present. Subjects who are acquainted prior to the experiment can initiate interaction easily; response rate should differ little from the alone condition. Strangers will have greater difficulty; response should, therefore, be somewhat lower than in the alone condition. Subjects placed with "passive confederates" face an insoluable problem. As the name suggests, passive confederates are confederates who refuse to respond to the subject. In this situation, polite exchange of information is impossible. We would therefore expect a considerable decline in response rate from that of the alone condition.

The obvious reason for a decline in response rate when subjects confront passive confederates is that the subject must dispense with attempts to form a group as he discovers that this will be time consuming. We suspect the situation is more complicated for two reasons:

1. The refusal of passive confederates to interact faces subjects with the new problem of explaining the passive confederate's behavior. This realization raises a variety of issues (e.g., determining whether the subject or confederate has been rude, whether the anomalous event really constitutes an emergency) that can distract attention from the emergency. In other words, the confederate's anomalous behavior acts as a "masking task."
2. A decision to dispense with the formation of a consensus requires some conscious awareness of the failure to initiate group interaction. Because group formation involves a process of interpersonal cueing that is probably heavily overlearned, conscious evaluation of this process may be difficult (Langer and Imber, 1979).

We are, therefore, suggesting that subjects tend to become "stuck" into trying to initiate interaction with passive confederates or, for that matter, recalcitrant fellow subjects. In the presence of passive confederates, we therefore expect an extremely low response rate, not because subjects decide not to help but because they never decide what to do (Latané and Darley, 1970:106).

In summary, this argument takes as given the response rate when subjects confront an anomalous event alone. We predict little or no decline in response rate when subjects are with at least one person who can obviously "take charge" or when they are with friends. We expect a greater decline when subjects are with strangers. We expect the greatest decline when subjects are with passive confederates.

All the conditions listed above are not present in any one of these three experiments; however, we shall find that all conditions occur at least once.

The Epileptic-seizure Experiment

In the epileptic-seizure experiment, male and female subjects were contacted and asked to take part in an unspecified psychology experiment. Upon arriving for the experiment, the subject is ushered into a room where he is given headphones and a microphone and told that he will be participating in a group discussion conducted with subjects separated to preserve anonymity. Subjects are told that only one subject will be able to use the communication network at a time, that they are to use the network sequentially, and that there are no outside listeners.

Actually, no group is present. All remarks on the network except those of the subject are prerecorded. During the discussion, one of the other "subjects" will seem to have an epileptic fit. Subjects will believe that there is a group present and that there are no outside listeners. Response to the emergency depends on some member of the group. Members of the discussion group cannot communicate, as the "victim" has tied up the communication network. Subjects have six minutes within which to respond.

There are three experimental conditions:

1. Two discussants—the subject believes the only other discussant present is the victim of an epileptic seizure;
2. Three discussants—the subject believes there is one other discussant besides himself and the victim;
3. Six discussants—the subject believes there are four other discussants besides himself and the victim.

Response rate for these three conditions is:

1. Two discussants:100%
2. Three discussants:85%
3. Six discussants:62% (Latané and Darley, 1970:97, Table 13).

These results are consistent with both Latané and Darley's diffusion of responsibility and our own group-structure explanation.

Latané and Darley's theory predicts that, as observed, response rate should decline as subjects are convinced that more people are present.

The group-structure argument suggests the highest response rate should occur when subjects are alone. This, in effect, is the two-discussant condition. Because forming a group structure is inherently impossible in this situation, as interpersonal interaction cannot occur (rather as if there were passive confederates present), the presence of others should depress responding. Subjects are probably not so likely, however, to experience themselves as being in an incipient group if the other group members are not physically present. The group nature of this situation probably becomes more salient when there are more subjects supposedly present. This would explain why the response rate is lower in the six- than in the three-discussant conditions.

Two variants of this experiment, however, are consistent with the group-formation, but not with the diffusion-of-responsibility explanation.

In one variant, the subject was female and was led to believe that two other subjects were present, both male. One of these "subjects" was described as a pre-med student. The other had the epileptic seizure.

Under these circumstances, a diffusion-of-responsibility theory should predict a very low response rate. Clearly, if anyone is responsible in the situation, it would be, not the female subject, but the male pre-med

TABLE 2.   Effects of Group Composition on Likelihood and Speed of Response[a]

Group Composition	N	Percent Responding by End of Fit	Time in Seconds
Female S, Male Other	13	62	94
Female S, Female Other	13	62	92
Female S, Male Medic Other	5	100[b]	60
Male S, Female Other	13	69	110

[a]This table clearly shows that there is no effect for gender characteristics of subject and supposed "other(s)."
[b]Note the anomaly in row 3, column 2 of this table. No statistical tests are reported.

student who presumably would have certain special skills applicable in this type of crisis.

The group-formation explanation, in contrast, would predict a very high response rate. As discussed in the previous section, the subject's problem of what to do next is immediately solvable: The pre-med student is obviously in charge, and the subject should obviously help him.

The group formation, not the diffusion-of-responsibility prediction, is correct. Fully 100% of subjects in this treatment respond (Latané and Darley, 1970:103, Table 14). (This important variant is reported in Table 2 [which is reproduced minus the final column which reports a "speed score"].)

In a second variant, the three-person condition is repeated, but with two friends acting as discussants. In other words, interaction involves a victim and two real bystanders who are mutually acquainted.

The group-formation explanation, but not the diffusion-of responsibility explanation, would predict a higher response rate in this condition. In fact, 100% of subjects respond in this condition, as opposed to 85% in the three-person condition (Latané and Darley, 1970:105, Table 15).

The Lady-in-distress Experiment

In the lady-in-distress experiment, male undergraduate subjects are met by a female "market-research representative" and asked into a small testing room separated by a collapsible folding curtain from another office. The female leaves the subjects to go to the adjoining room while they fill out some forms. Four minutes after the female has entered the other room, a tape recording is played which suggests that the female confederate has fallen and is in some pain. The tape recording is two minutes long; but after the first minute, the amount of pain suggested clearly declines. Thus, responding after the first minute seems less essential. The confederate returns after two minutes. Response is measured as the percentage of subjects going into the other room within two minutes.

There are four conditions in this experiment'

1. Subject is alone;
2. Two subjects, who are friends, wait together;
3. Two subjects, who do not know each other, wait together;
4. A subject waits with a passive confederate.

The diffusion-of-responsibility explanation would suggest a rather precipitous decline in response rate for any of the conditions in which the subject does not wait alone.

In contrast, the group-formation explanation predicts that there should be relatively little decline in response rate if two friends wait together, a greater decline if two strangers wait together, and the greatest decline if the subject waits with passive confederates.

Interpretation of these results depends on an appropriate standard of comparison for response rate. Latané and Darley argue that the appropriate measure of response rate for all conditions is given by $1 - (1 - p)^n$, where p is the percentage of subjects who have responded up to some particular point in time in the alone condition, and n is the number of naive subjects in the condition in question. This formula is meant to take into account the presence of different numbers of subjects who could respond for each trial. This formula is inappropriate if, as we argue, subjects are responding as a group. As Latané and Darley note in regard to the smoke-filled room experiment (p. 48), once one subject responds, the other feels no need to respond. We suggest a more appropriate measure is simply percentage of groups in which at least one subject responded.

By this measure, response rates are;

1. Alone condition:70%
2. Two-friends condition:70%
3. Two-strangers condition:40%
4. Subject-and-passive-confederate condition:7%:(pp. 60–62).

These results, particularly the identity of response rate in the "alone" and "two-friends" condition, are more consistent with the group structure than the diffusion-of-responsibility explanation.

The Smoke-filled Room Experiment

The smoke-filled-room experiment generally repeats the major manipulations of the lady-in-distress experiment, except that it omits a condition in which friends wait together.

Male undergraduate subjects are induced to enter a waiting room in order to fill out some forms before taking part in a supposed survey. While the subjects fill out the form, an acrid chemical smoke is introduced into the room. Subjects who leave the room within six minutes after the smoke begins to enter the room are considered to be responding to the emergency.

This experiment has three conditions:

1. The subject waits alone;
2. Three naive subjects wait together;
3. The subject waits with two passive confederates.

The diffusion-of-responsibility explanation predicts a similar decline in response rate in the last two conditions. The group-formation explanation, in contrast, predicts a considerably lower response rate in the condition in which passive confederates are present than in the three-naive-subjects condition. For reasons given in the last section, the group-formation explanation suggests the appropriate measure for comparison is the percentage of groups in which at least one subject responds.

By this measure, response rates are:

1. Alone condition:75%
2. Three-naive-subjects condition:37.5%
3. One-subject-and-two-passive-confederates condition:12.5%.
   (Lantané and Darley, 1970:49–50).

These results clearly confirm the group-formation predictions.

Attribution of Causal Influence in the Bystander-Intervention Experiments

In all three of these experiments, subjects seem unaware of the inhibiting effect that others have on their likelihood of responding to the emergency (Latané and Darley, 1970:52, 65, 100). This lack of awareness is not surprising if we see this inhibition as due primarily to a time-lag that results from unsuccessful or uncompleted attempts to form a group structure. As we believe groups are formed through a "conversation of cues" that is primarily reactive, it is not surprising to us that subjects cannot discover this process by introspection. In fact, subjects asked to explain this failure to respond in these experiments are in essentially the same position as subjects in the Festinger-Carlsmith experiment or dominance-order experiments who are asked to provide attributions or attitudes they do not possess. In all three cases, subjects will attempt to provide plausible but inaccurate explanations (e.g., they didn't really believe it was an emergency, the smoke was really "truth-gas").

OBEDIENCE TO AUTHORITY; THE MILGRAM EXPERIMENTS

Milgram (1974) reports a series of experiments on obedience to authority that have aroused considerable interest among social psychologists. The results of the experiment can be explained if they are seen as fundamentally similar to the various bystander-intervention experiments reported in the previous chapter.

Milgram's experiments all have basically similar characteristics. All can be seen as variations on one basic experiment (cf., Experiment 5; Milgram, 1974:55–57). In this experiment, a subject is told that he is to administer shocks to a confederate (the "victim") if the confederate errs in memorizing certain word sequences. The shocks are to be increased by 15 volts with each mistake.

The victim is taken to another room and strapped into a chair and shocks are administered. There is one window in this room from which the victim can look at the "experimenter" (actually another confederate) at his desk. The subject is placed at a desk facing a side wall and cannot see the stooge without moving. The victim is supposed to communicate with the subject by flashing lights on a signal board. Actually, the victim's voice is clearly audible to the subject.

The victim proves to be singularly inept at memorizing word pairs. Thus, although the shocks begin at a low 15 volts, they quickly become quite intense. Actually, no shocks are being administered to the victim; his reactions are feigned. The victim begins to display some discomfort when shocks reach the 75-volt level. His discomfiture becomes pronounced at the 120-volt level. At the 150-volt level, the victim demands that the experimenter end the experiment. These demands are accompanied by a reference to the victim's supposed heart condition. The demands continue with increased vehemence until the 300-volt shock is administered. The victim then refuses to provide more answers. The subject is told by the experimenter to treat nonanswers as wrong answers after allowing five to ten seconds for a response. After the 330-volt shock, the victim feigns unconsciousness. The experiment continues until the subject administers a 450-volt shock or refuses to continue. Milgram is interested in the compliance rate, that is, the proportion of subjects who administer all 30 shocks.

In this experiment, subjects frequently turn to the experimenter for instructions. The experimenter will react to all the subject's queries and demands by demanding continued compliance.

Four characteristics of the experiment should be noted:

1. Compliance rate is time dependent. It measures the proportion of subjects administering shocks for the *duration* of the experiment. Furthermore, the experiment is of relatively short duration, particularly once the victim refuses to respond to questions;
2. The victim and subjects are isolated from each other. The victim does not face the subject but the experimenter. The subject can see the victim only by turning his head. The victim is not in the same room with the subject. The victim addresses the experimenter, not the subject;
3. The problem faced by the subject is not straightforward. Although it may seem to the observer that the subject is faced with the simple issue of whether or not he should administer apparently dangerous shocks to the victim at the experimenter's request, the situation is far more ambiguous from the subject's point of view. A major contention of the victim—that the shocks he is enduring threaten his well-being—is continually denied by the experimenter, who can far more reasonably claim to have expert knowledge on the subject. Furthermore, the victim does continue the experiment, suggesting that he is withdrawing his complaints or is not entirely serious in making them;
4. During the duration of the experiment, the subject is engaged in performing the experimental task—administering a series of memory related questions to the victim.

Explaining the Milgram Experiments

Milgram explains compliance as the result of an "agentic state," a biogenetically based state in which individual's organization of behavior becomes controlled solely by the demands of some other person (Milgram, 1974:3).

This explanation cannot be considered very satisfactory if for no other reason than Milgram's failure to specify under what conditions the agentic state will be activated.[15]

We suggest that these experiments can be seen as fundamentally similar to the bystander-intervention experiments. In those experiments, some period of relative calm is followed by a seeming "emergency" which forces subjects to form a group or, if this is not possible, to ignore the presence of an incipient group. This decision or the group structure itself must be formed rapidly if the subject is to be counted as having responded. The experiment manipulates responsiveness by manipulating the difficulty of forming a group structure.

Milgram also manipulates the difficulty of making a decision in a time-dependent situation.

The social situation in which the subject is located can be treated as consisting of three distinct facets:

1. The subject's administration of the experimental task—which we shall label T';
2. The subject's interaction with the experimenter, centered around the demand that the experiment end—which we shall label E'';
3. The subject's interaction (frequently only indirect or potential) with the victim, concerning whether or not the subject should end the experiment—which we shall label V'.

The problem facing the subject is not the simple one of whether or not he should harm the victim at the experimenter's request. It is the more complicated one of whether or not the victim should be forced to take part in an experiment if he doesn't want to, whether or not the experiment is actually dangerous and whether or not he had previously agreed to take part. We will argue that subjects given time and opportunity to analyze this problem will usually decide to end the experiment. However, because: (a) the duration of the experiment is short; (b) the subject is engaged in performing the experimental task, T', which therefore functions as a "masking task" in relation to V'; relatively little time or opportunity is provided to analyze the plight of the victim (v'). Consequently, subjects frequently fail to end the experiment before it is ended by the experimenter.

If this interpretation of these experiments is correct, we would expect

---

[15]Milgram does argue that the agentic state occurs only when the individual perceives someone else to be in authority, himself to be subject to that authority, and that authority to be in the service of an institutionally sanctioned purpose which is legitimated by some ideology (Milgram, 1974:138–148). He does not, however, specify what conditions fulfill these requirements.

that subjects will be more likely to end the experiment when more time is allotted to them or the problem facing them is made more easily soluble.

More time would be available if the pace of the experiment were slowed down or the event-flow of the experimental task interrupted. No manipulations of the pace of the experiment have been performed by Milgram. However, we will find that subjects are most likely to end the experiment at those points in time at which the event-flow of the experiment is interrupted, thus creating time for an analysis of the plight of the victim.

The problem faced by the subject will be more easily solved if the victim's demands are more obviously directed to the subject or the situation increases the salience of the subject's role in the continuation of the experiment. Variations of Milgram's experiment that manipulate both of these factors are performed and do result in lowered compliance rates.

Manipulating Event-flow During the Experiment

In all treatments reported by Milgram, victims interrupt the event-flow of the experiment with verbal protests of varying length. Our explanation of the results in this experiment predicts that subjects' termination of the experiment should be associated with these interruptions and are more likely to occur the more extended the protest is.

The victim's protests are not constant over the course of the experiment. Fortunately, the operations underlying the data reported by Milgram do not typically randomize or vary the basic protest schedule. This provides an opportunity to use the data to directly test the prediction that interruption of the event-flow of the experiment will coincide with increased likelihood of the subjects' ending the experiment.

Milgram's treatments manipulate a variety of characteristics of interaction during the experiment. Some of these manipulations result in statistically significant alterations of compliance rate. If we combine data from those treatments we have judged to be procedurally similar, and which have failed to produce a statistically significant difference in overall compliance rate (cf. Ofshe, Saltz, and Christman, 1982a),[16] a "grand baseline" condition is created (reported as treatments 2, 3, 5, 6, 7, 8, and 9 (n = 280) in Milgram, 1974).

Two process theory yields the prediction that the points at which termination occur should be related to the length of disruption in the experiment. Since the length of disruption varies with the length of a victim's protest, protest length (number of words) can be used as a measure of

---

[16]See Ofshe, Saltz, and Christman (1982a), "Obedience to Authority: A Two-Process Explanation of the Milgram Experiments," for a complete re-analysis of Milgram's (1974) data. The results summarized here are fully presented in this paper.

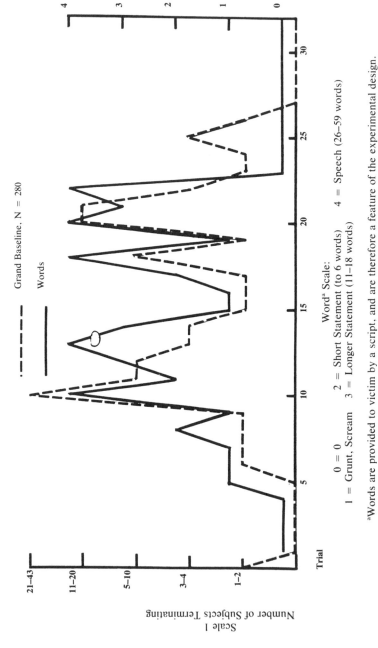

Scale 2
Length of Victim's Protest Words

Grand Baseline, N = 280

Words

Word[a] Scale:

0 = 0   2 = Short Statement (to 6 words)   4 = Speech (26–59 words)
1 = Grunt, Scream   3 = Longer Statement (11–18 words)

[a]Words are provided to victim by a script, and are therefore a feature of the experimental design.

FIGURE 1.   Subjects' Terminations as a Function of Victim's Verbal Activity.

Scale 1
Number of Subjects Terminating

Trial

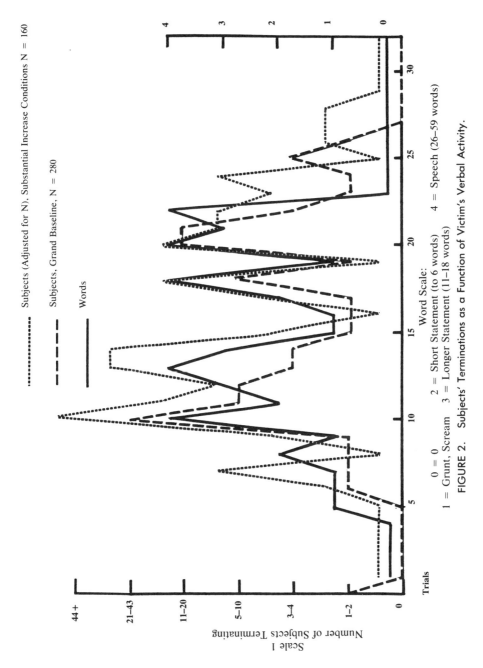

Scale 2
Length of Victim's Protest Words

Subjects (Adjusted for N), Substantial Increase Conditions N = 160
....

Subjects, Grand Baseline, N = 280
– – – –

Words
————

Word Scale:

0 = 0   2 = Short Statement (to 6 words)   4 = Speech (26–59 words)
1 = Grunt, Scream   3 = Longer Statement (11–18 words)

FIGURE 2.   Subjects' Terminations as a Function of Victim's Verbal Activity.

Scale 1
Number of Subjects Terminating

44 +
21–43
11–20
5–10
3–4
1–2
0

Trials

227

length of disruption. Figure 1 reports a graphic representation of the relationship between protest length and termination decision over the course
of the experiment. Figure 1 clearly shows a close relationship between
protest length and termination. Regression, using the same categories reported in Figure 1, reveals an r of .54 and .69 for raw and categorized
data, respectively, and a significance level beyond .01 (cf. Table 2).

If we augment this data with the results of procedurally similar treatments in which there is a significant difference in likelihood of termination
(treatments 4, 10, 12, 16, and 18; (n = 160) in Milgram, 1974 cf. Ofshe,
Saltz, and Christman, 1982a), similar results are obtained (cf. Figure 2).
R s of .58 and .70 for raw and categorized data, respectively, and a significance level beyond .01, are produced (cf. Table 2).

Directing Victim's Demands to the Subject

It has been predicted that compliance rate will decrease if the victim's
demands are made to seem more obviously directed to the subject. Four
experiments manipulate the conditions that isolate the victim from the
subject, and increase the likelihood that subjects will interpret the victim's
demands as directed to them.

Two of these experiments merely increase the physical proximity of
subject and victim. In the first, the victim is moved to a position only a
few feet behind the subject. In the second, the subject is actually made
to hold the victim's hand to a metal plate that presumably administers
the shock. Compliance rate fell to 40% and 30% respectively in these two
experiments (Milgram, 1974:34–35 Experiments 3, 4).[17]

In a rather interesting variant, the proximity of subject and victim
is not altered. However, the experimenter is removed from the room which
adjoins the victim's and which he and the subject occupy in other variants
of the experiment. The experimenter contacts the subject through a tele-
phone, but the experiment is otherwise unchanged. The subject will treat
the victim demands as directed to him as he is the only one that can hear
them. In this variant, only 20.5% of subjects comply throughout the experiment (Milgram, 1974:59–62, Experiment 7).

In another variant, there are two confederate-experimenters present
for the experiment. When the victim demands to be released, one experimenter orders the subject to end the experiment; the other orders the
subject to continue. The published transcript indicates both experimenters

---

[17]Experiments 3 and 4 omit the victim's reference to a heart condition. Experiment
2 is identical to the base-line experiment, except for a similar failure to mention a heart
condition, and produces a compliance rate virtually unchanged at 62.5%. Thus, this difference
seems to have little effect.

end up directing their demands to the subject (Milgram, 1974:106–107). Under these conditions, compliance rate falls to 0% (pp. 104–105, Experiment 15).

In the final variant of this type, a confederate who is initially presented as the experimenter agrees to be the "learner," i.e., victim, to reassure another confederate who is, seemingly, the person who should be the "learner." This second confederate attempts to take the role of the experimenter. It is he who will demand that the experiment continue. However, when the experimenter-turned-victim demands to be let out of the experiment, he addresses his demand to *both the subject and the victim-turned-experimenter*. Under these circumstances, there is no compliance (Milgram, 1974:99–104; Experiment 14, see transcript).

Increasing Subject Awareness of His Role in the Experiment

It has also been predicted that increasing the salience of the subject's role in the experiment will decrease compliance rate.

This is done in one experiment by providing the subject with two "helpers," also confederates, who, during the course of the experiment, refuse to continue. They make quite clear that the reason for their refusal to continue is the demands of the victim. Under these circumstances, only 10% of subjects comply throughout the entire experiment.

Interestingly, Milgram also provides an experiment in which the conceptually opposite manipulation occurs. A peer takes part in the experiment and ignores all the victim's demands. This variant leads to the highest compliance rate records—92.5% (Milgram, 1974:121–122, Experiment 18). The subject apparently infers that the victim's demands do not affect him because his "helper" is clearly unaffected.

Irrelevant Manipulations

If the present interpretation is correct, we should also be able to predict variations in the basic experiment that, by failing to manipulate the elements of the situation identified as crucial, have little or no effect on rate of compliance.

Milgram performs a series of experiments that manipulate variables we believe are irrelevant to compliance: (1) identity of the subject; (2) personal characteristics of the victim; (3) substance of the victim's demands. In none of these experiments does compliance vary greatly from the 65% observed in the standard experiment.

Milgram manipulates the identity of subjects by running the standard experiment with female subjects. Compliance rate is unchanged at 65% (Milgram, 1974:62, Experiment 8).

Milgram runs two experiments that vary the victim's characteristics. In the first, a confederate with a more impressive mien played the victim, while a considerably less physically impressive confederate acted as the experimenter. In the second, a confederate who was introduced as the experimenter took the role of victim, while another confederate, also introduced as an experimenter, actually acted as the experimenter. Compliance rates were 50% and 65%, respectively (Milgram, 1974:56–59, Experiment 6; 1974:197–212 Experiment 16).

Milgram also alters the substance of subject's demands by eliminating reference to a heart condition (Milgram, 1974:55–57 Experiment 2). Compliance rate is then 62.5%.

Post-hoc Attributions in the Milgram Experiment

Milgram provides transcripts of interviews with a number of subjects asked to explain why they comply with the demands of the experimenter throughout the experiment (Milgram, 1974, ch. 5, ch. 7). We view continued compliance as a result of failure to suppress strategically a reactive behavior. Because we do not believe the factors maintaining reactive behavior are available to introspection, we suggest subjects asked to explain their behavior are in the same position as the subjects discussed in the three previous sections when asked to provide information they do not possess. Thus, subjects' explanation of their continued compliance (e.g., "I was paid for doing this. I had to follow orders." [Milgram, 1974:47]; "He [the victim] agreed to it and must accept responsibility." [p. 51]) can be interpreted as plausible and, possibly, self-justificatory, reconstructions.

The Place of Time in the Milgram Experiments

Our interpretation of the Milgram experiment revolves around two conditions: (a) subject's continuation in the experiment requires no decision, but ending the experiment does; (b) they have only a short period of time to end the experiment. Once these two propositions are adopted, the explanation of Milgram's results becomes rather simple.

The explanation treats the Milgram experiment as manipulating conditions that lead to a subject's inability to a make decision in a short period of time. This manipulation drastically limits the scope of inference to be drawn from these experiments.

Milgram argues that these experiments shed light on processes that produced the holocaust, the My Lai massacre, and Andersonville (Milgram, 1974:179–184). All these events involved the operation of organizations over long periods of time. It is unlikely that individuals, because of an inability to reach a quick decision, continue to function obediently in an organizational hierarchy for years. It seems unlikely, therefore, that the Milgram experiment provides data of much use in understanding these events. This conclusion does not mean such events are not amenable to experimental research. We suspect that research, experimental and otherwise, on such topics as the development of ideologies and the effective administration of rewards and punishments in institutions would dramatically increase our understanding of these events (Ofshe et al., 1974; Ofshe, 1981). One must have some idea of the time-frame, however, in which social processes crucial to the existence of these events operate if one is to know the minimum time required to simulate them under laboratory conditions. One of the strengths of two-process theory is that, by allowing some appreciation of the role of time in social interaction, one allows an appreciation of the minimum amount of time required to simulate successfully some social phenomena.

AN ANALYSIS OF SUCCESS AND FAILURE IN INTERPERSONAL SIMULATIONS

Bem argues that subjects in the Festinger-Carlsmith and similar experiments, when asked to provide attitudes they do not possess, attempt to reconstruct these attitudes by using the same cognitive faculties and "internal 'program' " as would an outside observer.

To test this hypothesis, Bem and others have conducted a series of experiments in which subjects were given a description of the behavior and circumstances of subjects in a condition of the Festinger-Carlsmith (or related) experiment, and asked to estimate the subjects' attitudes. As predicted, these subjects provide essentially the same attitude as do subjects in the original experiment (Bem, 1972:25–26).

Bem terms this type of experiment, in which subjects are asked to "think themselves" into the place of subjects in an original experiment, an "interpersonal simulation."

Interestingly, interpersonal simulations, or their approximations, have been performed in three of the four research traditions discussed here. Using two-process theory, we can predict when subjects placed in an interpersonal simulation will successfully predict the behavior displayed or attributions provided by subjects in the original experiment. Our basic rule is simple: subjects can "think themselves" only into the place of subjects who, in the original experiment, were actually thinking. This rule is an extension of our contention that strategic processes provide the only model of behavior discoverable through introspection (cf. section on the Festinger-Carlsmith experiment). We predict subjects asked to predict the behavior or evaluations of others will, in effect, assume these others are behaving strategically. Thus, the prediction provided by subjects in an interpersonal simulation should be relatively accurate if the subjects whose behavior they predict were behaving strategically, but would be relatively inaccurate if those subjects were behaving reactively.

If we examine the situation encountered by subjects in the original Festinger-Carlsmith experiment and the information provided subjects in the interpersonal simulation, we can understand the latter's success. We have argued that, in the original Festinger-Carlsmith experiment, subjects at T4 make use of the information about previous behavior and environmental contingencies to reconstruct an attitude they do not possess. Subjects in the interpersonal simulation are placed in the same position as subjects in Festinger-Carlsmith at T4. They are asked to provide an estimate of attitudes they cannot discover by introspection (as they are presumably someone else's). They are aware of the behavior of and the environmental contingencies faced by the subject in the original experiment. We presume they are motivated to provide an accurate estimate of the Festinger-Carlsmith's subjects reported attitudes. They, therefore, also strategically reconstruct the attitudes of the original subjects, using, as Bem suggests, the same problem-solving algorithm which, interestingly, presumes the original subjects act strategically at T2.

Alexander and Lauderdale (1977) provide an example of an interpersonal simulation of one of the interpersonal influence experiments, reported in Berger et al. (1977), discussed in the section on dominance (cf. IV above). The Berger et al. experiments also precipitate strategic behavior on the part of subjects because they are given a novel (and, in fact, insoluble) problem to solve. The original subject attempts to solve the problem by employing the only relevant information available to him or her: the problem solutions of another subject and the other's supposed competence or social status. Alexander and Lauderdale's subjects solve the same problem in the same way. When asked how frequently they would have adopted the answer provided by the other, they estimate an influence rate comparable to that observed in the original experiment.

In contrast, when Milgram asks both lay-persons and professional psychiatrists how long subjects would comply in one of his experiments, we find that they grossly underestimate compliance (Milgram, 1974, ch. 3). We have argued that compliance in these experiments is due largely to a failure to suppress reactive behavior. It is therefore not surprising that neither psychiatrists nor laymen, attempting to think themselves into the place of subjects in the original experiment, take into account the factors that produce high compliance rates.

Although we are not aware of any experiment which attempts to "simulate interpersonally" a bystander-intervention experiment, we expect that subjects in such a simulation would not successfully predict response rates in the original experiment. Response rate in bystander-intervention experiments is crucially influenced by the largely reactive process of initiating group interaction. Subjects in a simulation should be unaware of this influence. Therefore, they should be unable to predict the effects on response rate of various types of bystanders (i.e., pre-med students, friends, strangers, passive confederates).

CONCLUSION

Most contemporary sociologists would agree with Parson's (1937) view that classic utilitarianism fails to recognize that individual behavior is governed by distinct moral rules or "norms." Unfortunately, sociologists have yet to address a number of questions that this criticism raises.

The ambiguity of Parson's criticism raises the first of these questions. It is not clear what it means to say that social behavior follows rules. A literal interpretation of this contention would be that individuals become acquainted with explicit, verbalizable, moral rules through socialization, and self-consciously use these rules to guide their behavior. However, although certain rules are both explicitly stated and learned (e.g., laws), few sociologists would claim that all or even most social behavior is governed by such explicit rules. Indeed, certain sociologists, most notably Goffman, have built careers on demonstrating that social behavior during face-to-face interaction follows distinct "rules" of which no one has been aware. So when sociologists claim that social behavior follows rules, their use of the term "rule" cannot be taken too literally. What they are, in fact, arguing is that social behavior is, to use Stinchecombe's apt phrase, "phenomenologically rule-like." In other words, social behavior follows predictable patterns. Furthermore, given the criticism of utilitarianism with which this claim has historically been paired, one must presume this pattern is not what one would expect, were individuals choosing behavior on the basis of a hedonistic evaluation of its probable consequences.

The contention that social behavior is phenomenologically rule-like raises a new question: What leads social behavior to be so structured? If we agree that such patterning implies some kind of mental state that, for lack of a better word, we can call a "rule," we immediately confront several new problems:

1. What is the cognitive status of these rules? How are they represented mentally?
2. Why do these rules influence behavior?
3. Are these rules verbalizable? If not, why not?
4. How are these rules acquired?

These are questions that sociologists have largely failed to address. Two-process theory is an attempt to use new research in cognitive psychology and cognitive social psychology to address this classic sociological problem: "Why is social behavior phenomenologically rule-like?" The answer provided is that classic utilitarianism provides an approximately correct account of much social behavior. When it does not—when social behavior seems to follow patterns not predictable using utilitarianism—an explanation can be found in the phenomena of automatic selective attention and over-learning. Through constant practice, individuals acquire a wide variety of over-learned behavioral strings which we call "routines." It is a characteristic of the human cognitive-behavioral apparatus that these routines can be activated without activating higher thought processes (experienced phenomenologically as "consciousness") when the appropriate cues are available in the environment. These higher thought processes will not intrude in familiar situations if major rewards or sanctions are not implicated in the behavior. In these situations, it is the parameters of the routines that have been learned that will pattern social behavior, and it is these parameters that will give social behavior its rule-like quality. Consequently, the mental states that give social behavior its rule-like quality in no sense approximate those mental states we normally call "rules:" they are not verbally encoded, they are not represented in a propositional format, and they cannot be verbalized. They are, in fact, behavioral skills and, we may assume, are encoded appropriately.

A pervasive tendency, to treat individuals as more cognitively active than they in fact are, has been noted. The tendency of sociologists to treat the structure of social interaction as resulting from "rules," conceived of as verbalizable propositions, is one example of this tendency. In 1972, Bem, in his now famous discussion of self-perception theory, noted a general turning away from models treating behavior as the results of general intellectual dispositions, and a trend towards more narrowly conceived information-processing models. Two-process theory reflects this trend. It is primarily an information-processing model that views the phenomenon of automatic selective attention in real time as crucial to explaining characteristics of social interaction. This paper has been devoted to demonstrating that the theory can explain a wide variety of extant research findings. We suggest that the theory is capable of answering most of the questions raised above.

1. The patterning of social behavior reflects not the activation of internalized "rules" but behavioral skills.
2. These behavioral skills structure social behavior not because of moral compulsion but because they are automatically activated by cues in the environment—cues that define social structure—

and the higher thought processes that might modify or control them typically are not activated.

3. These behavioral skills are not verbalizable because they are encoded as behavioral skills not as verbalizable propositions. In addition, they typically are not activated within consciousness, and so are typically unavailable to introspection.

REFERENCES

Abelson, Robert P.
1976 "Script processing in attitude formation and decision making." In J. S. Carroll and J. W. Payne (eds.), Cognition and Social Behavior. Hillsdale, NJ: Erlbaum.
Alexander, C. Norman, and Pat Lauderdale
1977 "Situated identities and social influence." Sociometry 40: 225–233.
Alston, William P.
1975 "Traits, consistency and conceptual alternatives for personality theory." Journal for the Theory of Social Behavior 5: 17–48.
Anderson, Barry F.
1975 Cognitive Psychology. New York: Academic Press.
Asch, S.
1946 "Forming impressions of personality." Journal of Abnormal and Social Psychology 41: 258–290.
Bales, R. F., F. L. Strodbeck, T. M. Mills, and M. E. Roseborough
1951 "Channels of communication in small groups." American Sociological Review 16: 461–468.
Bales, R. F., and P. Slater
1955 "Role differentiation in small decision-making groups." In T. Parsons and R. F. Bales (eds.), Family Socialization and Interaction Process. Glencoe, IL: The Free Press.
Bandura, Albert
1969 Principles of Behavior Modification. New York: Holt, Rinehart and Winston.
Bavelas, A., A. H. Hastorf, A. E. Gross, and W. E. Kite
1965 "Experiments on the alteration of group structure." Journal of Experimental Social Psychology 1: 55–70.
Bem, Dary J.
1972 "Self-perception theory." Pp. 1–62 in Leonard Berkowitz (ed.), Advances in Experimental Social Psychology, Vol. 6. New York: Academic Press.
Berger, Joseph, M. Hamit Fisek, Robert Z. Norman, and Morris Zelditch, Jr.
1977 Status Characteristics and Social Interaction. New York: Elsevier.
Berger, Peter L., and Thomas Luckman
1966 The Social Construction of Reality. Garden City, NY: Doubleday and Co.
Blau, P. M.
1965 Exchange and Power in Social Life. New York: Wiley.
Blaug, Mark
1968 Economic Theory in Retrospect. Homewood, IL: Richard D. Irwin.
Bobrow, Daniel G., and Donald A. Norman
1975 "Some principles of memory schemata." In Daniel G. Bobrow and Allan Collins (eds.), Representation and Understanding. New York: Academic Press.

Borgatta, E. F., and J. Stimson
1963   "Sex differences in interaction characteristics." Journal of Social Psychology 60: 89–100.

Boring, Edwin G.
1950   A History of Experimental Psychology. New York: Appleton-Century-Crofts.

Broadbent, D. E.
1958   Perception and Communication. London: Pergammon Press.

Burgess, R. L., and D. Bushell, Jr.
1969   Behavioral Sociology. New York: Columbia University Press.

Cantor, Nancy, and Walter Mischel
1977   "Traits as prototypes: Effects of recognition memoty." Journal of Personality and Social Psychology 35(1):38–48.

Carrol, John S., and John Payne (eds.)
1975   Cognition and Social Behavior. Hillsdale, NJ: Erlbaum.

Carver, Charles S.
1979   "A cybernetic model of self-attention processes." Journal of Personality and Social Psychology 37: 1251–1281.

Chanowitz, Benzion, and Ellen T. Langer
1980   "Premature cognitive commitment." Unpublished manuscript, The Graduate Center, City of New York.

Chaplin, James P., and T. S. Krawiec
1974   Systems and Theories of Psychology. (3rd ed.) New York: Holt, Rinehart and Winston.

Croog, S. H.
1956   "Patient government: Some aspects of participation and social background on two psychiatric wards." Psychiatry 19:203–207.

David, Kenneth H.
1972   "Generalization of operant conditioning of verbal output in three-man discussion groups." Journal of Social Psychology 87:245–249.

Dion, K., E. Berscheid, and E. Walster
1972   "What is beautiful is good." Journal of Personality and Social Psychology 24:285–290.

Downs, Anthony
1957   An Economic Theory of Democracy. New York: Harper & Row.

Duncan, Starkey, and Donald W. Fiske
1978   Face-to-face Interaction. Hillsdale, NJ: Erlbaum.

Duvall, S., and R. A. Wicklund
1972   A Theory of Objective Self-Awareness. New York: Academic Press.

Emerson, Richard M.
1972   "Exchange theory: Part I. A psychological basis for social exchange." In J. Berger, M. Zelditch, and B. Anderson (eds.), Sociological Theories in Progress, II. Boston, MA: Houghton, Mifflin.

Erdelyi, M. H.
1974   "A new look at the New Look; perceptual defence and vigilance." Psychological Review 81: 1–25.

Etkin, William (ed.)
1964   Social Behavior and Organization among Vertebrates. Chicago, IL: University of Chicago Press.

Exline, R. V., and B. J. Fehr
1978   "Application of semiotics to the study of visual interaction." In A. Stegman and S. Feldstein (eds.), Non-verbal Behavior and Communication. Hillsdale, NJ: Erlbaum.

Festinger, L., and J. M. Carlsmith
1959 "Cognitive consequences of forced compliance." Journal of Abnormal and Social Psychology, 203–210.

Fisek, M. Hamit, and Richard Ofshe
1970 "The process of status evolution." Sociometry 33:327–346.

Freese, Lee, and Milton Rokeach
1979 "On the use of alternative interpretation in contemporary social psychology." Social Psychology Quarterly 42:195–201.

Gitter, A. George, Harvey Black, and Janet C. Fishman
1975 "Effect of race, sex, nonverbal communication and verbal communication on perception of leadership." Sociology and Social Research 60(1):46–57.

Goffman, Erving
1974 Frame Analysis. Cambridge,MA: Harvard University Press.

Goffman, Erving
1969 Strategic Interaction. Philadelphia, PA: University of Pennsylvania Press.

Gold, M.
1958 "Power in the classroom." Sociometry 25:50–60.

Gold, R.
1952 "Janitors versus Tenants: A status-income dilemma." American Journal of Sociology 57:486–493.

Harré, K., and P. F. Secord
1972 The Explanation of Social Behavior. Oxford, England: Basil Blackwell.

Harvey, O. J.
1953 "An experimental approach to the study of status relations in informal groups." American Sociological Review 18:357–367.

Hatton, J.
1967 "Reactions of Negroes in biracial bargaining situations." Journal of Personality and Social Psychology 7:301–306.

Heath, Anthony
1976 Rational Choice and Social Exchange. New York: Cambridge University Press.

Heider, Fritz
1958 The Psychology of Interpersonal Relations. New York: Wiley.

Heinecke, C., and R. F. Bales
1953 "Developmental trends in the structure of small groups." Sociometry 16.

Heiss, J. S.
1962 "Degree of intimacy and male-female interaction." Sociometry 25: 197–208.

Herrnstein, Richard J.
1973 "Introduction to John B. Watson's comparative psychology." In Mary Henle, J. Jaynes, and J. Sullivan (eds.), Historical Conceptions of Psychology. New York: Springer.

Hess, E. H., and S. B. Petrovich
1978 "Pupillary behavior in communication." In A. Siesman and S. Feldstein (eds.), Nonverbal Behavior and Communication. Hillsdale, NJ: Erlbaum.

Hochschild, Arlie
1979 "Emotion word, feeling rules and social structure." American Journal of Sociology 85:551–575.

Homans, G. C.
1961 Social Behavior. Its Elementary Forms. London: Routledge and Kegan Paul.

Hurwitz, J. I., A. F. Zander, and B. Hymovitch
1960 "Some effects of power on the relations among group members." Pp. 800–806 in D. Cartwright and A. Zander (eds.), Group Dynamics. New York: Harper and Row.

Jaffee, Joseph
  1978   "Parliamentary procedure and the brain." In A. Siegman and S. Feldstein (eds.),
          Nonverbal Behavior and Communication. Hillsdale, NJ: Erlbaum.
Jaffe, Joseph, and S. Feldstein
  1970   Rhythms of Dialogue. New York: Academic Press.
Jaffee, Cabot L., Steven A. Richards, and Gerald W. McLaughlin
  1970   "Leadership selection under differing feedback conditions." Psychonomic Sci-
          ence 20:349–350.
Jaffee, Cabot L., and R. L. Lucas
  1969   "Effects of rates of talking and the correctness of decisions on leader choice in
          small groups." Journal of Social Psychology 79:247–254.
Kantor, J. R.
  1969   The Scientific Evolution of Psychology, II. Chicago, IL: Principia Press.
Katz, I., and L. Benjamin
  1960   "Effects of white authoritarianism in biracial work groups." Journal of Abnormal
          and Social Psychology 61:448–456.
Katz, I., E. Epps, and L. Axelson
  1964   "Effects upon Negro digit-symbol performance of anticipated comparison with
          whites and other Negroes." Journal of Abnormal and Social Psychology 69:77–
          83.
Katz, I., Judith Goldston, and Lawrence Benjamin
  1958   "Behavior and productivity in bi-racial work groups." Human Relations 11:122–
          141.
Kelley, H. H.
  1950   "The warm-cold variable in first impressions of persons." Journal of Personality
          18:431–439.
Kerr, Nancy, L. Meherson, and J. A. Michael
  1965   "A procedure for shaping vocalizations in a mute child." In L. P. Ullmann and
          L. Krasner (eds.), Case Studies in Behavior Modification. New York: Holt,
          Rinehart and Winston.
Kimble, Gregory A.
  1971   "Cogntive inhibition in classical conditioning." Pp. 69–88 in Howard Kendler
          and Janet T. Spence (eds.), Essays in Neobehaviorism, A Memorial Volume to
          Kenneth W. Spence. New York: Meredith.
Koomen, Willem, and Piet K. Sagel
  1977   "The prediction of participation in two-person groups." Sociometry 40(4):369–
          373.
Lachman, Roy, Janet L. Lachman, and Earl C. Butterfield
  1979   Cognitive Psychology and Information Processing. Hillsdale, NJ: Erlbaum.
Lakatos, Imre
  1970   "Falsification and the methodology of scientific research programs." Pp. 91–
          196 in Lakatos and Musgrave (eds.), Criticism and the Growth of Knowledge.
          Cambridge: Cambridge University Press.
Landreth, Harry
  1976   History of Economic Theory. Boston, MA: Houghton, Mifflin.
Langer, Ellen J.
  1978   "The role of mindlessness in the perception of deviance." Unpublished man-
          uscript, Harvard University.
Langer, Ellen J.
  1979a   "The illusion of incompetence." In L. Perlmutter and R. Monty (eds.), Choice
          and Perceived Control. Hillsdale, NJ: Erlbaum.
Langer, Ellen J.
  1979b   "Rethinking the role of thought in social interaction." In J. H. Harvey, W. J.

Ickes, and R. F. Kidd (eds.), New Directions in Attribution Research, 2. Hillsdale, NJ: Erlbaum.

Langer, Ellen J., Arthur Blank, and Benzion Chanowitz
1978   "The mindlessness of ostensibly thought action: The role of 'placebo' information in interpersonal interaction." Journal of Personality and Social Psychology 36(6):635–642.

Langer, Ellen J., and Lois G. Imber
1979   "When practice makes imperfect: Debilitating effects of overlearning." Journal of Personality and Social Psychology 378:2014–2024.

Langer, Ellen J., and Helen M. Newman
1979   "The role of mindlessness in a typical social psychological experiment." Personality and Social Psychology Bulleting 5:295–298.

Langer, Ellen J., and Cynthia Weinman
1979   "Mindlessness, confidence and accuracy." Unpublished manuscript, Harvard University.

Latané, Bibb, and John M. Darley
1970   The Unresponsive Bystander: Why Doesn't He Help? New York: Appleton-Century-Crofts.

Lee, Margaret, and Richard Ofshe
1981   "The impact of behavioral style and status characteristics on social influence: A test of two competing theories." Social Psychology Quarterly 44.

Lee, Margaret, and Richard Ofshe
1981   "Status and ability inferences based on behavioral style: Their creation and impact on social influence." Unpublished manuscript, University of California at Berkeley.

Leik, R. K.
1963   "Instrumentality and emotionality in family interaction." Sociometry 26:131–145.

Leik, R. K.
1965   " 'Irrelevant' aspects of stooge behavior: Implications for leadership studies and experimental methodologies." Sociometry 28:259–271.

Lewis, J. David
1979   "A social behaviorist interpretation of the median I." American Journal of Sociology 85:261–287.

Lippit, R., and M. Gold
1959   "Classroom social structure as a mental health problem." Journal of Social Issues 15:40–58.

Lucas, Richard L., and Cabot . Jaffee
1969   "Effects of high-rate talkers on group voting behavior in the leaderless-group problem-solving situation." Psychological Reports 25:471–477.

Mackworth, Jane F.
1970   Vigilance and Attention. Baltimore, MD: Penguin Books.

MacPherson, C. B.
1962   The Political Theory of Possessive Individualism. Oxford, England: Oxford University Press.

March, J. G.
1953   "Husband-wife interaction over political issues." Public Opinion Quarterly 13:461–470.

Markus, Hazel
1977   "Self-schemata and processing information about the self." Journal of Personality and Social Psychology 35(2):63–78.

Milgram, Stanley
1974   Obedience to Authority. New York: Harper and Row.

Miller, G. A., C. Galanter, and K. H. Pribram
  1960   Plans and the Structure of Behavior. New York: Holt, Rinehart and Winston.
Mischel, Walter
  1968   Personality Assessment. New York: Wiley.
Misiak, Henry K., and Virginia S. Sexton
  1966   History of Psychology, an Overview. New York: Grune and Stratton.
Moray, N.
  1959   "Attention in dichotic listening: Affective cues and the influence of instructions."
          Quarterly Journal of Experimental Psychology 11:56–60.
Moscovici, S., E. Lage, and M. Noffrechoux
  1969   "Influence of a consistent minority on the responses of a majority in a color
          perception task." Sociometry 32(4):365–381.
Moscovice, Serge, and Elizabeth Lage
  1976   "Studies in social influence III, majority vs. minority influence in a group."
          European Journal of Social Psychology 6(2):149–174.
Nadel, S. F.
  1957   The Theory of Social Structure. London, England: Cohen and West.
Neisser, Ulric
  1966   Cognitive Psychology. New York: Meredith.
Nemeth, Charlan, Mark Swendlund, and Barbara Kanki
  1974   "Patterning of the minority's responses and their influence on the majority."
          European Journal of Social Psychology 4(1):53–64.
Nemeth, Carlan, J. Endicott, and J. Wachtler
  1976   "From the 50's to the 70's: Women in jury deliberation." Sociometry 39:293–
          304.
Nemeth, Charlan, and J. Wachtler
  1974   "Creating the perception of consistency and confidence: A necessary condition
          for minority influence." Sociometry 37(4):529–540.
Nisbett, R., and C. Wilson
  1977   "Telling more than we can know; level of reports on mental processes." Psy-
          chological Review 84:231–259.
Norfleet, B.
  1948   "Interpersonal relations and group productivity." Journal of Social Issue
          4:66–69.
Ofshe, Richard
  1980   "The social development of the Synanon cult: The managerial strategy of or-
          ganizational transformation." Sociological Analysis 41(2).
Ofshe, Richard, Nancy C. Berg, Richard Coughlin, Gregory Dolinajee, Kathleen Gerson,
    and Avery Johnson
  1974   "Social structure and social control in Synanon." Journal of Voluntary Action
          Research 3:67–76.
Ofshe, Richard, and Lynne Ofshe
  1970   Utility and Choice in Social Interaction. Englewood Cliffs, NJ: Prentice-
          Hall.
Ofshe, Richard, Robert Saltz, and Kenneth Christman
  1982a   "Obedience to authority: A two-process explanation of the Milgram experi-
          ments." Unpublished manuscript, University of California at Berkeley.
Ofshe, Richard, Robert Saltz, and Kenneth Christman
  1982b   "Bystander intervention, the identity of bystanders, and the release of behavior."
          Unpublished manuscript, Unversity of California at Berkeley.
Olson, M.
  1965   The Logic of Collective Action: Public Goods and the Theory of Groups. Cam-
          bridge, MA: Harvard University Press.

Ostry, D., N. Moray, and G. Marks
   1976   "Attention, practice and semantic targets." Journal of Experimental Psychology: Human Perception and Performance 2:326–336.
Pash, Gordon
   1970   "Cognitive systems." Pp. 349–406 in Paul L. Garver (ed.), Cognition: A Multiple View. New York: Spartan Books.
Posner, M. I., and C. R. Snyder
   1974   "Attention and cognitive control." In R. L. Solso (ed.), Information Processing and Cognition: The Loyola Symposium. Potomac, MD: Erlbaum.
Preston, M., and J. Bayton
   1941   "Differential effects of a social variable upon three levels of aspiration." Journal of Experimental Psychology 29:351–369.
Regula, C. Robert, and James W. Julian
   1973   "The impact of quality and frequency of task contributions on perceived ability." Journal of Social Psychology 89:115–122.
Reilly, R. R., and C. L. Jaffee
   1970   "Influence of some task-irrelevant factors on leader selection." Psychological Record 20:535–539.
Richardson, James T., John R. Dugan, Louis Gray, and Bruce H. Mayhew
   1973   "Expert power: A behavioral interpretation." Sociometry 36(3):302–324.
Rosa, Eugene, and Allen Mazur
   1979   Incipient status in small groups." Social Forces 58:18–37.
Rosenfeld, Howard M.
   1978   "Coversational control functions of nonverbal behavior." In A. W. Siegman and S. Feldstein (eds.), Nonverbal Behavior and Communication. Hillsdale, NJ: Erlbaum.
Rosenthal, Robert
   1976   Experimenter Effects in Behavioral Research. New York: Halsted Press.
Ross, L. D.
   1977   "The intuitive psychologist and his shortcomings: Distortions in the attribution process." In L. Berkowitz (ed.), Advances in Experimental Social Psychology. New York: Adacemic Press.
Ross, L. E.
   1971   "Cognitive factors in conditioning the use of masking tasks in eyelid conditioning." In H. Kendler and J. Spence (eds.), Essays in Neobehaviorism, A Memorial Volume to Kenneth W. Spence (pp. 161–186). New York: Meredith.
Routh, G.
   1977   The Origin of Economic Ideas. New York: Vintage.
Schachter, S.
   1965   "The interaction of cognitive and physiological determinants of emotional state." In L. Berkowitz (ed.), Advances in Experimental Social Psychology. New York: Academic.
Schank, R., and R. Abelson
   1977   Scripts, Plans, Goals and Understanding. Hillsdale, NJ: Erlbaum.
Schein, M. W.
   1975   Social Hierarchy and Dominance. Stroudsburg, PA: Wiley (Halsted).
Schneider, Walters, and Richard M. Shiffrin
   1977   "Controlled and automatic human information processing, I. Detection search and attention." Psychological Review 84(1):1–66.
Schumpeter, Joseph A., History of Economic Analysis. New York: Oxford University Press.
Sherif, M., B. J. White, and O. J. Harvey
   1955   "Status in experimentally produced groups." American Journal of Sociology 60: 370–379.

Shiffrin, Richard M., and Walter Schneider
1977 "Controlled and automatic human information processing: II. Perceptual learning, automatic attending and a general theory." Psychological Review 84(2):127–190.
Siegel, Sidney, and Lawrence Foraker
1960 Bargaining and Group Decision-making. New York: McGraw-Hill.
Siegel, Sidney, Alberta Siegel, and Julia Andrews
1964 Choice Strategy and Utility. New York: McGraw-Hill.
Siegman, A. W., and S. Feldstein (eds.)
1978 Nonverbal Behavior and Communication. Hillsdale, NJ: Erlbaum.
Skinner, B. F.
1974 About Behaviorism. New York: Alfred A. Knopf.
Skinner, B. F.
1953 Science and Human Behavior. New York: The Free Press.
Slater, P.
1955 "Role differentiation in small groups." American Sociological Review 20:300–310.
Snyder, Mark
1978 "Self-monitoring processes." In L. Berkowitz (ed.), Advances in Experimental Social Psychology, Vol. 12. New York: Academic Press.
Solly, Charles M., and Murphy Gardner
1960 Development of the Perceptual World. New York: Basic Books.
Staats, Arthur W.
1975 Social Behaviorism. Homewood, IL: Dorsey Press.
Strodtbeck, Fred L.
1951 "Husband-wife interaction over revealed differences." American Sociological Review 16:468–473.
Strodtbeck, Fred L., R. James, and C. Hawkins
1957 "Social status in jury deliberation." American Sociological Review 22:713–719.
Strodtbeck, Fred L., and R. D. Mann
1956 "Sex role differentiation in jury deliberation." Sociometry 19:3–11.
Taylor, Overton, H.
1960 A History of Economic Thought. New York: McGraw-Hill.
Taylor, Shelley E., and Susan T. Fiske
1978 "Salience, attention and attribution: Top of the head phenomena." In L. Berkowitz (ed.), Advances in Experimental Social Psychology, Vol. 11. New York: Academic Press.
Taylor, Shelley, E., Jennifer Crocker, Susan T. Fiske, Merle Sprinter, and Joachim D. Winkler. "The generalizability of salience effects." Journal of Personality and Social Psychology 37:357–368.
Tesser, Abraham
1978 "Self-generated attitude change." In L. Berkowitz (ed.), Advances in Experimental Social Psychology, Vol. 11. New York: Academic Press.
Thibaut, J. W., and H. H. Kelley
1959 The Social Psychology of Groups. New York: Wiley.
Thorngate, W.
1976 "Must we always think before we act?" Personality and Social Psychology Bulletin 2:31–35.
Thorpe, W. H.
1966 "Ethology and consciousness." Pp. 470–505 in John C. Eccle (ed.), Brain and Conscious Experience. New York: Springer-Verlag.

Torrance, E. P.
1954   "Some consequences of power differences on desicion-making in permanent and temporary three-man groups." Research Studies 22:130–140.
Triesman, A. M.
1960   "Contextual cues in selective listening." Quarterly Journal of Experimental Psychology 12:242–248.
Tuddenham, R. D., P. Macbride, and V. Zahn
1951   "The influence of the sex composition of the group upon yielding to a distorted group norm." Journal of Psychology 46:243–251.
Underwood, G.
1974   "Moray vs. the rest: The effects of extended practice on shadowing." Quarterly Journal of Experimental Psychology 26:368–373.
Valins, S.
1966   "Cognitive effects of false heart-rate feedback." Journal of Personality and Social Psychology 4:400–408.
Whyte, W. F.
1943   Street Corner Society. Chicago, IL: University of Chicago Press.
Wicklund, R.
1975.   "Objective self-awareness." In L. Berkowitz (ed.), Advances in Experimental Social Psychology, Vol. 8. New York: Academic Press.
Willard, Don, and Fred L. Strodtbeck
1972   "Latency of verbal response and participation in small groups." Sociometry 35:161–175.
Wilson, E. O.
1975   Sociobiology. Cambridge, MA: Harvard University Press.
Woodworth, Robert S., and Mary R. Sheehan
1964   Contemporary Schools of Psychology. New York: Ronald Press.
Wundt, Wilhelm
1907   Lectures on Human and Animal Psychology. Translated by J. E. Creighton and E. B. Tichener. New York: Macmillan.
Zander, A., and A. R. Cohen
1955   "Attributed social power and group acceptance: A classroom experimental demonstration." Journal of Abnormal and Social Psychology 51:490–492.
Ziller, R. C., and R. V. Exline
1958   "Some consequences of age heterogencity in decision-making groups." Sociometry 21:198–201.
Zimbardo, P. G., A. Cohen, M. Weisenberg, C. Dworkin, and I. Firestone
1969   "The control of experimental pain." Pp. 100–125 in P. G. Zimbardo (ed.), The Cognitive Control of Motivation. Glenview, IL: Scott, Foresman.

Author Index

Italics indicate bibliographic citations.

245

Subject Index